AKSL

Leeds Trinity University

LIBRARY

**This book is due for return on or before
the last date stamped below**

WITHDRAWN FROM LIBRARY
LEEDS TRINITY

D0542201

250911 5

PROBLEMS IN EUROPEAN CIVILIZATION SERIES

General Editor
Merry E. Wiesner

Humanism and the Renaissance

Edited with an introduction by
Zachary S. Schiffman
Northeastern Illinois University

Houghton Mifflin Company   Boston   New York

2509115   940.21
SCH

LIBRARY
LRS

Sponsoring Editor: Nancy Blaine
Associate Editor: Julie Dunn
Associate Project Editor: Elisabeth Kehrer
Associate Production/Design Coordinator: Christine Gervais
Senior Manufacturing Coordinator: Marie Barnes
Marketing Manager: Sandra McGuire

Cover Image: School room scene from a 15th century Italian codice. Biblioteca Trivulziana, Milan, Italy/Art Resource, NY.

Credits:

Part I

p. 11: Excerpt from introduction from *The Civilization of the Renaissance in Italy,* Vols. I and II by Jacob Burckhardt and Introduction by Benjamin Nelson and Charles Trinkaus. Introduction and Notes to Introduction Copyright © 1958, renewed © 1986 by Harper & Row Publishers, Inc. Reprinted by permission of HarperCollins Publishers, Inc.

All other credits appear on page 253, which constitutes an extension of the copyright page.

Copyright © 2002 by Houghton Mifflin Company. All rights reserved.

No part of this work may be reproduced or transmitted in any form or by any means, electronic or mechanical, including photocopying and recording, or by any information storage or retrieval system without the prior written permission of the copyright owner unless such copying is expressly permitted by federal copyright law. With the exception of non-profit transcription in Braille, Houghton Mifflin is not authorized to grant permission for further uses of copyrighted selections reprinted in this text without the permission of their owners. Permission must be obtained from the individual copyright owners as identified herein. Address requests for permission to make copies of Houghton Mifflin material to College Permissions, Houghton Mifflin Company, 222 Berkeley Street, Boston, MA 02116-3764.

Printed in the U.S.A.

Library of Congress Control Number: 2001131549

ISBN: 0-618-11625-7

123456789-FFG-05 04 03 02 01

Contents

Preface

The Renaissance is such an inherently confusing period that debates about its nature have become the chief occasion for calling the whole enterprise of historical periodization into question. Some scholars avoid using the term *Renaissance* altogether, favoring instead more "value-free" expressions, like *Quattrocento, fifteenth century,* or *early modern.* Confusion over the term stems from attempts to extend it to virtually every aspect of life, with decidedly mixed results. The fruitless debates about whether there ever was such a thing as a "Renaissance monarchy" illustrate the limitations of a term that best applies to intellectual developments rather than political, social, or economic ones. By entitling this book *Humanism and the Renaissance,* I hope to have signaled my assumption that the Renaissance constitutes a period in intellectual history and high culture. I regard it as embedded in a political, social, and economic context that was less "early modern" than "late medieval," an expression best describing those aspects of life that remained fundamentally unchanged, despite intellectual developments.

Even when thus limited, the Renaissance remains a vast subject. Some of the scholars included in this volume can justifiably claim to have mastered large portions of the subject; however, I am not one of them, and thus I have incurred a number of debts in producing this work. I developed my conception of the book in close collaboration with the series editor, Merry Wiesner, who gently nudged me out of my intellectual ruts and onto new paths. Constantin Fasolt and Daniel Woolf, both better read than I, provided indispensable bibliographical guidance. Susan Rosa perused all my introductory materials with her usual discerning eye for clarity of thought and expression, sparing me many infelicities. I owe a special debt to the volume's reviewers — Jeffrey R. Watt (University of Mississippi), Brian W. Ogilvie (University of Massachusetts, Amherst), John B. Roney (Sacred Heart University), and Christopher DeRosa (University of California, Berkeley)—whose comments and suggestions curbed my intellectual excesses and lent greater focus to the work. Finally, I am grateful to Julie Dunn and Nancy Blaine at Houghton Mifflin for making the creation of this volume, from start to finish, a distinct pleasure.

Zachary S. Schiffman

Editor's Preface
to Instructors

There are many ways to date ourselves as teachers and scholars of history: the questions that we regard as essential to ask about any historical development, the theorists whose words we quote and whose names appear in our footnotes, the price of the books that we purchased for courses and that are on our shelves. Looking over my own shelves, it struck me that another way we could be dated was by the color of the oldest books we owned in this series, which used to be published by D.C. Heath. I first used a "Heath series" book—green and white, as I recall—when I was a freshman in college and taking a modern European history course. That book, by Dwight E. Lee on the Munich crisis, has long since disappeared, but several Heath books that I acquired later as an undergraduate are still on my shelves. Those that I used in graduate school, including ones on the Renaissance and Reformation, are also there, as are several I assigned my students when I first started teaching or have used in the years since. As with any system of historical periodization, of course, this method of dating a historian is flawed and open to misinterpretation. When a colleague retired, he gave me some of his even older Health series books, in red and black, which had actually appeared when I was still in elementary and junior high school, so that a glance at my shelves might make me seem ready for retirement.

The longevity of this series, despite its changing cover design and its transition from D.C. Heath to Houghton Mifflin, could serve as an indication of several things. One might be that historians are conservative, unwilling to change the way they approach the past or teach about it. The rest of the books on my shelves suggest that this conservatism is not the case, however, for many of the books discuss topics that were unheard of as subjects of historical investigation when I took that course as a freshman thirty years ago: memory, masculinity, visual culture, sexuality.

Another way to account for the longevity of this series is that several generations of teachers have found it a useful way for their students to approach historical subjects. As teachers, one of the first issues we confront in any course is what materials we will assign our students to read. (This decision is often, in fact, paramount for we have to order books months before the class begins.) We may include a textbook to provide an overview of the subject matter covered in the course and often have several from which to choose. We may use a reader of original sources, or several sources in their entirety, because we feel that it is important for our students to hear the voices of people of the past directly. We may add a novel from the period, for fictional works often give one details and insights that do not emerge from other types of sources. We may direct our students to visual materials, either in books or on the Web, for artifacts, objects, and art can give one access to aspects of life never mentioned in written sources.

Along with these types of assignments, we may also choose to assign books such as those in this series, which present the ideas and opinions of scholars on a particular topic. Textbooks are, of course, written by scholars with definite opinions, but they are designed to present material in a relatively bland manner. They may suggest areas about which there is historical debate (often couched in phrases such as "scholars disagree about . . .") but do not participate in those debates themselves. By contrast, the books in this series highlight points of dispute, and cover topics and developments about which historians often disagree vehemently. Students who are used to the textbook approach to history may be surprised at the range of opinion on certain matters, but we hope that the selections in each of these volumes will allow readers to understand why there is such a diversity. Each volume covers several issues of interpretive debate and highlights newer research directions.

Variety of interpretation in history is sometimes portrayed as a recent development, but the age of this series in its many cover styles indicates that this account is not accurate. Historians have long recognized that historical sources are produced by particular individuals with particular interests and biases that consciously and unconsciously shape their content. They have also long—one is tempted to say "always"—recognized that different people approach the past differently, making choices about which topics to study, which sources to use, which developments and individuals to highlight. This diversity in both sources and methodologies is part of what makes history exciting for those of us who study it, for new materials and new approaches allow us to see things that have never been seen before, in the same way that astronomers find new stars with better tools and new ways of looking.

The variety and innovation that is an essential part of good historical scholarship allow this series both to continue and to change. Some of the volumes now being prepared have the same titles as those I read as an undergraduate, but the scholarship on that topic has changed so much in the last several decades that they had to be completely redone, not simply revised. Some of the volumes now in print examine topics that were rarely covered in undergraduate courses when the series began publication, and a few former volumes are no longer in print because the topics they investigated now show up more rarely. We endeavor to keep the series up-to-date and welcome suggestions about volumes that would prove helpful for teaching undergraduate and graduate courses. You can contact us at http://college.hmco.com.

Merry E. Wiesner

Editor's Preface
to Students

History is often presented as facts marching along a timeline, and historical research is often viewed as the unearthing of information so that more facts can be placed on the timeline. Like geologists in caves or physicists using elaborate microscopes, historians discover new bits of data, which allow them to recover more of the past.

To some degree, this model is accurate. Like laboratory scientists, historians do conduct primary research, using materials in archives, libraries, and many other places to discover new things about the past. Over the last thirty years, for example, the timeline of history has changed from a story that was largely political and military to one that includes the experiences of women, peasants, slaves, children, and workers. Even the political and military story has changed and now includes the experiences of ordinary soldiers and minority groups rather than simply those of generals, rulers, and political elites. This expansion of the timeline has come in part through intensive research in original sources, which has vastly increased what we know about people of the past.

Original research is only part of what historians do, however, in the same way that laboratory or field research is only part of science. Historical and scientific information is useless until someone tries to make sense of what is happening, tries to explain why and how things developed the way they did. In making these analyses and conclusions, however, both historians and scientists often come to disagree vehemently about the underlying reasons for what they have observed or discovered, and sometimes about the observations themselves. Certain elements of those observations are irrefutable—a substance either caught fire or it did not, a person lived and died or he or she did not—but many more of them are open to debate: Was the event (whether historical or scientific) significant? Why and how did it happen? Under what circumstances might it not have happened? What factors influenced the way that it happened? What larger consequences did it have?

The books in this series focus on just those types of questions. They take one particular event or development in European history and present you with the analyses of several historians and other authors regarding this issue. In some cases the authors may disagree about what actually happened—in the same way that eyewitnesses of a traffic accident or crime may all see different things—but more often they disagree about the interpretation. Was the Renaissance a continuation of earlier ideas, or did it represent a new way of looking at the world? Was nineteenth-century European imperialism primarily political and economic in its origins and impact, or were cultural and intellectual factors more significant? Was ancient Athens a democracy worthy of emulation, an expansionary state seeking to swallow its neighbors, or both? Within each volume are often more specific points of debate, which add complexity to the main question and introduce you to further points of disagreement.

Each of the volumes begins with an introduction by the editor, which you should read carefully before you turn to the selections themselves. This introduction sets out the *historical* context of the issue, adding depth to what you may have learned in a textbook account or other reading, and also explains the *historiographical* context, that is, how historians (including those excerpted in the volume) have viewed the issue over time. Many volumes also include a timeline of events and several reference maps that situate the issue chronologically and geographically. These may be more detailed than the timelines and maps in your textbook, and consulting them as you read will help deepen your understanding of the selections.

Some of the volumes in the series include historical analyses that are more than a century old, and all include writings stretching over several decades. The editors include this chronological range not only to allow you to see that interpretations change, but also to see how lines of argument and analysis develop. Every historian approaching an issue depends not only on his or her own original research, but also on the secondary analyses of those who have gone before, which he or she then accepts, rejects, modifies, or adapts. Thus, within the book as a whole or within each section, the selections are generally arranged in chronological order; reading them in the order they are presented will allow you to get a better sense of the historiographical development and to make comparisons among the selections more easily and appropriately.

The description of the scholarly process noted above is somewhat misleading, for in both science and history, research and analysis are not sequential but simultaneous. Historians do not wander around archives looking for interesting bits of information but turn to their sources with specific questions in mind, questions that have often been developed by reading earlier historians. These questions shape where they will look, what they will pay attention to, and therefore what conclusions they will make. Thus, the fact that we now know so much more about women, peasants, or workers than we did several decades ago did not result primarily from sources on these people suddenly appearing where there had been none, but from historians, with new questions in mind, going back to the same archives and libraries that had yielded information on kings and generals. The same is true in science, of course; scientists examining an issue begin with a hypothesis and then test it through the accumulation of information, reaching a conclusion that leads to further hypotheses.

In both history and science, one's hypotheses can sometimes be so powerful that one simply cannot see what the sources or experiments show, which is one reason there is always opportunity for more research or a re-analysis of data. A scholar's analysis may also be shaped by many other factors, and in this volume the editor may have provided you with information about individual authors, such as their national origin, intellectual background, or philosophical perspective, if these factors are judged important to your understanding of their writings or points of view. You might be tempted to view certain of these factors as creating "bias" on the part of an author and thus to reduce the value of his or her analysis. It is important to recognize, however, that every historian or commentator has a particular point of view and writes at a particular historical moment; very often what scholars view as complete objectivity on their own part is seen as subjective bias by those who disagree. The central aim of this series over its forty-plus years of publication has been to help you and other students understand how and why the analyses and judgments of historians have differed and changed over time, to see that scholarly controversy is at the heart of the historical enterprise.

The instructor in your course may have provided you with detailed directions for using this book, but here are some basic questions that you can ask yourself as you read the selections:

- What is the author's central argument?
- What evidence does the author put forward to support this argument?
- What is the significance of the author's argument?
- What other interpretation might there be of the evidence that the author presents?
- How does each author's argument intersect with the others in the part? In the rest of the book?
- How convincing do you find the author's interpretation?

These questions are exactly the same as those that professional historians ask themselves, and in analyzing and comparing the selections in this book, you, too, are engaged in the business of historical interpretation.

Merry E. Wiesner

Introduction

The idea of the Renaissance, which predates the actual name for the period, originated with the earliest humanists, revealing the intimate connection between their movement and the notion of cultural "rebirth." The foremost of the early humanists, Petrarch (1304–1374), conceived of himself as reviving the glories of ancient Latin after a period of medieval "darkness" had obscured the light of classical eloquence. Petrarch's friend and admirer, Giovanni Boccaccio (1313–1375), subsequently extended this notion of renewal or rebirth to art as well as literature when he claimed that Giotto had done for painting what Dante had done for poetry. In the fifteenth century, the idea of a cultural revival encompassing both literature and art had become widespread in Italy. But not until the sixteenth century did Giorgio Vasari (1511–1574) invent the actual term *Renaissance* (*Rinascita*) in his *Lives of the Artists*, first published in 1550. Vasari limited his use of the term to the revival of art in Italy. By the seventeenth century, however, it had come to signify a European-wide cultural flowering, encompassing Latin, Greek, and vernacular literature, as well as the fine arts. Enlightenment thinkers further broadened the use of the term by conceiving of the Renaissance as a revolutionary break with the Gothic "barbarism" of the Middle Ages.

Although they helped enshrine the Petrarchan conception of a dark age separating antiquity from modernity, Enlightenment thinkers nonetheless began to separate "Renaissance" from "humanism." By regarding the Renaissance as having overturned medieval "ignorance" and "superstition," they initiated a process by which the term came to epitomize not just the rebirth of classical eloquence and of ancient naturalism in art but more broadly the emergence of an entirely new civilization. This process reached fruition in the mid-nineteenth century with the work of historians like Jules Michelet, Georg Voigt, and Jacob Burckhardt.

In one of the volumes of his massive *History of France*, entitled *The Renaissance* (1855), the fiery Michelet swept aside the linguistic, literary, and artistic rebirths as mere epiphenomena when compared to the real achievements of the age, namely, "the discovery of the world and the discovery of man." For Michelet, this twin discovery underlay and animated all that had previously been associated with the term *Renaissance*, giving unity to the entire age. Michelet's Renaissance brought the Middle Ages to a decisive close and heralded the triumph of modernity.

The sober Voigt echoed these same sentiments in his scholarly (and still useful) history of humanism, *The Revival of Classical Antiquity* (1859). Here he describes the subject of his book as the crest of a sea change that would sweep from Italy throughout all Europe, transforming civilization in its wake. At the heart of this change lay a notion of *humanitas*, a glorification of the human spirit and all it could accomplish in this world, which stood in stark contrast to the other-worldliness of the Middle Ages. The transformation of the term *Renaissance* thus entailed the redefinition of *humanism*. Not only did the latter signify the rebirth of classical language and literature but, more broadly (and vaguely), the reemergence of humanity from medieval darkness into the light of a new day.

More carefully considered than Michelet's impulsive work, and wider in scope than Voigt's scholarly study, Burckhardt's *The Civilization of the Renaissance in Italy* (1860) set the seal on the modern interpretation of the Renaissance. It betrays many debts—one of its sections bears the title, "The Discovery of the World and of Man," echoing Michelet's bold formulation—yet with the breadth and depth of its learning, the range of its coverage, and the seductiveness of its prose, Burckhardt's masterpiece eclipsed the work of his predecessors. Even today his Renaissance remains to a large extent our Renaissance.

Following in the footsteps of his predecessors, Burckhardt conceived of the Italian Renaissance as a cultural watershed marking the end of the Middle Ages and the beginning of modernity. But he went much farther than his predecessors in relegating humanism to the status of an effect rather than a cause of cultural transformation. Of course, humanists and humanism are everywhere apparent in his book. He utilized the movement to illustrate many distinctive aspects of Renaissance culture, and he constructed his account largely from the writings of the humanists themselves, which provided him with a wealth of primary source material. Yet he insisted that the roots of the Renaissance lay in the unique political and social climate of Italy, not in the revival of antiquity, and that a Renaissance—a turn toward modernity—could have occurred without such a revival. In Burckhardt's famous work, then, the Renaissance finally takes on a life of its own, apart from humanism.

The selections in this volume trace a story that necessarily begins with Burckhardt. For us, he is no straw man to be tossed aside after a cheap victory. His ideas have power and substance, and they resonate throughout our selections. But as scholars have reacted to his thesis, either by refining or rejecting it, they have tended to move humanism back to the center stage of the Renaissance. And in so doing, they have wittingly or unwittingly confirmed his fundamental insight into the nature of the Renaissance, all the while calling into question his distinction between that nature and the humanist movement. Our selections, then, embody an ironic subtext, for in contrast to Burckhardt, they ultimately show the extent to which his Renaissance (and by extension ours) stems in large part from the revival of antiquity.

Part I, "Originality and Continuity in the Renaissance," begins with the debate first sparked by Burckhardt's thesis, namely, whether the Italian Renaissance represents a rupture with the Middle Ages or an evolution from them. Burckhardt located the distinctive nature of the Renaissance in the development of the individual, not the revival of antiquity, and he argued that the idea of individuality sets the Renaissance apart from the Middle Ages. By the early twentieth century, medievalists had begun to attack this position. Most notably, Johan Huizinga argued for a medieval idea of individuality in his book, *The Waning of the Middle Ages*, where he also maintained that the Renaissance evolved directly from a decaying medieval civilization. In *The Renaissance of the Twelfth Century*, Charles Homer Haskins further undermined claims for the originality of the Italian Renaissance by identifying its antecedents in a medieval revival of classical literature and learning. This attack in particular forced Erwin Panofsky to reevaluate the Renaissance revival of antiquity, in order to distinguish it from its predecessors. In *Renaissance and Renascences in Western Art*, Panofsky basically refined Burckhardt's idea of individuality, using it to identify the unique nature of the Renaissance revival. The lineaments of our subtext are thus clear in Part I, which takes us from the Burckhardtian distinction between Renaissance and humanism toward their eventual reunion via Burckhardt's own central idea.

After having moved the classical revival back to center stage, we examine it more closely in Part II, "The Nature of Humanism." This part deals specifically with the humanist revival of classical language and literature that first suggested the notion of cultural rebirth. As we have already noted, nineteenth-century views of the Renaissance as "the discovery of the world and the discovery of man" tend to bathe humanism (a literary movement) in the diffuse light of *humanitas* (a reawakening of the human spirit). In the twentieth century, Paul Oskar Kristeller has been most responsible for restoring the original meaning of the term *humanism* as a literary curriculum. But his many essays on the subject, especially "Humanism and Scholasticism in the Italian Renaissance," have also sparked debate about the content and significance of that curriculum. Was it simply a phase in an ongoing Western rhetorical tradition extending back to the Middle Ages and antiquity, or did humanism signify the emergence of a new attitude toward the world? Whereas Kristeller tends toward the former opinion, Hanna H. Gray asserts the latter in her article, "Renaissance Humanism: The Pursuit of Eloquence," which finds the distinctive nature of humanism in its emphasis on the motive power of rhetoric. Charles Trinkaus and William J. Bouwsma elaborate the religious and philosophical content of humanist rhetoric in their respective works, *In Our Image and Likeness* and "The Two Faces of Humanism: Stoicism and Augustinianism in Renaissance Thought." And in "Book-Lined Cells: Women and Humanism in the Early Italian Renaissance," Margaret L. King shows how the nature of humanism was different for women than it was for men, despite their both practicing the same rhetorical art.

Burckhardt had attributed the advent of the Renaissance to the unique political situation in Italy. Part III, "Humanism and Politics," traces the fate of this interpretation in twentieth-century scholarship, which has given rise to the notion of "civic humanism." In *The Crisis of the Early Italian Renaissance*, Hans Baron describes the advent of civic humanism as the defining moment of the Renaissance, from which its originality and modernity stem. The influence of Baron's interpretation is arguably second only to Burckhardt's, and it has proven just as controversial. One of Baron's foremost critics, Jerrold E. Seigel, emphasizes the rhetorical over the civic aspects of humanism in his *Rhetoric and Philosophy in Renaissance Humanism*, where he describes civic themes as but a rhetorical adaptation to a republican audience. Quentin Skinner builds on this view in his *Foundations of Modern Political Thought*, where he also raises questions about the originality of the Renaissance by tracing civic themes back to the Middle Ages. And Anthony Grafton's "Humanism and Political Theory" sums up the debate over civic humanism and attempts to push beyond it, all the while asserting the fundamentally rhetorical nature of humanist political writings.

Parts II and III show how the study of humanism has become an arena for contentions about the originality of the Renaissance. In Part IV, "Humanism in Theory and Practice," we take a closer look at a distinctive feature of humanism—the ideal of *imitatio* (the imitation of classical models)—that has lately emerged as an element in the originality of the Renaissance. *Imitatio* is an especially important topic for modern readers, if only because the Renaissance notion of imitation is vastly different from our own. Thomas M. Greene's *The Light in Troy: Imitation and Discovery in Renaissance Poetry* shows how the most sophisticated forms of Renaissance imitation fostered self-expression, particularly as the humanists defined themselves over and against classical models from a lost culture. A sense of anachronism, of the differences between antiquity and modernity, is thus inherent in the humanist movement. Although humanism encouraged a new and more refined attitude toward the past, the system of education it inspired was anything but high-minded and sophisticated, as Anthony Grafton and Lisa Jardine argue in *From Humanism to the Humanities*. Here they show how humanist education emphasized the rote learning of classical Latin and the slavish following of classical models. Whereas Grafton and Jardine emphasize the instrumentalist nature of this educational system, which served the needs of the ruling elite, Paul F. Grendler sees higher ideals at work in his *Schooling in Renaissance Italy*.

The contrast between the theory and practice of humanism sets the stage for Part V, "Humanism and History," which recalls yet again Burckhardt's concept of individuality. As we have noted, the ideal of *imitatio* entails a sense of anachronism, an awareness of the differences between past and present. At the very least, this attitude spawned our now commonplace division of history into ancient, medieval, and modern periods, as Theodor E. Mommsen shows in "Petrarch's Conception of the 'Dark Ages'." And this attitude also engendered an acute sense of historical and cultural relativism, as Myron P. Gilmore shows in "The Renaissance Conception of the Lessons of History." But did the sense of relativism also bequeath our modern historical view of the world, as Donald R. Kelley maintains in "Guillaume Budé and the First Historical School of Law," or did it obstruct that view, as Zachary S. Schiffman argues in "Renaissance Historicism Reconsidered"? In wrestling with this question, we find ourselves ultimately grappling with Burckhardt, whose idea of individuality encompasses the notion of relativism. Here, in the topic of "Humanism and History," we once again confront the question of the originality of the Renaissance and its fundamentally Burckhardtian answer, revealed through the study of humanism.

PART

I Originality and Continuity in the Renaissance

At the sound of the word Renaissance *the dreamer of past beauty sees purple and gold. A festive world is bathed in mild clarity, rustling with sonorous tones. People move with grace and solemnity, untroubled by the distress of time and the beckonings of eternity. Everything is one ripe, full exuberance.*

The questioner says: Explain it in more detail. And the dreamer stammers: The Renaissance is altogether positive and it is undoubtedly in the key of C major. The questioner smiles. The dreamer recalls the things that he has learned determine the historical phenomenon we call the Renaissance . . . and half demurring, now that the terms force themselves upon him, he recites his credo. The Renaissance was the emergence of individualism, the awakening of the urge to beauty, the triumph of worldliness and joie de vivre, *the conquest of mundane reality by the mind, the revival of a pagan zest for life, the developing consciousness of the personality in its natural relation to the world.*

—Johan Huizinga, *"The Problem of the Renaissance"*

Huizinga's dreamer was Burckhardtian. In 1860, the Swiss art historian Jacob Burckhardt (1818–1897) published what is arguably the most influential of all cultural histories, *The Civilization of the*

Renaissance in Italy. At one and the same time, this work set the standard for the study of cultural history in general and of the Renaissance in particular. Its themes still resonate after almost 150 years and—regardless of Burckhardt's real intention—it remains the source for widespread preconceptions about the Renaissance as an age hued in purple and gold.

Unlike his teacher, the great "scientific" historian Leopold von Ranke (1795–1886), and in marked contrast to the vogue of Hegelian metahistory, Burckhardt sought to write cultural history, for which there existed no defined methodology. Thus, he refused to claim priority for his view of the Renaissance, which was simply a personal vision informed by his immersion in the literature, history, and art of the period. Yet this vision has attained great currency, in part because it presents so coherent a picture of the period. Between the opening section on politics and the concluding one on religion and morality lie sections on the development of the individual, the revival of antiquity, the discovery of the world and of man, and society and festivals. Inherent in the ordering of this six-part tableau is a simple but profound argument: that the dynamic political environment of an Italy filled with small, independent city-states fostered the development of the individual, marking the Renaissance Italian as "the first-born among the sons of modern Europe." The union of this distinctively Italian characteristic with the revival of antiquity constituted a cultural force that swept through the Western world, clearing the way for modernity.

Late nineteenth and early twentieth-century scholars subsequently explored the consequences of the Italian Renaissance for the countries of northern Europe, principally France, England, and Germany. They explained how the northward spread of the Renaissance, which altered its character with differing national circumstances, everywhere brought the Middle Ages to a close in the sixteenth century. Despite occasional dissenters, who traced the origins of the Renaissance to medieval and Christian roots, its status as the birthplace of modernity remained unquestioned until the Dutch-born Johan Huizinga (1872–1945) began to blur the dividing line between the death of the old civilization and the birth of the new one.

After Burckhardt, Huizinga is the most distinguished cultural historian of the modern era. Trained as a linguist and Sanskritist, he taught high school for a time in Haarlem, before eventually becoming a professor of history at the University of Leiden. Haarlem, with its visible medieval heritage, sparked a shift in Huizinga's interest from Indian to medieval civilization, a reorientation brought to fruition in his best-known work, *The Waning of the Middle Ages* (1919). Huizinga was inspired to write this book by the art of the brothers Van Eyck, whose intense realism and this-worldliness was traditionally regarded as a harbinger of the Renaissance in the north. Huizinga took an altogether different view, seeing in the intensity of their realism—they resolved every scene into its tiniest detail— a symptom of a medieval civilization in the advanced stages of decay. This insight suggested to Huizinga that much of what appears in the Renaissance as the birth of the new is really the death of the old, and that Renaissance is thus separated from Middle Ages not by some dramatic change in sensibility but by nuance only.

He explored this theme with reference to fourteenth- and fifteenth-century France, in particular the Duchy of Burgundy and its rich patrimony, Flanders. After Italy, Flanders was the most urbanized and wealthy region of Europe, a fact that supposedly accounted for its being in the vanguard of the Northern Renaissance. Indeed, in their chivalric ideals, the Burgundians evince for Huizinga a refined sense of individual glory and a love of antiquity that cedes nothing to the Italians, yet these very qualities stand in evidence of cultural decline, not renewal. By revealing the fundamentally medieval character of this vibrant urban culture, Huizinga implicitly undercut the Burckhardtian Renaissance's claim to originality.

Even more so than Huizinga, the American Charles Homer Haskins (1870–1937) popularized the idea of the continuity between Middle Ages and Renaissance in his famous work, *The Renaissance of the Twelfth Century* (1927). Indeed Haskins, who taught at both Johns Hopkins University and Harvard University, was a leading figure in what is sometimes termed "the revolt of the medievalists," who began to claim for their period much of the innovation that Burckhardt and his followers had attributed to the Renaissance. In *The Renaissance of the Twelfth Century,* Haskins decisively challenged the widespread notion that the Middle Ages knew little of classical learning and Latin style, which had previously been regarded as the province and preserve of the Italian humanists. Instead, Haskins details an extensive intellectual revival—encompassing classical and

contemporary Latin literature, law, history, science, and philosophy—at least as significant as that of the Italian Renaissance. Here
in the twelfth century lies the source of Huizinga's late medieval
classicism, from which Renaissance humanism would emerge like
a butterfly from its chrysalis.

Ninth-century Carolingian Renaissance, tenth-century Ottonian
Renaissance, twelfth-century Renaissance, Italian Renaissance—
Haskins acknowledged the bewildering proliferation of "renaissances" without distinguishing between them and without calling
the use of the term into question. Nor should he have. It was sufficient for him to study one of them—too long unappreciated—and
to reveal its affinities with the Italian one. Yet a logical problem
arises with the growing awareness of cultural continuity: if Italian
developments owe much to those of the twelfth century, does all
innovation stop here, or should we attribute twelfth-century developments to those of the tenth and, ultimately, ninth century? Is there
some ruling distinction between these phenomena, enabling us to
speak of *the* Renaissance (wherever one might care to locate it), or
are they akin to a series of cultural waves, distinct in time and space
but not in substance?

Erwin Panofsky (1892–1968), regarded by many as the foremost
art historian of the twentieth century, set for himself the task of distinguishing the Italian Renaissance from its predecessors. A professor of art history at the University of Hamburg, Panofsky rejected the
traditional stylistic approach to art and, instead, favored the use of
historical and anthropological techniques to show how art fit into a
culture and how a culture could produce the art it did. When Hitler
came to power, Panofsky fled to the United States, where he eventually became a member of Princeton's Institute for Advanced Study.

In the volume *Renaissance and Renascences in Western Art*
(1960), Panofsky brought together several essays about the distinctiveness of the Italian Renaissance as a cultural period. In the first
essay, he defends the concept of the Renaissance against growing
skepticism about the utility of historical periodization, a skepticism
deriving principally from the revolt of the medievalists and the subsequent proliferation of renaissances. He argues that the early humanists originated the idea of a cultural revival in literature, that they
soon extended the notion to art, and that we cannot blithely dismiss
this self-definition. Were they deluding themselves? Panofsky lays

this question to rest in the second essay, where he describes how the Renaissance made the whole of antiquity a permanent part of our cultural heritage, whereas previous revivals were limited in scope and duration. The notion of the Renaissance revival of art initially meant a return to nature, and in the third essay Panofsky relates this notion to the development of the idea of perspective in fourteenth-century Italian painting. In the final essay, he shows how the new perspectival art became joined with classical themes in the fifteenth century, evoking a distinctively modern nostalgia for antiquity. Thus, in the very act of resurrecting the whole of antiquity, *the* Renaissance engendered the realization that its beloved model was forever more dead and buried.

Jacob Burckhardt

The Civilization of the Renaissance in Italy

Burckhardt begins by declaring his work an "essay," a trial or attempt, and acknowledging that other forays into this complex subject would yield different interpretations. At the same time, he pleads that his six-part essay be judged as an organic whole. Unfortunately, the size and scope of the current work do not permit our honoring that plea, and we must limit ourselves to the argument laid out in the first three parts.

Although the term *Renaissance* signifies the "rebirth" of classical culture embodied in the humanist movement, Burckhardt launches the first part of his essay with an altogether different phenomenon, which he epitomizes as *der Staat als Kunstwerk*, "the state as a work of art." The term *Kunstwerk* denotes an artifice, like a clock, the creation of human calculation. Through the very structure of his work, Burckhardt thus pushes the revival of antiquity into the background and, instead, foregrounds the distinctive

From Jacob Burckhardt, *The Civilization of the Renaissance in Italy*. Intro. Benjamin Nelson and Charles Trinkaus. 2 vols. (New York: Harper & Row, 1958).

political situation in Italy, the cauldron of endlessly competing city-states and factions within cities, from which the culture of the Renaissance bubbled to the surface.

Still holding the revival of antiquity in the background, Burckhardt next showcases the "Development of the Individual" in the second part. This is the most controversial and misunderstood aspect of his thesis. To avoid confusion, we must distinguish between the modern notion of "individualism," embracing one's economic and social self-interest, and Burckhardt's notion of "individuality" as an enlivened sense of one's own uniqueness. Although the Renaissance sense of individuality was often accompanied by self-interested (if not willful) behavior, it did not point toward a doctrine of freedom from constraint but rather toward a fascination with a world filled with uniqueness. Burckhardt expressed the Renaissance appreciation of personal uniqueness in the now classic formulation, "man became a spiritual individual [*geistiges Individuum*] and recognized himself as such." The *geistiges Individuum* was an individual defined as such by the conception he had of himself as a distinct personality. Implicitly, this sense of one's own uniqueness extended to that of other individuals and entities in the world. Burckhardt signifies this extended meaning of the term by frequently employing the neuter form *das Individuelle* as he describes the individualizing perceptions of people conscious of their own uniqueness.

Only after exploring the consequences of Italian politics for the sense of individuality does Burckhardt finally arrive, in the third part, at a consideration of the "new birth" of antiquity, "which has been one-sidedly chosen as the name to sum up the whole period." In a remarkably subtle observation, he asserts that the general characteristics we associate with the Renaissance could have occurred entirely apart from a revival of antiquity, but he allows that it is only with and through this revival that these characteristics have manifested themselves to us.

Part I: The State as a Work of Art

. . . The struggle between the Popes and the Hohenstaufen left Italy in a political condition which differed essentially from that of other countries of the West. While in France, Spain, and England the feudal system was so organized that at the close of its existence it was naturally transformed into a unified monarchy, and while in Germany it helped to maintain, at least outwardly, the unity of the Empire, Italy had shaken it off almost entirely. The Emperors of the fourteenth century, even in the most favourable case, were no longer received and respected as feudal lords, but as possible leaders and supporters of powers already in existence; while the Papacy, with its creatures and allies, was strong enough to hinder national unity in the future, [it was] not strong enough itself to bring about that unity. Between the two lay a multitude of political units—republics and despots—in part of long standing, in part of recent origin, whose existence was founded simply on their power to maintain it. In them for the first time we detect the modern political spirit of Europe, surrendered freely to its own instincts, often displaying the worst features of an unbridled egoism, outraging every right, and killing every germ of a healthier culture. But wherever this vicious tendency is overcome or in any way compensated a new fact appears in history—the State as the outcome of reflection and calculation, the State as a work of art. This new life displays itself in a hundred forms, both in the republican and in the despotic states, and determines their inward constitution no less than their foreign policy. We shall limit ourselves to the consideration of the completer and more clearly defined type, which is offered by the despotic states. . . .

The Tyranny of the Fourteenth Century

. . . The deliberate adaptation of means to ends, of which no prince out of Italy had at that time a conception, joined to almost absolute power within the limits of the state, produced among the despots both men and modes of life of a peculiar character. The chief secret of government in the hands of the prudent ruler lay in leaving the incidence of taxation so far as possible where he found it, or as he had first arranged it. The chief sources of income were a land-tax, based on a valuation; definite taxes on articles of consumption and duties on exported and imported goods; together with the private fortune of the ruling house. The only possible increase was derived from the growth of business and of general prosperity. Loans, such as we find in the free cities, were here unknown; a well-planned confiscation was held a preferable means of raising money, provided only that it left public credit unshaken—an end attained, for example, by the truly Oriental practice of deposing and plundering the director of finances.

Out of this income the expenses of the little Court, of the bodyguard, of the mercenary troops, and of the public buildings were met, as well as of the buffoons and men of talent who belonged to the personal attendants of the prince. The illegitimacy of his rule isolated the tyrant and surrounded him with constant danger; the most honourable alliance which he could form was with intellectual merit, without regard to its origin. The liberality of the Northern princes of the thirteenth century was confined to the knights, to the nobility which served and sang. It was otherwise with the Italian despot. With his thirst for fame and his passion for monumental works it was talent, not birth, which he needed. In the company of the poet and the scholar he felt himself in a new position — almost, indeed, in possession of a new legitimacy. . . .

But whatever might be the brighter sides of the system, and the merits of individual rulers, yet the men of the fourteenth century were not without a more or less distinct consciousness of the brief and uncertain tenure of most of these despotisms. Inasmuch as political institutions like these are naturally secure in proportion to the size of the territory in which they exist, the larger principalities were constantly tempted to swallow up the smaller. Whole hecatombs of petty rulers were sacrificed at this time to the Visconti alone. As a result of this outward danger an inward ferment was in ceaseless activity; and the effect of the situation on the character of the ruler was generally of the most sinister kind. Absolute power, with its temptations to luxury and unbridled selfishness, and the perils to which he was exposed from enemies and conspirators, turned him almost inevitably into a tyrant in the worst sense of the word. Well for him if he could trust his nearest relations! But where all was illegitimate there could be no regular law of inheritance, either with regard to succession or to the division of the ruler's property; and consequently the heir, if incompetent or a minor, was liable in the interest of the family itself to be supplanted by an uncle or cousin of more resolute character. The acknowledgment or exclusion of the bastards was a fruitful source of contest; and most of these families in consequence were plagued with a crowd of discontented and vindictive kinsmen. This circumstance gave rise to continual outbreaks of treason and to frightful scenes of domestic bloodshed. . . .

The most complete and instructive type of the tyranny of the fourteenth century is to be found unquestionably among the Visconti of Milan, from the death of the Archbishop Giovanni onward (1354). The family likeness which shows itself between Bernabò and the worst of the Roman Emperors is unmistakable; the most important public object was the prince's boar-hunting; whoever interfered with it was put to death with torture; the terrified people were forced to maintain five thousand boar-hounds, with strict responsibility for their health and safety. The taxes were extorted by every conceivable sort of compulsion; seven daughters of the prince received a dowry of 100,000 gold florins apiece; and an enormous treasure was collected. On the death of his wife (1384) an order was issued "to the subjects" to share his grief, as once they had shared his joy, and to wear mourning for a year. The *coup de main* (1385) by which his nephew Giangaleazzo got him into his power—one of those brilliant plots which make the heart of even late historians beat more quickly—was strikingly characteristic of the man. Giangaleazzo, despised by his relations on account of his religion and love of science, resolved on vengeance, and, leaving the city under pretext of a pilgrimage, fell upon his unsuspecting uncle, took him prisoner, forced his way back into the city at the head of an armed band, seized on the government, and gave up the palace of Bernabò to general plunder.

In Giangaleazzo that passion for the colossal which was common to most of the despots shows itself on the largest scale. He undertook, at the cost of 300,000 golden florins, the construction of gigantic dikes, to divert in case of need the Mincio from Mantua and the Brenta from Padua, and thus to render these cities defenceless. It is not impossible, indeed, that he thought of draining away the lagoons of Venice. He founded that most wonderful of all convents, the Certosa of Pavia, and the cathedral of Milan, "which exceeds in size and splendour all the churches of Christendom." The palace in Pavia, which his father Galeazzo began, and which he himself finished, was probably by far the most magnificent of the princely dwellings of Europe. There he transferred his famous library and the great collection of relics of the saints, in which he placed a peculiar faith. King Winceslaus made him Duke (1395); he was hoping for nothing less than the kingdom of Italy or the Imperial crown, when (1402) he fell ill and died. His whole territories are said to have paid him in a single year, besides the regular contribution of 1,200,000 gold florins, no less than 800,000 more in extraordinary subsidies. After his death the dominions which he had brought together by every sort of violence fell to pieces; and for a time even the original nucleus could with difficulty be maintained by his successors. What might have become of his sons Giovanni Maria (d. 1412) and Filippo Maria (d. 1417), had they lived in a different country and among other traditions, cannot be said. But as heirs of their house they inherited that monstrous capital of cruelty and cowardice which had been accumulated from generation to generation.

Giovanni Maria, too, is famed for his dogs, which were no longer, however, used for hunting, but for tearing human bodies. Tradition has

preserved their names, like those of the bears of the Emperor Valentin-
ian I. In May 1409, when war was going on, and the starving populace
cried to him in the streets, "*Pace! Pace!*" he let loose his mercenaries
upon them, and two hundred lives were sacrificed; under penalty of the
gallows it was forbidden to utter the words *pace* and *guerra*, and the
priests were ordered, instead of *dona nobis pacem*, to say *tranquillitatem*!
At last a band of conspirators took advantage of the moment when
Facino Cane, the chief *condottiere* of the insane ruler, lay ill at Pavia,
and cut down Giovanni Maria in the church of S. Gottardo at Milan;
the dying Facino on the same day made his officers swear to stand by
the heir Filippo Maria, whom he himself urged his wife to take for a
second husband. His wife, Beatrice di Tenda, followed his advice. We
shall have occasion to speak of Filippo Maria later on.

And in times like these Cola di Rienzi was dreaming of founding
on the rickety enthusiasm of the corrupt population of Rome a new
state which was to comprise all Italy. By the side of rulers such as those
whom we have described he seems no better than a poor deluded fool.

The Tyranny of the Fifteenth Century

The despotisms of the fifteenth century show an altered character.
Many of the less important tyrants, and some of the greater, like the
Scala and the Carrara, had disappeared, while the more powerful ones,
aggrandized by conquest, had given to their systems each its characteristic development. Naples, for example, received a fresh and stronger
impulse from the new Aragonese dynasty. A striking feature of this
epoch is the attempt of the *condottieri* to found independent dynasties
of their own. Facts and the actual relations of things, apart from traditional estimates, are alone regarded; talent and audacity win the great
prizes. The petty despots, to secure a trustworthy support, begin to enter
the service of the larger states, and become themselves *condottieri*, receiving in return for their services money and impunity for their mis-
deeds, if not an increase of territory. All, whether small or great, must
exert themselves more, must act with greater caution and calculation,
and must learn to refrain from too wholesale barbarities; only so much
wrong is permitted by public opinion as is necessary for the end in view,
and this the impartial bystander certainly finds no fault with. No trace
is here visible of that half-religious loyalty by which the legitimate
princes of the West were supported; personal popularity is the nearest

approach we can find to it. Talent and calculation are the only means of advancement. A character like that of Charles the Bold, which wore itself out in the passionate pursuit of impracticable ends, was a riddle to the Italian. . . .

Good and evil lie strangely mixed together in the Italian states of the fifteenth century. The personality of the ruler is so highly developed, often of such deep significance, and so characteristic of the conditions and needs of the time that to form an adequate moral judgment on it is no easy task.

The foundation of the system was and remained illegitimate, and nothing could remove the curse which rested upon it. The Imperial approval or investiture made no change in the matter, since the people attached little weight to the fact that the despot had bought a piece of parchment somewhere in foreign countries, or from some stranger passing through his territory. If the Emperor had been good for anything—so ran the logic of uncritical common sense—he would never have let the tyrant rise at all. Since the Roman expedition of Charles IV the Emperors had done nothing more in Italy than sanction a tyranny which had arisen without their help; they could give it no other practical authority than what might flow from an Imperial charter. . . .

Closely connected with the political illegitimacy of the dynasties of the fifteenth century was the public indifference to legitimate birth, which to foreigners—for example, to Comines—appeared so remarkable. The two things went naturally together. In Northern countries, as in Burgundy, the illegitimate offspring were provided for by a distinct class of appanages, such as bishoprics and the like; in Portugal an illegitimate line maintained itself on the throne only by constant effort; in Italy, on the contrary, there no longer existed a princely house where, even in the direct line of descent, bastards were not patiently tolerated. . . . The bastards were often admitted to the succession where the lawful children were minors and the dangers of the situation were pressing; and a rule of seniority became recognized which took no account of pure or impure birth. The fitness of the individual, his worth and his capacity, were of more weight than all the laws and usages which prevailed elsewhere in the West. It was the age, indeed, in which the sons of the Popes were founding dynasties. . . .

But the highest and the most admired form of illegitimacy in the fifteenth century was presented by the *condottiere*, who, whatever may have been his origin, raised himself to the position of an independent ruler. At bottom, the occupation of Lower Italy by the Normans in the eleventh century was of this character. Such attempts now began to keep the peninsula in a constant ferment.

It was possible for a *condottiere* to obtain the lordship of a district even without usurpation, in the case where his employer, through want of money or troops, provided for him in this way; under any circumstances the *condottiere*, even when he dismissed for the time the greater part of his forces, needed a safe place where he could establish his winter quarters and lay up his stores and provisions. The first example of a captain thus portioned is John Hawkwood, who was invested by Gregory XI with the lordship of Bagnacavallo and Cotignola. When with Alberigo da Barbiano Italian armies and leaders appeared upon the scene the chances of founding a principality, or of increasing one already acquired, became more frequent. The first great bacchanalian outbreak of military ambition took place in the duchy of Milan after the death of Giangaleazzo (1402). The policy of his two sons was chiefly aimed at the destruction of the new despotisms founded by the *condottieri*; and from the greatest of them, Facino Cane, the house of Visconti inherited, together with his widow, a long list of cities, and 400,000 golden florins, not to speak of the soldiers of her first husband whom Beatrice di Tenda brought with her. From henceforth that thoroughly immoral relation between the Governments and their *condottieri* which is characteristic of the fifteenth century became more and more common. An old story—one of those which are true and not true, everywhere and nowhere—describes it as follows. The citizens of a certain town (Siena seems to be meant) had once an officer in their service who had freed them from foreign aggression; daily they took counsel how to recompense him, and concluded that no reward in their power was great enough, not even if they made him lord of the city. At last one of them rose and said, "Let us kill him and then worship him as our patron saint." And so they did, following the example set by the Roman Senate with Romulus. In fact, the *condottieri* had reason to fear none so much as their employers; if they were successful they became dangerous, and were put out of the way like Roberto Malatesta just after the victory he had won for Sixtus IV (1482); if they failed the vengeance of the Venetians on Carmagnola showed to what risks they were exposed (1432). It is characteristic of the moral aspect of the situation that the *condottieri* had often to give their wives and children as hostages and, notwithstanding this, neither felt nor inspired confidence. They must have been heroes of abnegation, natures like Belisarius himself, not to be cankered by hatred and bitterness; only the most perfect goodness could save them from the most monstrous iniquity. No wonder then if we find them full of contempt for all sacred things, cruel and treacherous to their fellows—men who cared nothing whether or no they died under the ban of the Church. At the same time, and through the force of the same conditions, the genius and capacity of many among them attained the highest conceivable development, and won for them the admiring devotion of their followers; their armies are the first in modern history in which the personal credit of the leader is the one moving power. . . .

The Greater Dynasties

. . . The despotism of the Dukes of Milan, whose government from the time of Giangaleazzo onward was an absolute monarchy of the most thoroughgoing sort, shows the genuine Italian character of the fifteenth century. The last of the Visconti, Filippo Maria (1412–47), is a character of peculiar interest, and of which fortunately an admirable description has been left us. What a man of uncommon gifts and high position can be made by the passion of fear is here shown with what may be called a mathematical completeness. All the resources of the State were devoted to the one end of securing his personal safety, though happily his cruel egoism did not degenerate into a purposeless thirst for blood. He lived in the citadel of Milan, surrounded by magnificent gardens, arbours, and lawns. For years he never set foot in the city, making his excursions only in the country, where lay several of his splendid castles; the flotilla which, drawn by the swiftest horses, conducted him to them along canals constructed for the purpose was so arranged as to allow of the application of the most rigorous etiquette. Whoever entered the citadel was watched by a hundred eyes; it was forbidden even to stand at the window, lest signs should be given to those without. All who were admitted among the personal followers of the Prince were subjected to a series of the strictest examinations; then, once accepted, were charged with the highest diplomatic commissions, as well as with the humblest personal services—both in this Court being alike honourable. And this was the man who conducted long and difficult wars, who dealt habitually with political affairs of the first importance, and every day sent his plenipotentiaries to all parts of Italy. His safety lay in the fact that none of his servants trusted the others, that his *condottieri* were watched and misled by spies, and that the ambassadors and higher officials were baffled and kept apart by artificially nourished jealousies, and in particular by the device of coupling an honest man with a knave. His inward faith too rested upon opposed and contradictory systems; he believed in blind necessity, and in the influence of the stars, and offering prayers at one and the same time to helpers of every sort; he was a student of the ancient authors, as well as of French tales of chivalry. And yet the same man, who would never suffer death to be mentioned in his presence, and caused his dying favourites to be removed from the castle, that no shadow might fall on the abode of happiness, deliberately hastened his own death by closing up a wound, and, refusing to be bled, died at last with dignity and grace.

His stepson and successor, the fortunate *condottiere* Francesco Sforza (1450–66), was perhaps of all the Italians of the fifteenth century the man most after the heart of his age. Never was the triumph of genius and individual power more brilliantly displayed than in him; and those who would not recognize his merit were at least forced to wonder at him as the spoilt child of fortune. The Milanese claimed it openly as an honour to be governed by so distinguished a master; when he entered the city the thronging populace bore him on horseback into the cathedral, without giving him the chance to dismount. Let us listen to the balance-sheet of his life, in the estimate of Pope Pius II, a judge in such matters:

> In 1459, when the Duke came to the congress at Mantua, he was sixty *[really fifty-eight]* years old; on horseback he looked like a young man; of a lofty and imposing figure, with serious features, calm and affable in conversation, princely in his whole bearing, with a combination of bodily and intellectual gifts unrivalled in our time, unconquered on the field of battle—such was the man who raised himself from a humble position to the control of an empire. His wife was beautiful and virtuous, his children were like the angels of heaven; he was seldom ill, and all his chief wishes were fulfilled. And yet he was not without misfortune. His wife, out of jealousy, killed his mistress; his old comrades and friends, Troilo and Brunoro, abandoned him and went over to King Alfonso; another, Ciarpollone, he was forced to hang for treason; he had to suffer it that his brother Alessandro set the French upon him; one of his sons formed intrigues against him, and was imprisoned; the March of Ancona, which he had won in war, he lost again in the same way. No man enjoys so unclouded a fortune that he has not somewhere to struggle with adversity. He is happy who has but few troubles.

With this negative definition of happiness the learned Pope dismisses the reader. Had he been able to see into the future, or been willing to stop and discuss the consequences of an uncontrolled despotism, one pervading fact would not have escaped his notice—the absence of all guarantee for the future. . . .

Part II: The Development of the Individual

In the character of these states, whether republics or despotisms, lies not the only but the chief reason for the early development of the Italian. To this it is due that he was the first-born among the sons of modern Europe.

In the Middle Ages both sides of human consciousness—that which was turned within as that which was turned without—lay dreaming or half awake beneath a common veil. The veil was woven of faith, illusion, and childish prepossession, through which the world and history were seen clad in strange hues. Man was conscious of himself only as a member of a race, people, party, family, or corporation—only through some general category. In Italy this veil first melted into air; an *objective* treatment and consideration of the State and of all the things of this world became possible. The *subjective* side at the same time asserted itself with corresponding emphasis; man became a spiritual *individual* [*geistiges Individuum*], and recognized himself as such. In the same way the Greek had once distinguished himself from the barbarian, and the Arabian had felt himself an individual at a time when other Asiatics knew themselves only as members of a race. It will not be difficult to show that this result was owing, above all, to the political circumstances of Italy.

In far earlier times we can here and there detect a development of free personality which in Northern Europe either did not occur at all or could not display itself in the same manner. The band of audacious wrongdoers in the sixteenth century described to us by Luidprand, some of the contemporaries of Gregory VII, and a few of the opponents of the first Hohenstaufen, show us characters of this kind. But at the close of the thirteenth century Italy began to swarm with individuality; the charm laid upon human personality was dissolved, and a thousand figures meet us each in its own special shape and dress. Dante's great poem would have been impossible in any other country of Europe, if only for the reason that they all still lay under the spell of race. For Italy the august poet, through the wealth of individuality [*die Fülle des Individuellen*] which he set forth, was the most national herald of his time. But this unfolding of the treasures of human nature in literature and art—this many-sided representation and criticism—will be discussed in separate chapters; here we have to deal only with the psychological fact itself. This fact appears in the most decisive and unmistakable form. The Italians of the fourteenth century knew little of false modesty or of hypocrisy in any shape; not one of them was afraid of singularity, of being and seeming unlike his neighbours.

Despotism, as we have already seen, fostered in the highest degree the individuality not only of the tyrant or *condottiere* himself, but also of the men whom he protected or used as his tools—the secretary, minister, poet, and companion. These people were forced to know all the inward resources of their own nature, passing or permanent; and their enjoyment of life was enhanced and concentrated by the desire to obtain the greatest satisfaction from a possibly very brief period of power and influence.

But even the subjects whom they ruled over were not free from the same impulse. Leaving out of account those who wasted their lives in secret opposition and conspiracies, we speak of the majority who were content with a strictly private station, like most of the urban population of the Byzantine Empire and the Mohammedan states. No doubt it was often hard for the subjects of a Visconti to maintain the dignity of their persons and families, and multitudes must have lost in moral character through the servitude they lived under. But this was not the case with regard to individuality; for political impotence does not hinder the different tendencies and manifestations of private life from thriving in the fullest vigour and variety. Wealth and culture, so far as display and rivalry were not forbidden to them, a municipal freedom which did not cease to be considerable, and a Church which, unlike that of the Byzantine or of the Mohammedan world, was not identical with the State—all these conditions undoubtedly favoured the growth of individual thought, for which the necessary leisure was furnished by the cessation of party conflicts. The private man, indifferent to politics, and busied partly with serious pursuits, partly with the interests of a *dilettante*, seems to have been first fully formed in these despotisms of the fourteenth century. Documentary evidence cannot, of course, be required on such a point. The novelists, from whom we might expect information, describe to us oddities in plenty, but only from one point of view and in so far as the needs of the story demand. Their scene, too, lies chiefly in the republican cities.

In the latter circumstances were also, but in another way, favourable to the growth of individual character. The more frequently the governing party was changed, the more the individual was led to make the utmost of the exercise and enjoyment of power. The statesmen and popular leaders, especially in Florentine history, acquired so marked a personal character that we can scarcely find, even exceptionally, a parallel to them in contemporary history, hardly even in Jacob van Artevelde.

The members of the defeated parties, on the other hand, often came into a position like that of the subjects of the despotic states, with the difference that the freedom or power already enjoyed, and in some cases the hope of recovering them, gave a higher energy to their individuality. Among these men of involuntary leisure we find, for instance, an Agnolo Pandolfini (d. 1446), whose work on domestic economy is the first complete programme of a developed private life. His estimate of the duties of the individual as against the dangers and thanklessness of public life is in its way a true monument of the age.

Banishment too has this effect above all, that it either wears the exile out or develops whatever is greatest in him. "In all our more populous cities," says Gioviano Pontano, "we see a crowd of people who have left their homes of their own free-will; but a man takes his virtues with him wherever he goes." And, in fact, they were by no means only men who had been actually exiled, but thousands left their native place voluntarily, because they found its political or economical condition intolerable. The Florentine emigrants at Ferrara and the Lucchese in Venice formed whole colonies by themselves.

The cosmopolitanism which grew up in the most gifted circles is in itself a high stage of individualism. Dante, as we have already said, finds a new home in the language and culture of Italy, but goes beyond even this in the words "My country is the whole world!" And when his recall to Florence was offered him on unworthy conditions he wrote back: "Can I not everywhere behold the light of the sun and the stars; everywhere meditate on the noblest truths, without appearing ingloriously and shamefully before the city and the people? Even my bread will not fail me!" The artists exult no less defiantly in their freedom from the constraints of fixed residence. "Only he who has learned everything," says Ghiberti, "is nowhere a stranger; robbed of his fortune and without friends, he is yet the citizen of every country, and can fearlessly despise the changes of fortune." In the same strain an exiled humanist writes: "Wherever a learned man fixes his seat there is home."

Part III: The Revival of Antiquity

Now that this point in our historical view of Italian civilization has been reached it is time to speak of the influence of antiquity, the "new birth" of which has been one-sidedly chosen as the name to sum up the whole period. The conditions which have been hitherto described would have sufficed, apart from antiquity, to upturn and to mature the national mind; and most of the intellectual tendencies which yet remain to be noticed would be conceivable without it. But both what has gone before and what we have still to discuss are coloured in a thousand ways by the influence of the ancient world; and though the essence of the phenomena might still have been the same without the classical revival, it is only with and through this revival that they are actually manifested to us. The Renaissance would not have been the process of world-wide significance which it is if its elements could be so easily separated from one another. We must insist upon it, as one of the chief propositions of this book, that it was not the revival of antiquity alone, but its union with the genius of the Italian people, which achieved the conquest of the Western world. The amount of independence which the national spirit maintained in this union varied according to circumstances. In the modern Latin literature of the period it is very small, while in plastic art, as well as in other spheres, it is remarkably great; and hence the alliance between two distant epochs in the civilization of the same people, because concluded on equal terms, proved justifiable and fruitful. The rest of Europe was free either to repel or else partly or wholly to accept the mighty impulse which came forth from Italy. Where the latter was the case we may as well be spared the complaints over the early decay of medieval faith and civilization. Had these been strong enough to hold their ground they would be alive to this day. If those elegiac natures which long to see them return could pass but one hour in the midst of them they would gasp to be back in modern air. That in a great historical process of this kind flowers of exquisite beauty may perish without being made immortal in poetry or tradition is undoubtedly true; nevertheless, we cannot wish the process undone. The general result of it consists in this—that by the side of the Church, which had hitherto held the countries of the West together (though it was unable to do so much longer), there arose a new spiritual influence, which, spreading itself abroad from Italy, became the breath of life for all the more instructed minds in Europe. The worst that can be said of the movement is that it was antipopular, that through it Europe became for the first time sharply divided into the cultivated and uncultivated classes. The reproach will appear groundless when we reflect that even now the fact, though clearly recognized, cannot be altered. The separation, too, is by no means as cruel and absolute in Italy as elsewhere. The most artistic of her poets, Tasso, is in the hands of even the poorest.

The civilization of Greece and Rome, which ever since the fourteenth century obtained so powerful a hold on Italian life, as the source and basis of culture, as the object and ideal of existence, partly also as an avowed reaction against preceding tendencies—this civilization had long been exerting a partial influence on medieval Europe, even beyond the boundaries of Italy. The culture of which Charles the Great was a representative was, in the face of the barbarism of the seventh and eighth centuries, essentially a Renaissance, and could appear under no other form. Just as in the Romanesque architecture of the North, beside the general outlines inherited from antiquity, remarkable direct imitations of the antique also occur, so too monastic scholarship had not only gradually absorbed an immense mass of materials from Roman writers, but the style of it, from the days of Eginhard onward, shows traces of conscious imitations.

But the resuscitation of antiquity took a different form in Italy from that which it assumed in the North. The wave of barbarism had scarcely gone by before the people, in whom the former life was but half effaced, showed a consciousness of its past and a wish to reproduce it. Elsewhere in Europe men deliberately and with reflection borrowed this or the other element of classical civilization; in Italy the sympathies both of the learned and of the people were naturally engaged on the side of antiquity as a whole, which stood to them as a symbol of past greatness. The Latin language, too, was easy to an Italian, and the numerous monuments and documents in which the country abounded facilitated a return to the past. With this tendency other elements—the popular character, which time had now greatly modified, the political institutions imported by the Lombards from Germany, chivalry and other

Northern forms of civilization, and the influence of religion and the Church—combined to produce the modern Italian spirit, which was destined to serve as the model and ideal for the whole Western world. . . .

But the great and general enthusiasm of the Italians for classical antiquity did not display itself before the fourteenth century. For this a development of civic life was required, which took place only in Italy, and there not till then. It was needful that noble and burgher should first learn to dwell together on equal terms, and that a social world should arise which felt the want of culture, and had the leisure and the means to obtain it. But culture, as soon as it freed itself from the fantastic bonds of the Middle Ages, could not at once and without help find its way to the understanding of the physical and intellectual world. It needed a guide, and found one in the ancient civilization, with its wealth of truth and knowledge in every spiritual interest. Both the form and the substance of this civilization were adopted with admiring gratitude; it became the chief part of the culture of the age. The general condition of the country was favourable to this transformation. The medieval Empire, since the fall of the Hohenstaufen, had either renounced, or was unable to make good, its claims on Italy. The Popes had migrated to Avignon. Most of the political Powers actually in existence owed their origin to violent and illegitimate means. The spirit of the people, now awakened to self-consciousness, sought for some new and stable ideal on which to rest. And thus the vision of the world-wide empire of Italy and Rome so possessed the popular mind that Cola di Rienzi could actually attempt to put it into practice. The conception he formed of his task, particularly when tribune for the first time, could end only in some extravagant comedy; nevertheless, the memory of ancient Rome was no slight support to the national sentiment. Armed afresh with its culture, the Italian soon felt himself in truth citizen of the most advanced nation in the world. . . .

Johan Huizinga

The Waning of the Middle Ages

Huizinga supervised the publication of an English translation and adaptation of *The Waning of the Middle Ages* in 1924. Although a new English translation, entitled *The Autumn of the Middle Ages* (1996), is more faithful to the letter of the Dutch original, we have utilized the 1924 edition, which better captures the lyrical spirit of Huizinga's writing. Those sufficiently intrigued by this spirit to undertake a detailed analysis of the work can consult the more precise (though less elegant) 1996 translation.

The book begins with a remarkable chapter on "The Violent Tenor of Life," which opens with the memorable line, "To the world when it was half a thousand years younger, the outlines of all things seemed more clearly marked than to us." Here Huizinga describes the "childlike" intensity of medieval experience, in which pleasure is always followed by pain (never, for example, by simple contentment). Subsequent chapters develop the ideal of the sublime life as the antidote to harsh realities, where the dream of the sublime took various forms, including the quest for personal glory and the veneration of antiquity. Our first selection is from this portion of the book, where Huizinga presents a counterpoise to Burckhardt's "development of the individual," for in the waning Middle Ages we find lives as self-consciously composed as any Renaissance Italian's.

The theme of the sublime life, developed through several chapters, ends abruptly with a consideration of "The Vision of Death," which tends toward the "macabre" (a word coined in fourteenth-century France). Vivid portrayals of suffering, death, and decay set the stage for Huizinga's consideration of religious thought, which treats the hypertrophy of Christian symbolism in the late Middle Ages, where even the most humble objects and practices of daily life have symbolic significance. After detailing the stultifying superabundance of religious images, Huizinga discusses the paintings of the brothers Van Eyck, showing how the hypertrophy of symbolic images in literature has its visual counterpoint in the hyper-detailed art of the period.

From Johan Huizinga, *The Waning of the Middle Ages* (Garden City, N.Y.: Doubleday & Co., 1954).

In the closing chapter, "The Advent of a New Form," excerpted in our second selection, Huizinga subtly undercuts the distinctiveness of Italian Renaissance developments in his discussion of the emergence of northern humanism. He admits that Italians lived in closer proximity to ancient culture and were thus better positioned to resurrect its spirit. But he cautions that this situation obscures the medieval aspects of their civilization, which lay just below the surface. In northern Europe, by contrast, medieval forms persisted more visibly, encrusting a deep and abiding classicism. That classical spirit eventually emerged in its own right as the medieval forms crumbled, when "by an inward ripening, the mind, after having been so long conversant with the forms of Antiquity, began to grasp its spirit." Humanism thus emerged not as a "new birth" but as a by-product of the process of decay.

. . . According to the celebrated Swiss historian [Jacob Burckhardt], the quest of personal glory was the characteristic attribute of the men of the Renaissance. The Middle Ages proper, according to him, knew honour and glory only in collective forms, as the honour due to groups and orders of society, the honour of rank, of class, or of profession. It was in Italy, he thinks, under the influence of antique models, that the craving for individual glory originated. Here, as elsewhere, Burckhardt has exaggerated the distance separating Italy from the Western countries and the Renaissance from the Middle Ages.

The thirst for honour and glory proper to the men of the Renaissance is essentially the same as the chivalrous ambition of earlier times, and of French origin. Only it has shaken off the feudal form and assumed an antique garb. The passionate desire to find himself praised by contemporaries or by posterity was the source of virtue with the courtly knight of the twelfth century and the rude captain of the fourteenth, no less than with the beaux-esprits of the *quattrocento*. When Beaumanoir and Bamborough fix the conditions of the famous combat of the Thirty, the English captain, according to Froissart, expresses himself in these terms: "And let us right there try ourselves and do so much that people will speak of it in future times in halls, in palaces, in public places and elsewhere throughout the world." The saying may not be authentic, but it teaches us what Froissart thought.

The quest of glory and of honour goes hand in hand with a hero-worship which also might seem to announce the Renaissance. The somewhat factitious revival of the splendour of chivalry that we find everywhere in European courts after 1300 is already connected with the Renaissance by a real link. It is a naïve prelude to it. In reviving chivalry the poets and princes imagined that they were returning to antiquity. In the minds of the fourteenth century, a vision of antiquity had hardly yet disengaged itself from the fairy-land sphere of the Round Table. Classical heroes were still tinged with the general colour of romance. On the one hand, the figure of Alexander had long ago entered the sphere of chivalry; on the other, chivalry was supposed to be of Roman origin. "And he maintained the discipline of chivalry well, as did the Romans formerly," thus a Burgundian chronicler praised Henry V of England. The blazons of Cæsar, of Hercules, and of Troilus, are placed in a fantasy of King René, side by side with those of Arthur and of Lancelot. Certain coincidences of terminology played a part in tracing back the origin of chivalry to Roman antiquity. How could people have known that the word *miles* with Roman authors did not mean a *miles* in the sense of medieval Latin, that is to say, a knight, or that a Roman *eques* differed from a feudal knight? Consequently, Romulus, because he raised a band of a thousand mounted warriors, was taken to be the founder of chivalry.

The life of a knight is an imitation; that of princes is so too, sometimes. No one was so consciously inspired by models of the past, or manifested such desire to rival them, as Charles the Bold. In his youth he made his attendants read out to him the exploits of Gauvain and of Lancelot. Later he preferred the ancients. Before retiring to rest, he listens for an hour or two to the "lofty histories of Rome." He especially admires Cæsar, Hannibal and Alexander, "whom he wished to follow and imitate." All his contemporaries attach great importance to this eagerness to imitate the heroes of antiquity, and agree in regarding it as the mainspring of his conduct. "He desired great glory"—says Commines—"which more than anything else led him to undertake his wars; and longed to resemble those ancient princes who have been so much talked of after their death." The anecdote is well known of the jester who, after the defeat of Granson, called out to him: "My lord, we are well Hannibaled this time!" . . .

Thus the aspiration to the splendour of antique life, which is the characteristic of the Renaissance, has its roots in the chivalrous ideal. Between the ponderous spirit of the Burgundian and the classical instinct of an Italian of the same period there is only a difference of nuance. The forms which Charles the Bold affected are still flamboyant Gothic, and he still read his classics in translations. . . .

The transition from the spirit of the declining Middle Ages to humanism was far less simple than we are inclined to imagine it. Accustomed to oppose humanism to the Middle Ages, we would gladly believe that it was necessary to give up the one in order to embrace the other. We find it difficult to fancy the mind cultivating the ancient forms of medieval thought and expression while aspiring at the same time to antique wisdom and beauty. Yet this is just what we have to picture to ourselves. Classicism did not come as a sudden revelation, it grew up among the luxuriant vegetation of medieval thought. Humanism was a form before it was an inspiration. On the other hand, the characteristic modes of thought of the Middle Ages did not die out till long after the Renaissance.

In Italy the problem of humanism presents itself in a most simple form, because there men's minds had ever been predisposed to the reception of antique culture. The Italian spirit had never lost touch with classic harmony and simplicity. It could expand freely and naturally in the restored forms of classic expression. The *quattrocento* with its serenity makes the impression of a renewed culture, which has shaken off the fetters of medieval thought, until Savonarola reminds us that below the surface the Middle Ages still subsist.

The history of French civilization of the fifteenth century, on the contrary, does not permit us to forget the Middle Ages. France had been the mother-land of all that was strongest and most beautiful in the products of the medieval spirit. All medieval forms—feudalism, the ideas of chivalry and courtesy, scholasticism, Gothic architecture— were rooted here much more firmly than ever they had been in Italy. In the fifteenth century they were dominating still. Instead of the full rich style, the blitheness and the harmony characteristic of Italy and the Renaissance, here it is bizarre pomp, cumbrous forms of expression, a worn-out fancy and an atmosphere of melancholy gravity which prevail. It is not the Middle Ages, it is the new coming culture, which might easily be forgotten.

In literature classical forms could appear without the spirit having changed. An interest in the refinement of Latin style was enough, it seems, to give birth to humanism. The proof of this is furnished by a group of French scholars about the year 1400. It was composed of ecclesiastics and magistrates, Jean de Monstreuil, canon of Lille and secretary to the king, Nicolas de Clemanges, the famous denouncer of abuses in the Church, Pierre et Gontier Col, the Milanese Ambrose de Miliis, also royal secretaries. The elegant and grave epistles they exchange are inferior in no respect—neither in the vagueness of thought, nor in the consequential air, nor in the tortured sentences, nor even in learned trifling—to the epistolary genre of later humanists. Jean de Monstreuil spins long dissertations on the subject of Latin spelling. He defends Cicero and Virgil against the criticism of his friend Ambrose de Miliis, who had accused the former of contradictions and preferred Ovid to the latter. On another occasion he writes to Clemanges: "If you do not come to my aid, dear master and brother, I shall have lost my reputation and be as one sentenced to death. I have just noticed that in my last letter to my lord and father, the bishop of Cambray, I wrote *proximior* instead of the comparative *propior*; so rash and careless is the pen. Kindly correct this, otherwise our detractors will write libels about it." . . .

It suffices to recall that we met Jean de Monstreuil and the brothers Col among the zealots of the *Roman de la Rose* and among the members of the Court of Love of 1401, to be convinced that this primitive French humanism was but a secondary element of their culture, the fruit of scholarly erudition, analogous to the so-called renaissances of classic latinity of earlier ages, notably the ninth and the twelfth century. The circle of Jean de Monstreuil had no immediate successors, and this early French humanism seems to disappear with the men who cultivated it. Still, in its origins it was to some extent connected with the great international movement of literary renovation. Petrarch was, in the eyes of Jean de Monstreuil and his friends, the illustrious initiator, and Coluccio Salutati, the Florentine chancellor who introduced classicism into official style, was not unknown to them either. Their zeal for classic refinement had evidently been roused not a little by Petrarch's taunt that there were no orators nor poets outside Italy. In France Petrarch's work had, so to say, been accepted in a medieval spirit and incorporated into medieval thought. He himself had personally known the leading spirits of the second half of the fourteenth century; the poet Philippe de Vitri, Nicolas Oresme, philosopher and politician , who had been a preceptor to the dauphin, probably also Philippe de Mézières. These men, in spite of the ideas which make Oresme one of the forerunners of modern science, were not humanists. As to Petrarch himself, we are always inclined to exaggerate the modern element in his mind and work, because we are accustomed to see him exclusively as the first of renovators.

It is easy to imagine him emancipated from the ideas of his century. Nothing is further from the truth. He is most emphatically a man of his time. The themes of which he treated were those of the Middle Ages: *De contemptu mundi, De otio religiosorum, De vita solitaria.* It is only the form and the tone of his work which differ and are more highly finished. His glorification of antique virtue in his *De viris illustribus* and his *Rerum memorandarum libri* corresponds more or less with the chivalrous cult of the Nine Worthies. There is nothing surprising in his being found in touch with the founder of the Brethren of the Common Life, or cited as an authority on a dogmatic point by the fanatic Jean de Varennes. Denis the Carthusian borrowed laments from him about the loss of the Holy Sepulchre, a typically medieval subject. What contemporaries outside Italy saw in Petrarch was not at all the poet of the Sonnets or the *Trionfi,* but a moral philosopher, a Christian Cicero.

In a more limited field Boccaccio exercised an influence resembling that of Petrarch. His fame too was that of a moral philosopher, and by no means rested on the *Decamerone.* He was honoured as the "doctor of patience in adversity," as the author of *De casibus virorum illustrium* and of *De claris mulieribus.* Because of these queer writings treating of the inconstancy of human fate "messire Jehan Bocace" had made himself a sort of *impresario* of Fortune. As such he appears to Chastellain, who gave the name of *Le Temple de Bocace* to the bizarre treatise in which he endeavoured to console Queen Margaret, after her flight from England, by relating to her a series of the tragic destinies of his time. In recognizing in Boccaccio the strongly medieval spirit which was their own, these Burgundian spirits of a century later were not at all off the mark.

What distinguishes nascent Humanism in France from that of Italy, is a difference of erudition, skill and taste, rather than of tone or aspiration. To transplant antique form and sentiment into national literature the French had to overcome far more obstacles than the people born under the Tuscan sky or in the shadow of the Coliseum. France too, had her learned clerks, writing in Latin, who were capable at an early date of rising to the height of the epistolary style. But a blending of classicism and medievalism in the vernacular, such as was achieved by Boccaccio, was for a long time impossible in France. The old forms were too strong, and the general culture still lacked the proficiency in mythology and ancient history which was current in Italy. Machaut, although a clerk, pitifully disfigures the names of the seven sages. Chastellain confounds Peleus with Pelias, La Marche Proteus with Pirithous. The author of the *Pastoralet* speaks of the "good king Scipio of Africa." But at the same time his subject inspires him with a description of the god Silvanus and a prayer to Pan, in which the poetical imagination of the Renaissance seems on the point of breaking forth. The chroniclers were already trying their hand at military speeches in Livy's manner, and adorning their narrative of important events by mentioning portents, in close imitation of Livy. Their attempts at classicism did not always succeed. Jean Germain's description of the Arras congress of 1435 is a veritable caricature of antique prose. The vision of Antiquity was still very bizarre. . . .

. . . Now, in Italy, where language and thought had never been entirely estranged from the pure Latin style, the social environment and the turn of mind were far more congenial to the humanistic tendencies than in France. Italian civilization had naturally developed the type of the humanist. The Italian language was not, like the French, corrupted by an influx of latinism; it absorbed it without difficulty. In France, on the contrary, the medieval foundations of social life were still solid; the language, much farther removed from Latin than Italian was, refused to be latinized. If, in English, erudite latinisms were to find an easy access, it was because of the very fact that here the language was not of Latin stock at all, so that no incongruity of expression made itself felt.

In so far as the French humanists of the fifteenth century wrote in Latin, the medieval subsoil of their culture is little in evidence. The more completely the classical style is imitated, the more the true spirit is concealed. The letters and the discourses of Robert Gaguin are not distinguishable from the works of other humanists. But Gaguin is, at the same time, a French poet of altogether medieval inspiration and of altogether national style. Whereas those who did not, and perhaps could not, write in Latin, spoiled their French by latinized forms, he, the accomplished latinist, when writing in French, disdained rhetorical effects. His *Débat du Laboureur, du Prestre et du Gendarme*, medieval in its subject, is also medieval in style. It is simple and vigorous, like Villon's poetry and Deschamps' best work.

Who are the true moderns in the French literature of the fifteenth century? Those, no doubt, whose works approach nearest to what the following century produced of beauty. Assuredly it is not, whatever their merits may have been, the grave and pompous representatives of the Burgundian style: not Chastellain, La Marche, Molinet. The novelties of form which they affected were too superficial, the foundation of their thought too essentially medieval, their classical whimsies too naïve. . . .

. . . If by moderns we understand those who have most affinity with the later development of French literature, the moderns are Villon, Charles of Orléans and the poet of *L'Amant rendu Cordelier,* just those who kept most aloof from classicism and who did not strain after over-nice forms. The medieval character of their motifs robs them not in the least of their aspect of youth and of promise. It is the spontaneity of their expression which makes them moderns.

Classicism then was not the controlling factor in the advent of the new spirit in literature. Neither was paganism. The frequent use of pagan expressions or tropes has often been considered the chief characteristic of the Renaissance. This practice, however, is far older. As early as the twelfth century mythological terms were employed to express concepts of the Christian faith, and this was not considered at all irreverent or impious. Deschamps speaking of "Jupiter come from paradise," Villon calling the Holy Virgin "high goddess," the humanists referring to God in terms like "princeps superum" and to Mary as "genetrix tonantis," are by no means pagans. Pastorals required some admixture of innocent paganism, by which no reader was duped. The author of the *Pastoralet* who calls the Celestine church at Paris "the temple in the high woods, where people pray to the gods," declares, to dispel all ambiguity, "If, to lend my Muse some strangeness, I speak of the pagan gods, the shepherds and myself are Christians all the same." In the same way Molinet excuses himself for having introduced Mars and Minerva, by quoting "Reason and Understanding," who said to him: "You should do it, not to instil faith in gods and goddesses, but because Our Lord alone inspires people as it pleases Him and frequently by various inspirations." . . .

To find paganism, there was no need for the spirit of the waning Middle Ages to revert to classic literature. The pagan spirit displayed itself, as amply as possible, in the *Roman de la Rose.* Not in the guise of some mythological phrases; it was not there that the danger lay, but in the whole erotic conception and inspiration of this most popular work of all. From the early Middle Ages onward Venus and Cupid had found a refuge in this domain. But the great pagan who called them to vigorous life and enthroned them was Jean de Meun. By blending with Christian conceptions of eternal bliss the boldest praise of voluptuousness, he had taught numerous generations a very ambiguous attitude towards Faith. He had dared to distort Genesis for his impious purposes by making Nature complain of men because they neglect her commandment of procreation, in the words: "So help me God who was crucified / I much repent that I made man."

It is astonishing that the Church, which so rigorously repressed the slightest deviations from dogma of a speculative character, suffered the teaching of this breviary of the aristocracy (for the *Roman de la Rose* was nothing less) to be disseminated with impunity.

But the essence of the great renewal lies even less in paganism than in pure Latinity. Classic expression and imagery, and even sentiments borrowed from heathen Antiquity, might be a potent stimulus or an indispensable support in the process of cultural renovation, they never were its moving power. The soul of Western Christendom itself was outgrowing medieval forms and modes of thought that had become shackles. The Middle Ages had always lived in the shadow of Antiquity, always handled its treasurers, or what they had of them, interpreting it according to truly medieval principles: scholastic theology and chivalry, asceticism and courtesy. Now, by an inward ripening, the mind, after having been so long conversant with the forms of Antiquity, began to grasp its spirit. The incomparable simpleness and purity of the ancient culture, its exactitude of conception and of expression, its easy and natural thought and strong interest in men and in life, —all this began to dawn upon men's minds. Europe, after having lived in the shadow of Antiquity, lived in its sunshine once more.

This process of assimilation of the classic spirit, however, was intricate and full of incongruities. The new form and the new spirit do not yet coincide. The classical form may serve to express the old conceptions: more than one humanist chooses the sapphic strophe for a pious poem of purely medieval inspiration. Traditional forms, on the other hand, may contain the spirit of the coming age. Nothing is more erroneous than to identify classicism and modern culture.

The fifteenth century in France and the Netherlands is still medieval at heart. The diapason of life had not yet changed. Scholastic thought, with symbolism and strong formalism, the thoroughly dualistic conception of life and the world still dominated. The two poles of the mind continued to be chivalry and hierarchy. Profound pessimism spread a general gloom over life. The gothic principle prevailed in art. But all these forms and modes were on the wane. A high and strong culture is declining, but at the same time and in the same sphere new things are being born. The tide is turning, the tone of life is about to change.

Charles Homer Haskins

The Renaissance of the Twelfth Century

The following selections are taken from the preface and first chapter of *The Renaissance of the Twelfth Century*, where Haskins argues most strongly for continuity from the twelfth century to the Italian Renaissance. In the body of the work, he delineates the broad extent of the twelfth-century revival of learning, encompassing the Latin classics and Roman law on the one hand, and contemporary literature, science, and philosophy on the other. One should note that Haskins does not outwardly deny the existence of the Italian Renaissance, but his blurring of the distinction between Middle Ages and Renaissance calls the distinctiveness of the latter period into question. At issue here is his assertion that the twelfth-century Renaissance "partook of the same character as the better known movement of the fifteenth century," for if both movements share the same character, precedence naturally goes to the earlier one.

The title of this book will appear to many to contain a flagrant contradiction. A renaissance in the twelfth century! Do not the Middle Ages, that epoch of ignorance, stagnation, and gloom, stand in the sharpest contrast to the light and progress and freedom of the Italian Renaissance which followed? How could there be a renaissance in the Middle Ages, when men had no eye for the joy and beauty and knowledge of this passing world, their gaze ever fixed on the terrors of the world to come? Is not this whole period summed up in Symonds' picture of St. Bernard, blind to the beauties of Lake Leman as he bends "a thought-burdened forehead over the neck of his mule," typical of an age when "humanity had passed, a careful pilgrim, intent on the terrors of sin, death, and judgment, along the highways of the world, and had scarcely known that they were sightworthy, or that life is a blessing"?

From Charles Homer Haskins, *The Renaissance of the Twelfth Century* (New York: Meridian Books, 1957).

The answer is that the continuity of history rejects such sharp and violent contrasts between successive periods, and that modern research shows us the Middle Ages less dark and less static, the Renaissance less bright and less sudden, that was once supposed. The Middle Ages exhibit life and color and change, much eager search after knowledge and beauty, much creative accomplishment in art, in literature, in institutions. The Italian Renaissance was preceded by similar, if less wide-reaching movements; indeed it came out of the Middle Ages so gradually that historians are not agreed when it began, and some would go so far as to abolish the name, and perhaps even the fact, of a renaissance in the Quattrocentro.

To the most important of these earlier revivals the present volume is devoted, the Renaissance of the Twelfth Century which is often called the Mediaeval Renaissance. This century, the very century of St. Bernard and his mule, was in many respects an age of fresh and vigorous life. The epoch of the Crusades, of the rise of towns, and of the earliest bureaucratic states of the West, it saw the culmination of Romanesque art and the beginnings of Gothic; the emergence of the vernacular literatures; the revival of the Latin classics and of Latin poetry and Roman law; the recovery of Greek science, with its Arabic additions, and of much of Greek philosophy; and the origin of the first European universities. The twelfth century left its signature on higher education, on the scholastic philosophy, on European systems of law, on architecture and sculpture, on the liturgical drama, on Latin and vernacular poetry. The theme is too broad for a single volume, or a single author. Accordingly, since the art and the vernacular literature of the epoch are better known, we shall confine ourselves to the Latin side of this renaissance, the revival of learning in the broadest sense—the Latin classics and their influence, the new jurisprudence and the more varied historiography, the new knowledge of the Greeks and Arabs and its effects upon Western science and philosophy, and the new institutions of learning, all seen against the background of the century's centres and materials of culture. The absence of any other work on this general theme must be the author's excuse for attempting a sketch where much must necessarily rest upon second-hand information. . . .

The European Middle Ages form a complex and varied as well as a very considerable period of human history. Within their thousand years of time they include a large variety of peoples, institutions, and types of culture, illustrating many processes of historical development and containing the origins of many phases of modern civilization. Contrasts of East and West, of the North and the Mediterranean, of old and new, sacred and profane, ideal and actual, give life and color and movement to this period, while its close relations alike to antiquity and to the modern world assure it a place in the continuous history of human development. Both continuity and change are characteristic of the Middle Ages, as indeed of all great epochs of history.

This conception runs counter to ideas widely prevalent not only among the unlearned but among many who ought to know better. To these the Middle Ages are synonymous with all that is uniform, static, and unprogressive; "mediaeval" is applied to anything outgrown, until, as Bernard Shaw reminds us, even the fashion plates of the preceding generation are pronounced "mediaeval." The barbarism of Goths and Vandals is thus spread out over the following centuries, even to that "Gothic" architecture which is one of the crowning achievements of the constructive genius of the race; the ignorance and superstition of this age are contrasted with the enlightenment of the Renaissance, in strange disregard of the alchemy and demonology which flourished throughout this succeeding period; and the phrase "Dark Ages" is extended to cover all that came between, let us say, 476 and 1453. Even those who realize that the Middle Ages are not "dark" often think of them as uniform, at least during the central period from *ca.* 800 to *ca.* 1300, distinguished by the great mediaeval institutions of feudalism, ecclesiasticism, and scholasticism, and preceded and followed by epochs of more rapid transformation. Such a view ignores the unequal development of different parts of Europe, the great economic changes within this epoch, the influx of the new learning of the East, the shifting currents in the stream of mediaeval life and thought. On the intellectual side, in particular, it neglects the mediaeval revival of the Latin classics and of jurisprudence, the extension of knowledge by the absorption of ancient learning and by observation, and the creative work of these centuries in poetry and in art. In many ways the differences between the Europe of 800 and that of 1300 are greater than the resemblances. Similar contrasts, though on a smaller scale, can be made between the culture of the eighth and the ninth centuries, between conditions *ca.* 1100 and those *ca.* 1200, between the preceding age and the new intellectual currents of the thirteenth and fourteenth centuries.

For convenience' sake it has become common to designate certain of these movements as the Carolingian Renaissance, the Ottonian Renaissance, the Renaissance of the Twelfth Century, after the fashion of the phrase once reserved exclusively for the Italian Renaissance of the fifteenth century. Some, it is true, would give up the word renaissance altogether, as conveying false impressions of a sudden change and an original and distinct culture in the fifteenth century, and, in general, as implying that there ever can be a real revival of something past; Mr. Henry Osborn Taylor prides himself on writing two volumes on *Thought and Expression in the Sixteenth Century* without once using this forbidden term. Nevertheless, it may be doubted whether such a term is more open to misinterpretation than others, like the Quattrocento or the sixteenth century, and it is so convenient and so well established that, like Austria, if it had not existed we should have to invent it. There was an Italian Renaissance, whatever we choose to call it, and nothing is gained by the process which ascribes the Homeric poems to another poet of the same name. But—thus much we must grant—the great Renaissance was not so unique or so decisive as has been supposed. The contrast of culture was not nearly so sharp as it seemed to the humanists and their modern followers, while within the Middle Ages there were intellectual revivals whose influence was not lost to succeeding times, and which partook of the same character as the better known movement of the fifteenth century. To one of these this volume is devoted, the Renaissance of the Twelfth Century, which is also known as the Mediaeval Renaissance.

The renaissance of the twelfth century might conceivably be taken so broadly as to cover all the changes through which Europe passed in the hundred years or more from the late eleventh century to the taking of Constantinople by the Latins in 1204 and the contemporary events which usher in the thirteenth century, just as we speak of the Age of the Renaissance in later Italy; but such a view becomes too wide and vague for any purpose save the general history of the period. More profitably we may limit the phrase to the history of culture in this age—the complete development of Romanesque art and the rise of Gothic; the full bloom of vernacular poetry, both lyric and epic; and the new learning and new literature in Latin. The century begins with the flourishing age of the cathedral schools and closes with the earliest universities already well established at Salerno, Bologna, Paris, Montpellier, and Oxford. It starts with only the bare outlines of the seven liberal arts and ends in possession of the Roman and canon law, the new Aristotle, the new Euclid and Ptolemy, and the Greek and Arabic physicians, thus making possible a new philosophy and a new science. It sees a revival of the Latin classics, of Latin prose, and of Latin verse, both in the ancient style of Hildebert and the new rhymes of the Goliardi, and the formation of the liturgical drama. New activity in historical writing reflects the variety and amplitude of a richer age—biography, memoir, court annals, the vernacular history, and the city chronicle. A library of *ca.* 1100 would have little beyond the Bible and the Latin Fathers, with their Carolingian commentators, the service books of the church and various lives of saints, the textbooks of Boethius and some others, bits of local history, and perhaps certain of the Latin classics, too often covered with dust. About 1200, or a few years later, we should expect to find, not only more and better copies of these older works, but also the *Corpus Furis Civilis* and the classics partially rescued from neglect; the canonical collections of Gratian and the recent Popes; the theology of Anselm and Peter Lombard and the other early scholastics; the writings of St. Bernard and other monastic leaders (a good quarter of the two hundred and seventeen volumes of the Latin *Patrologia* belong to this period); a mass of new history, poetry, and correspondence; the philosophy, mathematics, and astronomy unknown to the earlier mediaeval tradition and recovered from the Greeks and Arabs in the course of the twelfth century. We should now have the great feudal epics of France and the best of the Provençal lyrics, as well as the earliest works in Middle High German. Romanesque art would have reached and passed its prime, and the new Gothic style would be firmly established at Paris, Chartres, and lesser centres in the Île de France. . . .

Chronological limits are not easy to set. Centuries are at best but arbitrary conveniences which must not be permitted to clog or distort our historical thinking: history cannot remain history if sawed off into even lengths of hundreds of years. The most that can be said is that the later eleventh century shows many signs of new life, political, economic, religious, intellectual, for which, like the revival of Roman law and the new interest in the classics, specific dates can rarely be assigned, and that, if we were to choose the First Crusade in 1096 as a convenient turning-point, it must be with a full realization that this particular event has in itself no decisive importance in intellectual history, and that the real change began some fifty years earlier. At the latter end the period is even less sharply defined. Once requickened, intellectual life did not slacken or abruptly change its character. The fourteenth century grows out of the thirteenth as the thirteenth grows out of the twelfth, so that there is no real break between the mediaeval renaissance and the Quattrocento. . . .

Erwin Panofsky

Renaissance and Renascences in Western Art

In the title essay of *Renaissance and Renascences in Western Art,* Panofsky distinguishes between various medieval "renascences" and the Italian Renaissance. Starting with the so-called Carolingian Renaissance of the ninth century (an administrative and ecclesiastical reform fostered by Charlemagne), Panofsky shows how it drew on only a limited range of late antique and early Christian models, which were salvaged but not reactivated. In other words, antiquity did not become a force that shaped culture and, in so doing, was itself reshaped. In Panofsky's homey analogy, the Carolingians had turned to the not-so-distant past in search of cultural reform, just as one whose car has broken down might refurbish an older vehicle that still worked.

Quickly dismissing the so-called Ottonian and Anglo-Saxon Renaissances of the tenth century as Christian rather than classical revivals, he moves on to his main subject, the so-called twelfth-century Renaissance. This he divides into two phenomena, the "proto-Renaissance" encompassing the three-dimensional arts in southern France, Italy, and Spain, and "proto-humanism" encompassing the literary products of France, the Netherlands, Germany, and England. These phenomena signify full-scale revivals in their respective areas, utilizing models of greater antiquity than the Carolingian Renaissance and infusing classical themes with new meaning. In other

From Erwin Panofsky, *Renaissance and Renascences in Western Art* (New York: Harper & Row, 1969).

words, antiquity was not just copied passively but became a dynamic force in twelfth-century culture, shaping it and being reshaped by it.

In the selections below, Panofsky discusses the "principle of disjunction" that for him conclusively distinguishes the proto-Renaissance and proto-humanism of the twelfth century from the Italian Renaissance of the fourteenth and fifteenth centuries. The twelfth century evinces a tendency to "compartmentalize" ancient culture, to borrow its content without its form, or its form without its content—hence, for example, the medieval depiction of Virgil as a cloistered schoolman or monk seated at a writing desk. By contrast, the Italian Renaissance reintegrates classical form with classical content, portraying Virgil as a Roman poet, clad in a toga and crowned with laurel.

According to Panofsky, twelfth-century developments cannot even stand as the prelude to the Italian Renaissance, for they are separated from it by the "Gothic counterrevolution." By the fourteenth century, the Gothic style has absorbed and disguised the classical elements of proto-Renaissance art, and scholasticism has superseded proto-humanism, utilizing Latin in an entirely new (and decidedly unclassical) way. Thus, for Panofsky, a divide separates the twelfth-century disjunction of classical form and content from their reintegration in the Italian Renaissance.

Panofsky's idea about the Renaissance reintegration of classical form and content dovetails with Burckhardt's central theme about individuality. Recall that the "development of the individual" entails an awareness of one's own uniqueness *and* that of others. From this viewpoint, Virgil's uniqueness resides in, among other things, the fact that he lived, spoke, and dressed like an ancient Roman. Panofsky's reintegration of form and content in art thus represents a refinement of Burckhardt's Renaissance idea of individuality.

. . . As far as the representational arts are concerned, the influence of proto-humanism, diffusing from North to South, interpenetrated with that of the proto-Renaissance which, as has been seen, spread in the opposite direction; and the combined effect of these two complementary movements resulted in what may be called the "reactivation" of classical motifs as well as classical concepts.

Carolingian art, we remember, revived and re-employed scores of "images" in which classical form was happily united with classical content and often not only endowed these images with an expressive power entirely foreign to their prototypes but also, as I have phrased it, "permitted them to escape from their original context without abandoning their original nature". . . .

Nowhere in Carolingian art, however, do we seem to encounter an effort to infuse into a given classical image a meaning other than that with which it had been invested from the outset: an Atlas or a river-god in the Utrecht Psalter may immeasurably surpass his model in animation and expressiveness, but he remains an Atlas or a river-god; we are confronted with quotations or paraphrases, however skillful and spirited, rather than with reinterpretations. Conversely—and this is even more important—nowhere in Carolingian art do we seem to encounter an effort to devise a formula that might translate a given classical (or otherwise secular) text into a new picture: where illustrations of such texts were available, they were copied and recopied without cease; where none were available, none were invented.

In both these respects the simultaneous rise of proto-Renaissance and proto-humanism effected an essential change. As we have seen, the sculptors of the eleventh, twelfth and thirteenth centuries repeated on a new level what the Early Christian artists had so extensively done but what their Carolingian heirs had so conspicuously refrained from doing: they subjected classical originals to an *interpretatio Christiana*, the term *Christiana* here meant to include, in addition to that which can be found in Scripture or in hagiology, all kinds of concepts that come under the heading of Christian philosophy. Antoninus Pius, we recall, was transformed into St. Peter, Hercules into Fortitude, Phaedra into the Virgin Mary, Dionysus into Simeon; *Venus Pudica* could be changed into Eve, and *Terra* into Luxury.

At the same time, however, classical concepts as well as classical characters (real or imaginary) and classical narratives (historical or mythical) came to be picturalized in a manner entirely independent from classical representational sources. The Four Elements and the Seven Liberal Arts, Socrates and Plato, Aristotle and Seneca, Pythagoras and Euclid, Homer and Alexander the Great, Pyramus and Thisbe, Narcissus and Europa, the heroes of the Trojan war and all the classical gods were depicted either according to the conventions familiar to the artist from the life and art of his day or on the basis of verbal descriptions. . . .

All these illustrations bear witness to a curious and, in my opinion, fundamentally important phenomenon which may be described as the "principle of disjunction": wherever in the high and later Middle Ages a work of art borrows its form from a classical model, this form is almost invariably invested with a non-classical, normally Christian, significance; wherever in the high and later Middle Ages a work of art borrows its theme from classical poetry, legend, history or mythology, this theme is quite invariably presented in a non-classical, normally contemporary, form.

To some extent this "principle of disjunction" would seem to operate even in literature. Short poems as convincingly "antique" as Matthew of Vendôme's *Hermaphroditus* are not too frequent, and epics classical in language and meter as well as in content are in a minority as compared to treatments of classical myth and fable in very mediaeval Latin or one of the vernacular languages. . . .

In the representational arts of the high and later Middle Ages . . . the "principle of disjunction" applies almost without exception, or only with such exceptions as can be accounted for by special circumstances; from which results the paradox that—quite apart from the now familiar generic difference between sculpture and painting—an intentionally classicizing style is found in the ecclesiastical rather than in the secular sphere, in the decoration of churches, cloisters and liturgical objects rather than in the representations of mythological or other classical subjects which adorned the walls of sumptuous private dwellings and enliven the interesting "Hansa Bowls" not to mention the miniatures in secular manuscripts.

In the pictures accompanying Remigius of Auxerre's *Commentary on Martianus Capella* . . . Jupiter is represented in the guise of a ruler enthroned, and the raven which, according to the text, belongs to him as his sacred bird of augury is surrounded by a neat little halo because the illustrator involuntarily assimilated the image of a ruler enthroned and accompanied by a sacred bird to that of Pope Gregory visited by the dove of the Holy Spirit. Apollo—he, too, faithfully represented according to the indications of the text—rides on what looks like a peasant's cart and carries in his hands a kind of nosegay from which emerge the figures of the Three Graces as little busts. The Greek and Trojan heroes and heroines, referred to as "barons" and "damsels" in the vernacular accounts of the Trojan cycle, invariably move in a mediaeval environment, act according to mediaeval customs and are clad in mediaeval armor or dress. Achilles and Patroclus as well as Medea and Jason and Dido and Aeneas are shown engaged in playing chess. Laocoön, the "priest", appears tonsured. Thisbe converses with Pyramus through a wall separating two abbreviated Gothic buildings and waits for him on a Gothic tomb slab whose inscription ("Hic situs est Ninus rex") is preceded by the then indispensable cross. Pygmalion is represented as a practitioner of *la haute couture*, putting the finishing touches to an elaborate mediaeval dress which he has provided for his beautiful statue. . . .

From the eleventh and twelfth centuries, then, mediaeval art made classical antiquity assimilable by way of decomposition, as it were. It was for the Italian Renaissance to reintegrate the separated elements. Rendering unto Caesar the things which are Caesar's, Renaissance art not only put an end to the paradoxical mediaeval practice of restricting classical form to non-classical subject matter but also broke the monopoly of architecture and sculpture with regard to classicizing stylization (though painting did not catch up with their "maniera antica" until the second half of the fifteenth century). And we need only to look at Michelangelo's *Bacchus* and *Leda*, Raphael's Farnesina frescoes, Giorgione's *Venus*, Correggio's *Danae*, or Titian's mythological pictures to become aware of the fact that in the Italian High Renaissance the visual language of classical art had regained the status of an idiom in which new poems could be written—just as, conversely, the emotional content of classical mythology, legend and history could come to life in the dramas (nonexistent as such throughout the Middle Ages), epics and, finally, operas devoted to such subjects as Orpheus and Eurydice, Cephalus and Procris, Venus and Adonis, Lucrece and Tarquin, Casear and Brutus, Antony and Cleopatra.

When thirteenth-century Mantua resolved to honor its secular patron saint, Virgil, by public monuments, the poet was portrayed, like the representatives of the liberal arts on the Portail Royal at Chartres, as a mediaeval scholar or canonist seated before his desk and busily engaged in writing [Fig. 1]. . . . But when in 1499, at the very threshold of the High Renaissance, Mantegna was asked to design a statue of Virgil—meant to replace another monument said to have been on the Piazza d'Erbe and to have been destroyed by Carlo Malatesta almost exactly one century before—he conceived of Virgil as a truly classical figure, proudly erect, clad in a toga and addressing the beholder with the timeless dignity of a Demosthenes or Sophocles [Fig. 2].

This reintegration was, however, preceded—and, in my opinion, predicated upon—a general and radical reaction against the classicizing tendencies that had prevailed in proto-Renaissance art and proto-humanistic writing. In Italy the seals and coins postdating the *Augustales* of Frederick II and what I have called the "deceptively antique" cameos produced in the thirteenth century became progressively less rather than

FIGURE 1   Benedetto Antelami (?), Statue of Virgil, Mantua, Palazzo Ducale, *ca.* 1215 (Massimo Listri/Corbis).

FIGURE 2   Andrea Mantegna (after), Project for the Statue of Virgil. Planned in 1499, Paris, Louvre (Reunion des Musees Nationaux/Art Resource, NY).

more classical in style. Nicolo Pisano's own son, Giovanni, while keenly responding to the expressive value of classical art and even daring to employ a *Venus pudica* type for the representation of Prudence in his Pisa pulpit, repudiated the formal classicism of his father and started what may be called a Gothic counterrevolution which, in spite of certain fluctuations, was to win out in the second half of the fourteenth century; and it was from this Trecento Gothic rather than from the lingering tradition of Nicolo's classicism that the *buona maniera moderna* of Jacopo della Quercia, Ghiberti and Donatello arose.

In France the classicizing style of Reims was—with such rare exceptions as the Auxerre reliefs just mentioned—submerged by an altogether different current exemplified by the *Mary Annunciate* right next to the famous *Visitation* and nearly contemporary with it; and next to this *Mary Annunciate* there can be seen the figure of the Angel Gabriel, produced only about ten or fifteen years later, in which classical equilibrium has been abandoned in favor of what is known as the "Gothic sway". . . .

. . . [T]hat sway or lilt which determines the High Gothic conception of human movement is nothing but a classical *contrapposto* in disguise. It is, however, precisely this disguise that matters. In a figure posed *all'antica*, the shoulder above the standing leg (the latter's function being comparable to that of a column supporting the load of the entablature), sags; in a figure dominated by the Gothic sway, the shoulder above the standing leg (the latter's function being comparable to that of a pier transmitting energy to the vault-ribs) rises. What had been the result of two natural forces in balance becomes the result of one preternatural force ruling supreme: the classical element is so completely absorbed as to become indiscernible.

Analogous observations can be made in other fields, especially in that of literature. In the course of the thirteenth century the content of classical philosophy, historiography and poetry, though enormously augmented and popularized, came to be as completely absorbed in the high-mediaeval system of thought, imagination and expression as was the classical *contrapposto* in the "Gothic sway", and the linguistic form of Latin writing completely emancipated itself from classical models. Unlike Bernard of Chartres, John of Salisbury, Bernardus Silvestris, or Alanus de Insulis, the great scholastics of the thirteenth and fourteenth centuries no longer modelled their style upon the prose of Cicero or Suetonius, much less upon the verse of Virgil, Horace, Lucan, or Statius. It was, in fact, the very ascendancy of scholasticism, pervading and molding

all phases of cultural life, which more than any other single factor contributed to the extinction of "proto-humanistic" aspirations: scholastic
thinking demanded and produced a new language—new not only with
respect to syntax but also to vocabulary—which could do justice to the
principle of *manifestatio* (or, as I once ventured to express it, "clarification
for clarification's sake") but would have horrified the classics—as it was to
exasperate Petrarch, Lorenzo Valla, Erasmus, and Rabelais. . . .

In short, before the Italian High Renaissance performed its task of reintegration, that undulating curve which, as I said, may serve to describe
the fluctuations of classicizing tendencies in postclassical art had reached
the zero mark in all genres as well as in all countries. The later phases
of the Middle Ages had not only failed to unify what the Antique itself had
left to its heirs as a duality—visible monuments on the one hand, texts on
the other—but even dissolved those representational traditions which the
Carolingian *renovatio* had managed to revive and to transmit as a unity.

The "principle of disjunction" . . . would seem to express a fundamental tendency or idiosyncrasy of the high-mediaeval mind which we
shall re-encounter on several later occasions: an irresistible urge to "compartmentalize" such psychological experiences and cultural activities as
were to coalesce or merge in the Renaissance; and, conversely, a basic
inability to make what we would call "historical" distinctions. And this
leads us back to the question which was posed at the beginning of this
chapter: can the three phenomena which we have been considering—
the Italian *rinascita*, the Carolingian *renovatio* and the twin movement
known as proto-Renaissance and proto-humanism—be shown to differ
from each other not only in scale but also in structure? And, if so, is it
still possible to distinguish, within this triad of phenomena, between the
Renaissance with a capital "*R*" and the two mediaeval revivals which I
propose to call "renascences"? This question, too, deserves, I think, an
affirmative answer; for, to put it briefly, the two mediaeval renascences
were limited and transitory; the Renaissance was total and permanent.

The Carolingian *renovatio* pervaded the whole of the empire and
left no sphere of civilization untouched; but it was limited in that it re-
claimed lost territory rather than attempting to conquer new lands. It
did not transcend a monastic and administrative *Herrenschicht* directly
or indirectly connected with the crown; its artistic activities did not include major sculpture in stone; the models selected for imitation were
as a rule productions of the minor arts and normally did not antedate
the fourth and fifth centuries A.D.; and the classical values—artistic as

well as literary—were salvaged but not "reactivated" (as we have seen, no effort was made either to reinterpret classical images or to illustrate classical texts *de novo*).

The classical revival of the eleventh and twelfth centuries, on the other hand, penetrated many strata of society. In art it sought and achieved monumentality, selecting models of greater antiquity than those normally chosen by the Carolingian masters, and emancipated classical images from what I have called the stage of quotation and paraphrase (it did precisely what the Carolingian *renovatio* had failed to do in that new meanings were infused into classical images and a new visual form was given to classical themes). But it was limited in several other respects: it represented only a special current within the larger stream of contemporary civilization (whereas Carolingian civilization as a whole was coextensive with the *renovatio* movement) and was restricted to particular regions; there was, according to these regions, a basic difference between a recreative and a literary or antiquarian response to the Antique; the proto-Renaissance in the arts was virtually restricted to architecture and sculpture as opposed to painting; and in art as well as literature classical form came to be divorced from classical content. Both these mediaeval renascences, finally, were transitory in that they were followed by a relative or—in the Northern countries—absolute estrangement from the aesthetic traditions, in art as well as literature, of the classical past.

How things were changed by the real, Italian Renaissance can be illustrated by a small but significant incident. The Carolingian *Aratea* manuscript . . . had been left untouched for about four hundred years. Then a well-meaning scribe saw fit to repeat the entire text in the script of the thirteenth century [Fig. 3] because he evidently thought that the Carolingian "Rustic Capital" would stump his contemporaries, as well as future generations. But the twentieth-century reader finds Carolingian script easier to decipher than Gothic, and this ironic fact tells the whole story.

Our own script and letter press derive from the Italian Renaissance types patterned, in deliberate opposition to the Gothic, upon Carolingian and twelfth-century models which in turn had been evolved on a classical basis. Gothic script, one might say, symbolizes the transitoriness of the mediaeval renascences; our modern letter press, whether "Roman" or "italic", testifies to the enduring quality of the Italian Renaissance. Thereafter, the classical element in our civilization could be opposed (though it should not be forgotten that opposition is only another form of dependence); but it could not entirely disappear again. In the Middle Ages

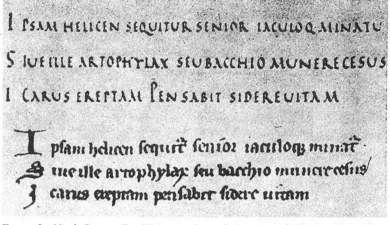

FIGURE 3   Ninth-Century Text Written in *Capitalis Rustica*, with Thirteenth-Century Transliteration (Leiden, University Library, Cod. lat. Voss. 79. fol, 7).

there was in relation to the Antique a cyclical succession of assimilative and non-assimilative stages. Since the Renaissance the Antique has been constantly with us, whether we like it or not. It lives in our mathematics and natural sciences. It has built our theatres and cinemas as opposed to the mediaeval mystery stage. It haunts the speech of our cab driver — not to mention the motor mechanic or radio expert — as opposed to that of the mediaeval peasant. And it is firmly entrenched behind the thin but thus far unbroken glass walls of history, philology and archaeology.

The formation and, ultimately, formalization of these three disciplines — foreign to the Middle Ages in spite of all the Carolingian and twelfth-century "humanists" — evince a fundamental difference between the mediaeval and the modern attitude towards classical antiquity, a difference which makes us understand the essential strength and the essential weakness of both. In the Italian Renaissance the classical past began to be looked upon from a fixed distance, quite comparable to the "distance between the eye and the object" in that most characteristic invention of this very Renaissance, focused perspective. As in focused perspective, this distance prohibited direct contact — owing to the interposition of an ideal "projection plane" — but permitted a total and rationalized view. Such a distance is absent from both mediaeval renascences. "The Middle Ages", as has recently been said, "never knew that they were mediaeval.

The men of the twelfth century had none of that awareness of a Cimmerian night from which—as Rabelais wrote his friend Tiraqueau in 1532—humanity had emerged".

The Carolingian revival had been started because it was felt that a great many things needed overhauling: the administrative system, the liturgy, the language, and the arts. When this was realized, the leading spirits turned to antiquity, both pagan and Christian (and even with a strong initial emphasis on the latter), much as a man whose motor car has broken down might fall back on an automobile inherited from his grandfather which, when reconditioned . . . will still give excellent service and may even prove more comfortable than the newer model ever was. In other words, the Carolingians approached the Antique with a feeling of legitimate heirs who had neglected or even forgotten their property for a time and now claimed it for precisely those uses for which it had been intended.

In contrast to this untroubled sense of legitimacy, the high-mediaeval attitude toward the Antique is characterized by an ambivalence. . . .

 . . . [T]here was, on the one hand, a sense of unbroken continuity with classical antiquity that linked the "Holy Roman Empire of the Middle Ages" to Caesar and Augustus, mediaeval music to Pythagoras, mediaeval philosophy to Plato and Aristotle, mediaeval grammar to Donatus—and, on the other, a consciousness of the insurmountable gap that separated the Christian present from the pagan past (so that in the case of Aristotle's writings a sharp distinction was made, or at least attempted, between what was admissible and what should be condemned). The classical world was not approached historically but pragmatically, as something far-off yet, in a sense, still alive and, therefore, at once potentially useful and potentially dangerous. . . .

For want of a "perspective distance" classical civilization could not be viewed as a coherent cultural system within which all things belonged together. . . . Every phenomenon of the classical past, instead of being seen in context with other phenomena of the classical past, thus had to have one point of contact, and one of divergence, with the mediaeval present: it had to satisfy both the sense of continuity and the feeling of opposition. . . .

Now we can see why the union of classical form and classical content, even if retained in the images revived in Carolingian times, was bound to break apart, and why this process of "disjunction" was so much more radical in the arts—where the very fact that they provided a visual rather than intellectual experience entailed the danger of *curiositas* or even idolatry—than in literature. To the high-mediaeval mind Jason and Medea (even though she tended to perform her tricks of rejuvenation with the aid of the "water of Paradise") were acceptable as long as they were depicted as Gothic aristocrats playing chess in a Gothic chamber. Classical gods and goddesses were acceptable as long as they lent their beautiful presence to Christian saints, to Eve or to the Virgin Mary. But a Thisbe clad in classical costume and waiting for Pyramus by a classical mausoleum would have been an archaeological reconstruction incompatible with the sense of continuity; and an image of Mars or Venus classical in form as well as significance was either, as we have seen, an "idol" or talisman or, conversely, served to personify a vice. . . .

The "distance" created by the Renaissance deprived antiquity of its realness. The classical world ceased to be both a possession and a menace. It became instead the object of a passionate nostalgia which found its symbolic expression in the re-emergence—after fifteen centuries—of that enchanting vision, Arcady. Both mediaeval renascences, regardless of the differences between the Carolingian *renovatio* and the "revival of the twelfth century", were free from this nostalgia. Antiquity, like the old automobile in our homely simile, was still around, so to speak. The Renaissance came to realize that Pan was dead—that the world of ancient Greece and Rome . . . was lost like Milton's Paradise and capable of being regained only in the spirit. The classical past was looked upon, for the first time, as a totality cut off from the present; and, therefore, as an ideal to be longed for instead of a reality to be both utilized and feared.

The Middle Ages had left antiquity unburied and alternately galvanized and exorcised its corpse. The Renaissance stood weeping at its grave and tried to resurrect its soul. And in one fatally auspicious moment it succeeded. This is why the mediaeval concept of the Antique was so concrete and at the same time so incomplete and distorted; whereas the modern one, gradually developed during the last three or four hundred years, is comprehensive and consistent but, if I may say so, abstract. And this is why the mediaeval renascences were transitory; whereas the Renaissance was permanent. Resurrected souls are intangible but have the advantage of immortality and omnipresence. Therefore the role of classical antiquity after the Renaissance is somewhat elusive but, on the other hand, pervasive—and changeable only with a change in our civilization as such.

II The Nature of Humanism

Undoubtedly Huizinga's dreamer would find the word *humanism* as beguiling as *Renaissance*, evoking the image of a pagan worldliness inspired by the glories of ancient Greece and Rome, the original ages of purple and gold. Indeed, the dreamer might even be hard pressed to distinguish between the two terms, so closely would they intertwine in his imagination. And when confronted by a skeptical questioner, the dreamer would likely retreat into yet another Burckhardtian credo, pronouncing humanism the secular, worldly, practical philosophy that used classical culture to free the mind from the stranglehold of the Church and of feudal ideals, ending the medieval night of the soul and releasing the modern spirit. Of course, we now know that this caricature belies the complexities of Burckhardt's vision, which rigorously distinguishes between the substance of the Renaissance and the classical form it took. But by epitomizing that substance as the development of the individual, Burckhardt in effect fostered the notion of humanism as a secular philosophy of man, a view that held sway until the mid–twentieth century.

Paul Oskar Kristeller (1905–1999) devoted much of his scholarly career to correcting this misconception. Trained in classical philology and philosophy at the University of Heidelberg, Kristeller fled Nazi

Germany for Italy, where he launched a lifelong project of ferreting out uncatalogued humanistic manuscripts. Forced eventually to leave Italy, he came to the United States in 1939, ultimately to become a professor of philosophy at Columbia University. With an encyclopedic knowledge of even the most obscure humanistic writings, Kristeller was the acknowledged dean of Renaissance studies in America and perhaps the world's foremost authority on humanism, combining a detailed understanding of the subject with an exceptional ability to communicate it to a broad audience.

In his most widely read work, *Renaissance Thought: The Classic, Scholastic, and Humanist Strains* (1961), Kristeller gathered together a series of public lectures and essays interpreting humanism as a phase in a long rhetorical tradition extending back to antiquity. Far from being a philosophy, it was, for Kristeller, a curriculum pure and simple, comprising grammar, rhetoric, history, poetry, and moral philosophy—the *studia humanitatis,* progenitor of what we now know as the "humanities." In this essentially literary curriculum, rhetoric held pride of place as the key to effective speaking and writing, the best examples of which derived from antiquity. The emphasis on classical models encouraged the elevation of history, poetry, and moral philosophy to the status of disciplines within the *studia humanitatis,* a position they had not held in the medieval curriculum. According to Kristeller, the humanists differed from their predecessors, medieval teachers of rhetoric known as *dictatores,* chiefly in this classical emphasis. He showed that humanism not only evolved from the practice and profession of medieval rhetoric but that it also coexisted with scholasticism rather than superseding it. Indeed, the humanists did much to advance the study of Aristotle, the prince of the scholastics. By overturning the traditional conception of humanism as a philosophy at odds with the medieval past, Kristeller lent powerful support to the notion that the intellectual fruits of the Renaissance grew from medieval soil.

While not disagreeing with Kristeller's overall assessment of humanism as a curriculum rather than a philosophy, Hanna H. Gray sought to modify his view that the humanists differed from the *dictatores* merely in their insistence upon a more classical style. Gray, professor emerita of history at the University of Chicago (where she served as president for fifteen years), specializes in the history of humanism, among other areas. In her path-breaking article, "Renaissance Humanism: The Pursuit of Eloquence" (1963), she isolates the intellectual shift distinguishing the humanists from the *dictatores,* namely, the belief in the power and efficacy of eloquence for human life. The humanists thus differed from their predecessors not merely by emphasizing classical style but by espousing an ideal of eloquence that marked a new existential stance, one better suited to the world than the abstractions of scholastic philosophy. Without denying the many continuities between Middle Ages and Renaissance, Gray nonetheless insists that the humanists' own claims to have broken with the past must be taken seriously if we are to assess properly the nature of their movement.

Charles Trinkaus (1911–1999) further modified Kristeller's vision of humanism in his compendious work, *In Our Image and Likeness: Humanity and Divinity in Italian Humanist Thought* (1970). Trinkaus studied at Columbia University in the 1930s, before Kristeller's arrival there, and he subsequently taught at both Sarah Lawrence College and the University of Michigan. He was one of the first Americans to devote himself wholeheartedly to the subject of humanism. From the start, he bent to the task of overturning Burckhardt's assertion, in the closing section on religion in *The Civilization of the Renaissance in Italy,* that humanism was basically pagan in its outlook, even for those humanists who openly professed their religion. *In Our Image and Likeness* not only lays this Burckhardtian misconception to rest but, in the process, also shows how the humanists articulated what we might loosely term a Christian philosophy of man. Their belief in the power of eloquence led the humanists to a deep consideration of philosophical and theological matters, of how men might best live in the real world as creatures made in the image of God. In spirit, then, humanism extended beyond the narrow scope of Kristeller's *studia humanitatis* to encompass fundamental concerns about human existence.

In his masterful essay, "The Two Faces of Humanism: Stoicism and Augustinianism in Renaissance Thought" (1975), William J. Bouwsma further refines Trinkaus's vision of the humanists as engaged with philosophical and theological rather than just rhetorical concerns. Educated at Harvard University and past president of the American Historical Association, Bouwsma is emeritus professor of history at the University of California at Berkeley and the author of many volumes and articles on both the Renaissance and the Reformation. Whereas Trinkaus showed how humanism combined Stoical and Augustinian visions of the human condition to spur man toward virtue, Bouwsma portrays Stoicism and Augustinianism more as conflicting traditions within the humanist movement. In "The Two Faces of Humanism," he illustrates this conflict, both between and within authors, as they struggled to reconcile the ancient Stoics' fundamentally rational and ordered view of the human condition with Augustine's altogether messier view, in which man was a mysterious amalgam of reason and will, with the latter often predominating, for better or worse. According to Bouwsma, the conflict between these two traditions engendered the remarkable durability of the humanist movement, which adapted itself over time not only to a wide range of spiritual needs but also to changing political, social, and intellectual realities. Ultimately, Bouwsma deepens Kristeller's insight into the rhetorical nature of the humanist movement by showing how the humanists' concerns extended beyond the practice and profession of rhetoric to encompass formative issues in the history of European culture, issues inherent in the rhetorical tradition itself.

It is worth noting that "The Two Faces of Humanism" originally appeared in a *Festschrift* honoring Kristeller on the occasion of his seventieth birthday, one of ultimately seven *Festschriften* celebrating a lifetime of scholarly achievement. Though Gray, Trinkaus, and Bouwsma all seek to refine Kristeller's vision of humanism, none questions his fundamental insight into the rhetorical nature of the movement. And this insight represents only one aspect of his many contributions to the study of the Renaissance. Another resides in his assiduous unearthing and cataloguing of humanistic manuscripts. By bringing to light several striking works by and about women humanists, Kristeller has helped inspire the work of another scholar, Margaret L. King, professor of history at Brooklyn College and the Graduate Center of the City University of New York. In her penetrating article, "Book-Lined Cells: Women and Humanism in the Early Italian Renaissance" (1980), King builds on Kristeller's work by examining how women fared in the overwhelmingly male world of humanism.

She reveals that the nature of humanism was different for women than it was for men, despite the fact that they both practiced the same art of rhetoric. Adolescent girls from elite and professional families in northern Italian cities often received humanist training, but once they reached marriageable age, the male world of humanism left them little practical outlet for their literary and scholarly talents. Furthermore, according to King, those who persisted in the life of learning found themselves marginalized, a condition due only in part to a lack of opportunities for learned women. Indeed, King shows how they often willingly isolated themselves, partially out of a generic insecurity with their sex, partially out of a desire to retreat to confines more within their control, and partially in response to subtle (and not so subtle) messages they received from their male counterparts, who did not know quite what to make of them. All these factors conspired to encourage their withdrawal into "book-lined cells," an ideal of female intellectual solitude that stands in marked contrast to the active life of moral and social engagement that rhetoric supposedly fostered for men. Yet despite their isolation, King suggests, these women humanists were likely the first examples of a model of female learning that is still with us, for better or worse. Strangely, then, even in the experiences of women humanists, the Renaissance stands as a prelude to modernity.

Paul Oskar Kristeller

Humanism and Scholasticism in the Italian Renaissance

Kristeller's essay, "Humanism and Scholasticism in the Italian Renaissance," epitomizes the interpretation of humanism he advanced in *Renaissance Thought: The Classic, Scholastic, and Humanist Strains.* The essay begins with a nod to Burckhardt and the debates about originality and continuity in the Renaissance that his thesis stirred. Kristeller notes that assertions of a

From Paul Oskar Kristeller, *Renaissance Thought: The Classic, Scholastic, and Humanist Strains* (New York: Harper & Row, 1961).

medieval revival have called into question the very existence of the Renaissance as a viable historical period, thus forcing proponents of the Renaissance back on a new line of defense, that the humanists themselves claimed to have revived learning. In addition to granting that the term had subjective meaning for the humanists, Kristeller suggests that it also has objective meaning as a period standing in contrast not to the high culture of the French Middle Ages but to the more modest culture of the Italian Middle Ages. While medieval France stood in the vanguard of a revival of learning that included classical scholarship as well as philosophy, medieval Italy remained by comparison an intellectual backwater. Thus, one may safely speak of an Italian Renaissance within the context of Italian history, where a genuine revival of learning occurred in the fourteenth and fifteenth centuries, relative to what had gone before.

In the selections below, Kristeller shows how humanism emerged from rhetoric, the area of learning that most flourished in the Italian Middle Ages. Medieval teachers of rhetoric, the *dictatores*, first championed the ideal of eloquence. By the end of the thirteenth century, the Italian emphasis on rhetorical eloquence merged with an interest in classical studies imported from medieval France, thus giving rise to the humanist movement. Concurrently with the advent of humanism, scholasticism began filtering down into Italy. Developing side by side, rhetoric and philosophy operated in different intellectual arenas and hence, according to Kristeller, the disputes between their proponents were not battles to the death between competing systems of thought but mere academic disputes, devoid of larger significance. Humanism thus constitutes, for Kristeller, not a new philosophy superseding an old one but a curriculum centering on a study of rhetoric newly invigorated by classicizing tendencies.

. . . The most characteristic and most pervasive aspect of the Italian Renaissance in the field of learning is the humanistic movement. I need hardly say that the term "humanism," when applied to the Italian Renaissance, does not imply all the vague and confused notions that are now commonly associated with it. Only a few traces of these may be found in the Renaissance. By humanism we mean merely the general tendency of the age to attach the greatest importance to classical studies, and to consider classical antiquity as the common standard and model by which to guide all cultural activities. It will be our task to understand the meaning and origin of this humanistic movement which is commonly associated with the name of Petrarch. . . .

The humanistic movement did not originate in the field of philosophical or scientific studies, but it arose in that of grammatical and rhetorical studies. The humanists continued the medieval tradition in these fields, as represented, for example, by the *ars dictaminis* and the *ars arengandi*, but they gave it a new direction toward classical standards and classical studies, possibly under the impact of influences received from France after the middle of the thirteenth century. This new development of the field was followed by an enormous growth, both in the quantity and in the quality, of its teaching and its literary production. As a result of this growth, the claims of the humanists for their field of study also increased considerably. They claimed, and temporarily attained, a decided predominance of their field in elementary and secondary education, and a much larger share for it in professional and university education. This development in the field of grammatical and rhetorical studies finally affected the other branches of learning, but it did not displace them. After the middle of the fifteenth century, we find an increasing number of professional jurists, physicians, mathematicians, philosophers, and theologians who cultivated humanistic studies along with their own particular fields of study. Consequently, a humanistic influence began to appear in all these other sciences. It appears in the studied elegance of literary expression, in the increasing use made of classical source materials, in the greater knowledge of history and of critical methods, and also sometimes in an emphasis on new problems. This influence of humanism on the other sciences certainly was important, but it did not affect the content or substance of the medieval traditions in those sciences. For the humanists, being amateurs in those other fields, had nothing to offer that could replace their traditional content and subject matter. . . .

Yet if the humanists were amateurs in jurisprudence, theology, medicine, and also in philosophy, they were themselves professionals in a number of other fields. Their domains were the fields of grammar, rhetoric, poetry, history, and the study of the Greek and Latin authors. They also expanded into the field of moral philosophy, and they made some attempts to invade the field of logic, which were chiefly attempts to reduce logic to rhetoric. . . .

. . . [T]he vast majority of humanists exercised either of two professions, and sometimes both of them. They were either secretaries of princes or cities, or they were teachers of grammar and rhetoric at universities or at secondary schools. The opinion so often repeated by historians that the humanistic movement originated outside the schools and universities is a myth which cannot be supported by factual evidence. Moreover, as chancellors and as teachers, the humanists, far from representing a new class, were the professional heirs and successors of the medieval rhetoricians, the so-called *dictatores*, who also made their career exactly in these same two professions. The humanist Coluccio Salutati occupied exactly the same place in the society and culture of his time as did the *dictator* Petrus de Vineis one hundred and fifty years before. Nevertheless there was a significant difference between them. The style of writing used by Salutati is quite different from that of Petrus de Vineis or of Rolandinus Passagerii. Moreover, the study and imitation of the classics which was of little or no importance to the medieval *dictatores* has become the major concern for Salutati. Finally, whereas the medieval *dictatores* attained considerable importance in politics and in administration, the humanists, through their classical learning, acquired for their class a much greater cultural and social prestige. Thus the humanists did not invent a new field of learning or a new professional activity, but they introduced a new, classicist style into the traditions of medieval Italian rhetoric. . . .

The same result is confirmed by an examination of the literary production of the humanists if we try to trace the medieval antecedents of the types of literature cultivated by the humanists. If we leave aside the editions and translations of the humanists, their classical interests are chiefly represented by their numerous commentaries on ancient authors and by a number of antiquarian and miscellaneous treatises. Theoretical works on grammar and rhetoric, mostly composed for the school, are quite frequent, and even more numerous is the literature of humanist historiography. Dialogues and treatises on questions of moral philosophy, education, politics, and religion have attracted most of the attention of modern historians, but represent a comparatively small proportion of humanistic literature. By far the largest part of that literature, although relatively neglected and partly unpublished, consists of the poems, the speeches, and the letters of the humanists.

If we look for the medieval antecedents of these various types of humanistic literature, we are led back in many cases to the Italian grammarians and rhetoricians of the later Middle Ages. This is most obvious for the theoretical treatises on grammar and rhetoric. Less generally recognized, but almost equally obvious is the link between humanist epistolography and medieval *ars dictaminis*. The style of writing is different, to be sure, and the medieval term *dictamen* was no longer used during the Renaissance, yet the literary and political function of the letter was basically the same, and the ability to write a correct and elegant Latin letter was still a major aim of school instruction in the Renaissance as it had been in the Middle Ages.

The same link between humanists and medieval Italian rhetoricians which we notice in the field of epistolography may be found also in the field of oratory. Most historians of rhetoric give the impression that medieval rhetoric was exclusively concerned with letter-writing and preaching, represented by the *ars dictaminis* and the somewhat younger *ars praedicandi*, and that there was no secular eloquence in the Middle Ages. On the other hand, most historians of Renaissance humanism believe that the large output of humanist oratory, although of a somewhat dubious value, was an innovation of the Renaissance due to the effort of the humanists to revive ancient oratory and also to their vain fancy for speech-making. Only in recent years have a few scholars begun to realize that there was a considerable amount of secular eloquence in the Middle Ages, especially in Italy. I do not hesitate to conclude that the eloquence of the humanists was the continuation of the medieval *ars arengandi* just as their epistolography continued the tradition of the *ars dictaminis*. It is true, in taking up a type of literary production developed by their medieval predecessors, the humanists modified its style according to their own taste and classicist standards. Yet the practice of speech-making was no invention of the humanists, of course, since it is hardly absent from any human society, and since in medieval Italy it can be traced back at least to the eleventh century.

Even the theory of secular speech, represented by rules and instructions as well as by model speeches, appears in Italy at least as early as the thirteenth century. Indeed practically all types of humanist oratory have their antecedents in this medieval literature: wedding and funeral speeches, academic speeches, political speeches by officials or ambassadors, decorative speeches on solemn occasions, and finally judicial speeches. Some of these types, to be sure, had their classical models, but others, for example, academic speeches delivered at the beginning of the year or of a particular course or upon conferring or receiving a degree, had no classical antecedents whatsoever, and all these types of oratory were rooted in very specific customs and institutions of medieval Italy. The humanists invented hardly any of these types of speech, but they merely applied their standards of style and elegance to a previously existing form of literary expression and thus satisfied a demand, both practical and artistic, of the society of their time. . . .

In their historiography, the humanists succeeded the medieval chroniclers, yet they differ from them both in their merits and in their deficiencies. Humanist historiography is characterized by the rhetorical concern for elegant Latin and by the application of philological criticism to the source materials of history. In both respects, they are the predecessors of modern historians. To combine the requirements of a good style and those of careful research was as rare and difficult then as it is at present. However, the link between history and rhetoric that seems to be so typical of the Renaissance was apparently a medieval heritage. Not only was the teaching of history in the medieval schools subordinate to that of grammar and rhetoric, but we also find quite a few medieval historiographers and chronists who were professional grammarians and rhetoricians. Even the Renaissance custom of princes and cities appointing official historiographers to write their history seems to have had a few antecedents in medieval Italy.

Most of the philosophical treatises and dialogues of the humanists are really nothing but moral tracts, and many of them deal with subject matters also treated in the moralistic literature of the Middle Ages. There are, to be sure, significant differences in style, treatment, sources, and solutions. However, the common features of the topics and literary patterns should not be overlooked either. A thorough comparative study of medieval and Renaissance moral treatises has not yet been made so far as I am aware, but in a few specific cases the connection has been pointed out. Again it should be added that the very link between rhetoric and moral philosophy which became so apparent in the Renaissance had its antecedents in the Middle Ages. Medieval rhetoric, no less than ancient rhetoric, was continually quoting and inculcating moral sentences that interested the authors and their readers for the content as well as for their form. Moreover, there are at least a few cases in which medieval rhetoricians wrote treatises on topics of moral philosophy, or argued about the same moral questions that were to exercise the minds and pens of their successors, the Renaissance humanists.

Less definite is the link between humanists and medieval Italian rhetoricians in the field of Latin poetry. On the basis of available evidence, it would seem that in the Italian schools up to the thirteenth century verse-making was less cultivated than in France. Throughout the earlier Middle Ages, historical and panegyric epics as well as verse epitaphs were composed abundantly in Italy, yet prior to the thirteenth century her share in rhythmical and in didactic poetry seems to have been rather modest. It is only after the middle of the thirteenth century that we notice a marked increase in the production of Latin poetry in Italy, and the appearance of the teaching of poetry in the schools and universities. This development coincides with the earliest traces of Italian humanism, and it is tempting to ascribe it to French influences.

The same may be said with more confidence of the literature of commentaries on the Latin classics, which are the direct result of school teaching. It is often asserted that, Italy throughout the Middle Ages was closer to the classical tradition than any other European country. Yet if we try to trace the type of the humanistic commentary back into the Middle Ages, we find hardly any commentary on a Latin poet or prose writer composed in Italy prior to the second half of the thirteenth century, whereas we find many such commentaries, from the ninth century on, written in France or in the other Western countries that followed the French development. Only after 1300, that is, after the earliest phase of humanism, did Italy produce an increasing number of such commentaries. Also of antiquarian studies there is very little evidence in Italy prior to the latter part of the thirteenth century. Whereas we have abundant information about the reading of the Latin poets and prose writers in the medieval schools of France and of other Western countries, and whereas such centers as Chartres and Orléans in the twelfth and early thirteenth centuries owed much of their fame to the study of the Latin classics, the sources for Italy are silent during the same period and begin to speak only after the middle of the thirteenth century. It was only after the beginning of the fourteenth century that the teaching of poetry and of the classical authors became firmly established in the Italian schools and universities, to continue without interruption throughout the Renaissance. Italian libraries, with the one exception of Monte Cassino, were not so well furnished with Latin classical poets as were some French and German libraries, and it has been noticed that the humanists of the fifteenth century made most of their manuscript discoveries not in Italy, but in other countries. The conclusion seems inevitable that the study of classical Latin authors was comparatively neglected in Italy during the earlier Middle Ages and was introduced from France after the middle of the thirteenth century. The Italian humanists thus took up the work of their medieval French predecessors just about the time when classical studies began to decline in France, and whereas the classical scholarship of the earliest humanists in its range and method was still close to the medieval tradition, that of the later Renaissance developed far beyond anything attained during the Middle Ages. Consequently, if we consider the entire literary production of the Italian humanists we are led to the conclusion that the humanistic movement seems to have originated from a fusion between the novel interest in classical studies imported from France toward the end of the thirteenth century and the much earlier traditions of medieval Italian rhetoric.

We have seen that the humanists did not live outside the schools and universities, but were closely connected with them. The chairs commonly held by the humanists were those of grammar and rhetoric, that is, the same that had been occupied by their medieval predecessors, the *dictatores*. Thus it is in the history of the universities and schools and of their chairs that the connection of the humanists with medieval rhetoric becomes most apparent. However, under the influence of humanism, these chairs underwent a change which affected their name as well as their content and pretenses. About the beginning of the fourteenth century poetry appears as a special teaching subject at Italian universities. After that time, the teaching of grammar was considered primarily as the task of elementary instructors, whereas the humanists proper held the more advanced chairs of poetry and of eloquence. For eloquence was the equivalent of prose writing as well as of speech. The teaching of poetry and of eloquence was theoretical and practical at the same time, for the humanist professor instructed his pupils in verse-making and in speech-making both through rules and through models. Since classical Latin authors were considered as the chief models for imitation, the reading of these authors was inseparably connected with the theoretical and practical teaching of poetry and of eloquence.

Thus we may understand why the humanists of the fourteenth and fifteenth centuries chose to call their field of study poetry and why they were often styled poets even though they composed no works that would qualify them as poets in the modern sense. Also the coronation of poets in the Renaissance must be understood against this background. It had been originally understood as a kind of academic degree, and it was granted not merely for original poetic compositions, but also for the competent study of classical poets.

History was not taught as a separate subject, but formed a part of the study of rhetoric and poetry since the ancient historians were among the prose writers commonly studied in school. Moral philosophy was always the subject of a separate chair and was commonly studied from the *Ethics* and *Politics* of Aristotle. However, after the beginning of the fifteenth century, the chair of moral philosophy was often held by the humanists, usually in combination with that of rhetoric and poetry. This combination reflects the expansion of humanistic learning into the field of moral philosophy. The chairs of Greek language and literature which were an innovation of the fourteenth century were also commonly held by humanists. . . .

Later on the fields of study cultivated by the humanists were given a new and even more ambitious name. Taking up certain expressions found in Cicero and Gellius, the humanists as early as the fourteenth century began to call their field of learning the humane studies or the studies befitting a human being (*studia humanitatis, studia humaniora*). The new name certainly implies a new claim and program, but it covered a content that had existed long before and that had been designated by the more modest names of grammar, rhetoric, and poetry. Although some modern scholars were not aware of this fact, the humanists certainly were, and we have several contemporary testimonies showing that the *studia humanitatis* were considered as the equivalent of grammar, rhetoric, poetry, history, and moral philosophy.

These statements also prove another point that has been confused by most modern historians: the humanists, at least in Italy or before the sixteenth century, did not claim that they were substituting a new encyclopaedia of learning for the medieval one, and they were aware of the fact that their field of study occupied a well defined and limited place within the system of contemporary learning. To be sure, they tended to emphasize the importance of their field in comparison with the other sciences and to encroach upon the latter's territory, but on the whole they did not deny the existence or validity of these other sciences. This well defined place of the *studia humanitatis* is reflected in the new term *humanista* which apparently was coined during the latter half of the fifteenth century and became increasingly popular during the sixteenth century. The term seems to have originated in the slang of university students and gradually penetrated into official usage. It was coined after the model of such medieval terms as *legista, jurista, canonista,* and *artista,* and it designated the professional teacher of the *studia humanitatis*. The term *humanista* in this limited sense thus was coined during the Renaissance, whereas the term *humanism* was first used by nineteenth century historians. If I am not mistaken, the new term *humanism* reflects the modern and false conception that Renaissance humanism was a basically new philosophical movement, and under the influence of this notion the old term humanist has also been misunderstood as designating the representative of a new *Weltanschauung*. The old term *humanista*, on the other hand, reflects the more modest, but correct, contemporary view that the humanists were the teachers and representatives of a certain branch of learning which at that time was expanding and in vogue, but well limited in its subject matter. Humanism thus did not represent the sum total of learning in the Italian Renaissance.

If we care to look beyond the field of the humanities into the other fields of learning as they were cultivated during the Italian Renaissance, that is, into jurisprudence, medicine, theology, mathematics, and natural philosophy, what we find is evidently a continuation of medieval learning and may hence very well be called scholasticism. . . . It is well known that the content of scholastic philosophy, since the thirteenth century, was largely based on the writings of Aristotle, and that the development of this philosophy, since the twelfth century, was closely connected with the schools and universities of France and England, especially with the universities of Paris and of Oxford. The place of Italy is, however, less known in the history and development of scholastic philosophy. . . . Whereas Italy had flourishing schools of rhetoric, of jurisprudence, and of medicine during the twelfth and early thirteenth century, she had no native center of philosophical studies during the same period. . . .

Aristotelian philosophy, although not entirely unknown at Salerno toward the end of the twelfth century, made its regular appearance at the Italian universities after the middle of the thirteenth century and in close connection with the teaching of medicine. I think it is safe to assume that Aristotelian philosophy was then imported from France as were the study of classical authors and many other forms of intellectual activity. After the beginning of the fourteenth century, this Italian Aristotelianism assumed a more definite shape. The teaching of logic and natural philosophy became a well established part of the university curriculum and even spread to some of the secondary schools. An increasing number of commentaries and questions on the works of Aristotle reflect this teaching tradition, and numerous systematic treatises on philosophical subjects show the same general trend and background. During the fourteenth and fifteenth centuries, further influences were received from Paris in the field of natural philosophy and from Oxford in the field of logic; and from the latter part of the fourteenth century on we can trace an unbroken tradition of Italian Aristotelianism which continued through the fifteenth and sixteenth century and far into the seventeenth century.

The common notion that scholasticism as an old philosophy was superseded by the new philosophy of humanism is thus again disproved by plain facts. For Italian scholasticism originated toward the end of the thirteenth century, that is, about the same time as did Italian humanism, and both traditions developed side by side throughout the period of the Renaissance and even thereafter.

However, the two traditions had their locus and center in two different sectors of learning: humanism in the field of grammar, rhetoric, and poetry and to some extent in moral philosophy, scholasticism in the fields of logic and of natural philosophy. Everybody knows the eloquent attacks launched by Petrarch and Bruni against the logicians of their time, and it is generally believed that these attacks represent a vigorous new movement rebelling against an old entrenched habit of thought. Yet actually the English method of dialectic was quite as novel at the Italian schools of that time as were the humanistic studies advocated by Petrarch and Bruni, and the humanistic attack was as much a matter of departmental rivalry as it was a clash of opposite ideas or philosophies. Bruni is even hinting at one point that he is not speaking quite in earnest. Such controversies, interesting as they are, were mere episodes in a long period of peaceful coexistence between humanism and scholasticism. Actually the humanists quarreled as much among each other as they did with the scholastics. Moreover, it would be quite wrong to consider these controversies as serious battles for basic principles whereas many of them were meant to be merely personal feuds, intellectual tournaments, or rhetorical exercises. Finally, any attempt to reduce these controversies to one issue must fail since the discussions were concerned with many diverse and overlapping issues. Therefore, we should no longer be surprised that Italian Aristotelianism quietly and forcefully survived the attacks of Petrarch and his humanist successors.

But the Aristotelianism of the Renaissance did not remain untouched by the new influence of humanism. Philosophers began to make abundant use of the Greek text and of the new Latin translations of Aristotle, of his ancient commentators, and of other Greek thinkers. The revival of ancient philosophies that came in the wake of the humanistic movement, especially the revival of Platonism and of Stoicism, left a strong impact upon the Aristotelian philosophers of the Renaissance. Yet in spite of these significant modifications, Renaissance Aristotelianism continued the medieval scholastic tradition without any visible break. It preserved a firm hold on the university chairs of logic, natural philosophy, and metaphysics, whereas even the humanist professors of moral philosophy continued to base their lectures on Aristotle. . . .

Thus we may conclude that the humanism and the scholasticism of the Renaissance arose in medieval Italy about the same time, that is, about the end of the thirteenth century, and that they coexisted and developed all the way through and beyond the Renaissance period as different branches of learning. Their controversy, much less persistent and violent than usually represented, is merely a phase in the battle of the arts, not a struggle for existence. We may compare it to the debates of the arts in medieval literature, to the rivaling claims of medicine and of law at the universities, or to the claims advanced by Leonardo in his *Paragone* for the superiority of painting over the other arts. Humanism certainly had a tendency to influence the other sciences and to expand at their expense, but all kinds of adjustments and combinations between humanism and scholasticism were possible and were successfully accomplished. It is only after the Renaissance, through the rise of modern science and modern philosophy, that Aristotelianism was gradually displaced, whereas humanism became gradually detached from its rhetorical background and evolved into modern philology and history. . . .

Hanna H. Gray

Renaissance Humanism: The Pursuit of Eloquence

Gray introduces her essay with an important qualifier, that humanism contained many schools of thought. Although she intended to discuss an attitude toward eloquence characteristic of the movement as a whole, she did not intend to explain humanism by means of this common denominator. Rather, she hoped that her discussion of what makes humanists alike would help throw the differences between them into high relief. It is essential for

From Hanna H. Gray, "Renaissance Humanism: The Pursuit of Eloquence," *Journal of the History of Ideas* 24 (1963): 497–514.

us to keep this qualifier in mind, for Gray's insight into humanism's common denominator is so elegant that we might mistake it for an explanation of an inherently diverse and complex movement.

In the selections below, Gray begins by announcing her intention to take both the rhetorical form and the intellectual substance of humanist writings seriously, despite the modern tendency to dismiss the former in favor of the latter. This modern tendency is especially misleading in the analysis of humanist writings because their substance was in many cases slender, leading some commentators to dismiss them as "mere" rhetoric. But for Gray, an assessment of their rhetorical form is essential to a proper understanding of their historical significance. In this regard, she advances beyond Kristeller, who (despite asserting the rhetorical nature of the humanist movement) did not give adequate weight to the humanists' own loud protestations that theirs was the pursuit of eloquence and that eloquence was the highest form of wisdom. (Ironically, then, we may regard him as dismissing these protestations as "mere" rhetoric.) After showing how the pursuit of eloquence constituted a new existential stance in the world, Gray goes on to consider how the humanists used various rhetorical forms—such as disputation and dialogue—as integral parts of their consideration of important issues. And she closes by showing how the humanists fused rhetorical ideals, like that of *decorum*, with the substance of their arguments, allowing the form of their writings to illuminate life's issues.

. . . Modern commentators have too often distinguished between "form" and "substance" in their consideration of humanist literature. In their anxiety to penetrate to the significant ideas of humanism, they have regarded these as separable from the formal structures within which those ideas were expressed. So, paradoxically, the conventions which, to the humanists, created an intelligible and constant frame of reference through which they could communicate clearly with their audience have been cast aside by a later age as irrelevant to the exposition and comprehension of their mode of thought. As a result, the particular assumptions underlying the humanists' own stress on form have not always been treated sufficiently as an integral dimension of their thought. It is curious that many interpreters who have pointed out the humanists' insistence on reading classical works as a whole and in context should not have drawn from such assertions the conclusion that the humanists intended their works to be approached in the same spirit; that their writings were, perhaps, designed with that specific expectation in mind.

It may be objected that much humanist writing is wordy, tedious, repetitive, so that the historian of ideas can justifiably abstract what is really interesting. Or it may be objected that much humanist writing cannot be taken seriously as literature. But in the analysis of the humanists' thought and work, their pretensions must be considered, their stated purposes kept in mind. To that end, it is essential to understand the humanists' reiterated claim, that theirs was the pursuit of eloquence. That claim, indeed, reveals the identifying characteristic of Renaissance humanism. The bond which united humanists, no matter how far separated in outlook or in time, was a conception of eloquence and its uses. Through it, they shared a common intellectual method and a broad agreement on the value of that method. Classical rhetoric—or classical rhetoric as interpreted and adapted in the Renaissance—constituted the main source for both. It provided the humanists with a body of precepts for the effective communication of ideas and, equally important, with a set of principles which asserted the central role of rhetorical skill and achievement in human affairs.

In pointing to the rhetorical concerns of Renaissance humanism, it is not necessary to conclude, as has sometimes been done, that humanist writing was "merely rhetorical" or that humanism was a "merely literary" movement. The term "rhetoric" must be divorced from its pejorative associations. By "rhetoric" the humanists did not intend an empty pomposity, a willful mendacity, a love of display for its own sake, an extravagant artificiality, a singular lack of originality, or a necessary subordination of substance to form and ornament. Nor did the humanists identify rhetoric with "sophistry" in the popular sense, as the specious manipulation of language and argument for purposes of deception. They distinguished carefully between "true eloquence" and "sophistry," perceiving in the latter a perversion, not a consequence, of the former. True eloquence, according to the humanists, could arise only out of a harmonious union between wisdom and style; its aim was to guide men toward virtue and worthwhile goals, not to mislead them for vicious or trivial purposes. It was this conception of eloquence which the humanists placed in opposition to scholastic philosophy. Scholasticism they criticized both on aesthetic grounds and for its failure to concentrate on "wisdom," on really essential matters. In this controversy, the humanists were not contrasting one finished philosophical system with another, but neither were they simply opposing literary form to philosophical substance.

Professor Kristeller has demonstrated conclusively that the interpretation of humanism as a new system of thought locked in mortal combat with scholasticism cannot be maintained. Systematic philosophy, as he points out, was precisely what the earlier humanists did not profess; their interest lay rather in the realm of the *studia humanitatis*, or of the liberal arts, understood generally as comprising the studies of grammar, rhetoric, poetry, history, and moral philosophy. Hence the term "humanist" originally had reference to this preoccupation with the "humanities" and was first used to describe the professional teacher of the *studia humanitatis*. Professor Kristeller has argued also—and here his emphasis seems to me somewhat misleading—that in their capacity as teachers and practitioners of this largely literary culture, the humanists belonged to and continued an older profession, that of the medieval *dictatores*; that their concerns can be understood to a considerable extent as an outgrowth of their calling as rhetoricians; and that their contribution lay not in the creation of a new field of activity, but rather in their insistence on the cultivation of a more classical style, on the imitation of classical models, within the forms already prescribed and followed by their medieval predecessors. Thus the humanists emerge as a professional group whose activities and ideas can be explained as a function of their calling, and their conflicts with scholastics may be seen as typical academic disputes between disciplines which were always struggling to achieve a larger jurisdiction without questioning one another's existence.

That Renaissance humanism falls into the larger rhetorical tradition of the West, a tradition which persisted in the Middle Ages, is beyond doubt. The humanists did not invent rhetoric, and many of their ideas, including their stress on classicism, had been anticipated in the thirteenth-century *ars dictaminis*. It is true, too, that the rhetorical tradition carries with it certain kinds of writing, certain types of educational activities, a tendency toward certain beliefs. But with internal variations accompanying that tradition there may come important shifts in the specific convictions which define the intellectual outlook of its adherents. Those variations may not be so great objectively as they appeared subjectively to those who developed them, but the subjective consciousness of novelty is of some historical significance. To say that the humanists merely introduced a more classical tone into a fixed series of activities does not indicate why it appeared so essential to them to return to the classical models of the *studia humanitatis*, or why they failed to recognize, indeed disclaimed, continuity with medieval practice. To suggest that their attitudes are explicable in terms of their professional concerns, which are naturally in competition with those of other professions, does not explain how they articulated those concerns, how and why in a particular age men should have turned to rhetoric and claimed for it a special educational and cultural role.

A given Renaissance humanist might be in the technical sense a professional rhetorician; the humanist as such need not be. Certainly the term "humanist," as first applied in the later fifteenth and earlier sixteenth centuries, referred specifically to the professional teachers of the humanities, and these teachers often occupied chairs of rhetoric. Yet many who participated in the humanist movement would not come under this description. Before the word "humanist" gained general currency, the humanists were referring to themselves and to their colleagues by other names—sometimes "philosophers," often "poets." Most frequently, however, they called themselves "orators." By this, they meant not that they made a living by the teaching or practice of oratory, but that they wished to be known as men of eloquence. An "orator" could have made his career in government, in the Church, in leisured study and collecting, in teaching or writing or scholarship. He might have written poetry or history or commentaries on classical texts; he might have composed treatises on moral or political philosophy; he might have devoted himself to translation or editing. Usually, of course, his work included a variety of these activities. The orator was, by definition and inclination, a non-specialist. Further, the humanist's attack on scholasticism and his defense of the studies of the humanities represented more than a struggle for academic precedence, even though it was not an all-out war of displacement. While the humanists did not oppose a new systematic philosophy to the systems of the scholastics, they did oppose to the method of the scholastics another method, and to the values which they believed implied in scholastic method, a different ideal of the aims of knowledge and debate.

The Renaissance humanists believed that education should equip a man to lead a good life, and that therefore the function of knowledge was not merely to demonstrate the truth of given precepts, but to impel people toward their acceptance and application. They believed also that men could be molded most effectively, and perhaps only, through the art of eloquence, which endowed the precept with life, immediacy, persuasive effect, and which stimulated a man's will as well as informing his reason. In attacking scholastic logic and scholastic Latin, the humanists were condemning at once an attitude toward knowledge which appeared to stress the abstract and intellectual, to have no true utility or direct relevance for human life, and criticizing what they regarded as the failure of the scholastics to communicate important truths with persuasive effect. The humanists had a horror of abstract speculation carried on for its own sake, of specialization which led to absorption in purely "theoretical' questions or in the elaboration of exclusively "technical" concerns. Their orientation was toward rhetoric rather than logic, ethics rather than metaphysics; their interest lay in questions of education rather than of epistemology, in the subject matter of literature rather than of natural philosophy. The humanists were contrasting a general and practical culture to the professional and academic activities and attitudes which, in their interpretation, were symbolized by scholasticism. Whether their understanding of scholasticism was correct is, for the moment, immaterial. What matters is the image of scholasticism which they built up and the ideal of eloquence which they proposed to substitute. The central point of this contrast was formulated in terms of the "merely intellectual" on the one side, the "actively persuasive" on the other.

Always, in comparing and preferring the classical author of eloquence to the scholastic philosopher, the humanist states that the first not only makes one see what virtue is, but makes one feel and will to practice it. "The object of the will," Petrarch maintained, "is to be good; that of the intellect is truth. It is better to will the good than to know the truth." Against the Aristotle of the scholastics, from whom one may gain a greater learning, but not a more intense desire for virtue, Petrarch asserts the claims of the great Roman authors, Cicero, Seneca, and Horace in particular:

> . . . they stamp and drive deep into the heart the sharpest and most ardent stings of speech, by which the lazy are startled, the ailing are kindled, and the sleepy aroused, the sick healed, and the prostrate raised, and those who stick to the ground lifted up to the highest thoughts and to honest desire. Then earthly things become vile; the aspect of vice stirs up an enormous hatred of vicious life; virtue and 'the shape, and as it were, the face of honesty,' are beheld by the inmost eye 'and inspire miraculous love' of wisdom and of themselves, 'as Plato says.'

. . . For the humanists, it was of course the studies of the liberal arts which affected will as well as intellect in the appropriate way. These studies had been given eloquent expression in classical literature; they were concretely embodied in a series of texts. The ancient texts as they stood proved, to the humanist, that knowledge and eloquence were necessarily related. The *studia humanitatis* could be pursued through the masterpieces of the past. Their relevance to human experience needed no demonstration. Their capacity to teach men, to spur them to achievement, had been tested. While individually the *studia humanitatis* possessed different subject matters and aims, together they represented an interconnected whole, sharing the common purposes and methods of eloquence. What was needed was a return to those sources which exemplified the humanists' ideals. The liberal arts were to be re-endowed with eloquence through the imitation of the classical models. They would become again the basis of a general education and of an integrated culture, replacing the arid specialization of contemporary learning. The modern orator, reviving ancient tradition, would become a teacher of life as well as of letters.

The humanists' stand on eloquence implied an almost incredible faith in the power of the word. The sweeping claims which ancient writers on rhetoric had made for the impact of oratory were reiterated by the humanists for the written as for the spoken word. The classical precepts governing the art of oratory were now applied to all forms of literature. The process of merging rhetoric and literature within a generalized view of eloquence had been initiated already in later antiquity, and the humanists continued and extended this development. For them, after all, the existing models of eloquence were precisely the surviving texts. The written word of the past still possessed vital authority, still enclosed the essential material of useful knowledge and right action, still enabled men to visualize and benefit from the heroes, institutions, and ideas of the ancient world. Antiquity had life and force because of its perpetuation in literature.

For Petrarch and his successors, Cicero's oration *Pro Archia* was a sacred text. They often cited or adapted the passage which celebrated the role of letters as bestowing glory upon subject and author alike, maintaining that letters provide the best, even the exclusive vehicle of immortality for men, deeds, and ideas. The speech might be invoked in its original sense to apply to poetry, as by Petrarch in his coronation oration, but it was also used to expound the claims of eloquence as a whole. And a favorite commonplace of the fifteenth century was to deplore the darkness of the Middle Ages, dark not because they lacked men of talent or noble acts, but because the light of eloquence had not illuminated and so preserved them. Hence they languished *in tenebris.*

The humanists followed the Ciceronian tradition also in their portrait of the orator as hero. The true orator, they maintained, should combine wide learning, extensive experience—and, according to most humanists, good character—with persuasive capacity. His role was to instruct, to delight, and to move men toward worthwhile goals. His eloquence would represent a unity of content, structure, and form, without ever losing sight of the sovereignty of substance or of the didactic aims which were to be realized, and could only be realized, through the cooperation of argument and style. Without his eloquence, truth would lie mute, knowledge would never serve the reality of human affairs or speak to the needs of worldly existence. The other arts would be lost, society ill-organized; justice might not triumph nor evil be vanquished. The humanists' *uomo universale,* if such there was, is to be found in their picture of the ideal orator, master of many arts and governor of his fellowmen, through the force of his eloquence forging a link between the intellectual and practical spheres of human experience. . . .

. . . The persistence of this image of the orator's power reveals the persistence of those assumptions which in the fourteenth century had inspired, and which in the sixteenth century continued to guide, the humanist pursuit of eloquence. Those assumptions grew out of the conviction that knowledge should serve practical ends, that human learning ought to have utility for human life, that education should instruct both will and intellect, and that in persuasion and eloquent discussion lie the effective means of conveying truth. In turning to rhetoric as the teacher of these means, the humanists derived from it more than literary formulae, slogans about education, or aesthetic satisfaction. The subjects which seemed to them of interest were just those which, according to the ancient rhetorician, fell within the province of eloquence. Equally important, rhetoric provided a source for the humanists' basic modes of argument and analysis. Ancient doctrine held that it was the function of rhetoric to argue over matters which presented alternative possibilities, problems about which different points of view could be maintained, questions open to debate because they could be judged only in terms of probable truth and were not susceptible to scientific demonstrations of irrefutable validity. The principal questions to which the humanists addressed themselves could be ascribed to this category. Thus they developed their ideas in the framework of rhetorical argumentation not only because of their artistic and didactic ideals, but also because their discussions appeared to fall naturally within the area to which rhetorical analysis was applicable.

Several tendencies of humanist thought and expression may be cited to illustrate the pervasive influence of rhetoric. The humanist's modes of argument from example and from authority, their emphasis on "verisimilitude," on variety, and on vividness, their insistence on representing general types or conveying universal lessons through the concrete, the visual, the emotionally convincing—all these bear both a formal and a substantive relation to rhetoric. The humanists applied to their analysis of many disciplines the ideas and the vocabulary of rhetoric. Alberti, for instance, adapted the teachings of ancient rhetoric to the formulation of an "art" of painting. In their discussions of the "art" of history, Renaissance humanists utilized rhetorical doctrines in describing the structure and purposes of historical writing and defined history within the classification of eloquence. The humanists also assimilated the concepts of rhetoric to precepts of another nature. The terms "*decorum*" and "*imitatio*," for example, are central in both rhetoric and moral philosophy, and the humanists often appear to fuse their meanings whatever the context. Thus, the imitations of stylistic and of ethical models are spoken of in identical terms; or the idea of always speaking appropriately, of suiting style and manner to subject, aim, and audience, is treated as the exact analogue of behaving with *decorum*, of choosing the actions and responses which are best in harmony with and most appropriate to individual character and principles on the one hand, the nature of circumstances on the other.

Their presuppositions about eloquence identified the humanists with no one school of philosophy. The same general assumptions could be adopted and developed by men who maintained quite different positions on the role of human will and reason, the relative value of the active and contemplative lives, or the relationship between secular learning and religious concerns. However, in reflecting on such issues the humanists recognized certain common boundaries, outlined by their concern with rhetoric and by the structure of belief which underlay it, and these in turn influenced both the form and the substance of their theoretical discussions. For the majority of humanists, philosophy signified ethics, or practical philosophy, as opposed to pure logic or metaphysics. It belonged to the liberal arts, to the studies of eloquence, and it required, in return, the support and the voice of eloquence.

Moral philosophy was connected with poetry, which taught ethical truths under the guise of fiction, and with history, which showed how its precepts had actually been, and should always be, applied in practice. The other branches of speculation had value especially in their relation to ethics, or should at least be directed toward the problem of how to find and lead the best life; studied for their own sake, they became merely academic.

For consigning moral philosophy, understood in its widest sense as including political and social theory, to the hands of the "orator," the humanists could find precedents in a number of ancient sources. When they turned to other aspects of philosophy, they usually attempted to apply, to some degree at least, the tools and concepts of rhetoric. Their efforts were ordinarily directed at simplifying, or even popularizing, the philosophical systems of antiquity. They were more interested in showing essential similarities and compatibilities among ideas than in making close discriminations among different schools of thought, and they were typically eclectic in their views. All these tendencies were reinforced by the humanists' rhetorical-didactic concerns. It was regarded as the task of eloquence to take what was at hand, to make it generally intelligible and useful. Overattention to precise contrasts could be criticized as word splitting and concentration on points of little import. Virtue and vice, prudence and folly, might, after all, be described in different languages and exemplified in a variety of ways while remaining substantially the same for all. The moralist had, of course, to declare what was unacceptable and erroneous, what could not be reconciled with the true standards of ethics and religious teaching, but his major aim must be to instruct by constructive synthesis. . . .

The literary forms and the modes of argumentation associated with eloquence were applied by the humanists to a great diversity of issues. Their choice of form did not shackle originality, nor was it incidental to the expression of their ideas. Thus the humanist oration could be a stultifying and imitative stringing together of expected clichés, but it could also become an elegant, imaginative, and serious argument. The compelling motive behind its use was the humanists' belief in the importance of moving, swaying, and entertaining as a part of persuasive instruction, in the necessity of lending immediacy, color, concrete force, to their appeals. The fixed conventions of the oration could be adopted to underscore meaning, as Erasmus used the rules of panegyric in the *Praise of Folly*. The conventions of oratory might also give an author the

80 Hanna H. Gray

opportunity to state arguments which he could then claim had not been meant literally. Thus Valla, attacking the authenticity of the Donation of Constantine, called his work a "declamation," the term for an oratorical exercise. In the practice of declamation, ancient orators were supposed to be able to construct equally convincing cases for opposing sides of the same question. . . .

The structure of Valla's *Declamation*, the fictitious speeches within the speech, and the appeal to the emotions of his audience are all clearly rhetorical. So, too, is the nature of Valla's argument. Its concern is with verisimilitude, with what may be convincingly believed, with what may be reasonably taken to have occurred. Surely, Valla argues, Constantine would scarcely have been likely to have made the donation, his sons to have permitted it, the senate or people to have tolerated it, or Sylvester to have accepted it. Surely Roman emperors and early Popes would not have behaved in so extraordinary a manner, and clearly others would have dissuaded them from such conduct, had they proposed it. With these rhetorical deductions Valla combines argument from authority and example in establishing a case built up by a mounting chain of probable truths and moral indignation. He presents the philological and documentary evidence which to us may appear conclusive as one persuasive argument in a series. Valla's *Declamation* demonstrates the way in which rhetorical analysis could serve as an approach to historical analysis. Rhetoric offered a kind of rigorous common-sense method of ascertaining what was or is or will most probably be true; it also described procedures by which these findings might be rendered persuasive. Typically, the mode of "historical criticism" characteristic of Renaissance humanism is founded on rhetorical argumentation. Humanist philology, too, played a role. It created instruments for precise textual investigations; it may have implied a "historical" conception of language and its uses. But the ideas and methods of philological criticism were not ordinarily, and not systematically, applied to history directly, except in partnership with, or at the behest of, rhetorical analysis. Valla's *Declamation* shows the creative results of rhetoric, and not only of philology, in the service of humanist historiography. . . .

In dialogue, the humanists found the most flexible form for discussing issues of all sorts. In their view, dialogue could bring to life and dramatize with persuasive effect the actual process of exposition, analysis, and debate appropriate to the matters under discussion. Rational thinking about such subjects was regarded as in itself a mental dialogue; the form, through externalizing, could help to teach the method of thought. The development of a dialogue could demonstrate how questioning was essential to the illumination of truth. The humanist, presenting his interlocutors as men of firm reputation and experience, could attach at once authority and a concrete, personal tone to the ideas which he had them express. Otherwise he might employ invented interlocutors, or stage a simple question and answer session between himself and some disciple or friend, again on the assumption that to "see" and "hear" individuals engaged in discourse would have a greater effect on the audience than would the reading of a straightforward treatise. In dialogue, a humanist could state a clear position or refuse to take one. Some dialogues were left deliberately without explicit conclusion, either because the author wished to point out what could be said on different sides of doubtful or complex matters, not to assert one final decision, or with the purpose of allowing the reader to render his own judgment. It was possible in dialogue to take up a number of issues, sometimes quite unrelated ones, without sacrificing its unity. Dialogue, according to humanist practice, should show busy men engaged in thoughtful leisure, it should be nonformalistic, ostensibly casual; in setting and atmosphere it should be natural and unhurried. All this required careful design.

To dialogue as to the other types of eloquence the humanists applied the principle that form and content must be fused, that language and tone must suit both the speaker and his argument. In Erasmus' *Ciceronianus*, we have a humanist dialogue which provides both an example of, and a rumination on, that tradition. Through the fictitious characters in his dialogue, Erasmus pictures the schools they typify. He intends to bring to life, as an object lesson to be shunned, the so-called Ciceronians and their views, and to present a model of the lessons that ought to be followed. The argument is developed rhetorically; the style is everywhere meant to reflect, to afford concrete proof and exemplification of its theme. Erasmus argues that literary imitation should be based on many models rather than one alone and that it consists in following the spirit rather than the letter of the model texts. He argues further that eloquence is not a matter of external devices but that it is "wisdom speaking copiously" and rests in a true appreciation of *decorum*, the appropriate suiting of language and form to subject and ideas, which can come only out of a deep understanding of issues. Erasmus argues, finally, that the eloquent man through imitation has learned not to re-produce the exact style of others, but has learned to represent himself through eloquence. Clearly, Erasmus intended that his own style should stand as a striking model of the practical application of all these precepts, to confirm and to illustrate his own precise understanding of the nature of imitation. So, for instance, Erasmus quotes and paraphrases passages from numerous ancient authors, and not Cicero alone, and weaves them into a pattern distinctively his own. His teachings on *decorum*, on the in-appropriateness of clothing Christian ideas in pagan dress, are paralleled by the language he employs in referring to Christian themes. The pre-cept that the object of imitation is ultimately to represent one's self is followed here as elsewhere by Erasmus, whose aim was always to picture himself, his mind, his opinions. The lack of any individual characteriza-tion in the dialogue is a direct result of this Erasmian aim: he wishes to delineate not other individuals, but himself.

In the *Ciceronianus*, Erasmus is arguing over doctrines of rhetoric. But these doctrines, like that of eloquence, are carried beyond the con-fines of technical rhetoric. In maintaining, for instance, that eloquence must look always to the *decorum*, and that a mechanical, externalized classicism is inconsistent with that goal, Erasmus is discussing the spir-itual and historical distance between the facts of antiquity and the re-quirements of modern Christianity. In urging the application of eloquence to Christian truth, he is urging a particular program of theol-ogy and education. Finally, in seeing the nature of "true Ciceronian-ism" to lie in understanding and following the spirit rather than the letter of authority, Erasmus is indicating his whole approach to doctrine and is pointing to the area where he believes the actual reconciliation of past and present, paganism and Christianity, to be both possible and necessary. . . .

Rhetoric has been called "the greatest barrier between us and our ancestors." Too often, the attempt is made to destroy that barrier by regarding rhetorical form as the chaff which can be separated from the wheat of humanist thought. "What subject," asked Melanchthon, "can possibly be richer than that of the dignity and utility of eloquence?" The question was, of course, rhetorical, but the answer was clear. It was the pursuit of eloquence which united humanists of all shades. To ig-nore the impact of eloquence and of the ideas associated with it is to dis-tort the mentality of humanism and to disregard a vital dimension of Renaissance thought and method.

Charles Trinkaus

In Our Image and Likeness

Although Trinkaus conceived of the Renaissance along Burckhardtian lines—see his introduction (with Benjamin Nelson) to the 1958 Harper Torchbook edition of *The Civilization of the Renaissance in Italy*—he devoted much of his scholarly career to studying the religious and philosophical dimensions of humanism, themes that Burckhardt had largely ignored. According to Trinkaus, the humanist movement articulated a philosophy of will consistent with the "development of the individual." But instead of endorsing a pagan or secular view of man, this philosophy constituted a drive toward a new theology that celebrated man as emulator of divinity, as making his own world much as God made him. While not denying that the Renaissance may have had some nonreligious or even antireligious aspects, Trinkaus devotes *In Our Image and Likeness* to elaborating the predominantly religious view of human existence that shaped the humanist movement.

Trinkaus's exhaustive coverage of this theme encompasses most of the major intellectual figures of fourteenth- and fifteenth-century Italy, as well as many minor ones. Our selections below are drawn from his first chapter on Petrarch, specifically from the section entitled, "Humanism and the Intellectual Traditions: The Pursuit of Christian Selfhood from St. Augustine to the Renaissance." This section epitomizes the point about humanism and spirituality that Trinkaus later elicits from a host of writers. It shows that the humanists, though not philosophers in any traditional sense, could not avoid philosophical issues about human existence, issues that (as Christians) they inevitably viewed through a spiritual lens. Furthermore, it shows how an ideal of eloquence—shades of Gray—lies at the heart of their new spirituality, which aims not to instruct the mind but move the will toward God.

The *self*, in the history of philosophy, is built around the *will*. Though the Socrates of the *Phaedo*, though Seneca and Cicero, all were seeking within their intellectual and philosophical bounds to realise the concept of selfhood, it remained for Christianity, and especially for St. Augustine,

From Charles Trinkaus, *In Our Image and Likeness: Humanity and Divinity in Italian Humanist Thought*, 2 Vols. (Chicago: University of Chicago Press, 1970).

to develop it. There is no work like the *Confessions* in entire antiquity. There the *self*, Augustine's self, is made manifest as pure subject in search of a vision of the world that corresponds to its own inner experience of truth. It is this great achievement of St. Augustine—his delineation of the will and construction of a philosophy based on it—that attracted Petrarch, a man of lesser intellect, more limited education and far weaker character. But with Augustine as his mentor and model he was able to feel his way towards a new vision of Christianity adjusted to the new needs of his own time and re-synthesised with classical moral thought and the teachings of ancient rhetoric and poetic (three branches of ancient culture that were in essential harmony with each other).

Augustine and the Latin fathers had achieved an earlier synthesis that worked tolerably well for them and was far more resilient and subtle than the Middle Ages required, although twelfth-century cathedral humanism began once again to comprehend it. Scholasticism produced a number of new syntheses with what was then felt to be a crucial need, the cosmological, physical and logical writings of the ancients, and there emerged a number of attempts to state ecclesiastical ethics and theology with the aid of Aristotelian naturalistic doctrine, in many respects a forced marriage which compromised both sides. Ockhamism exposed the logical and epistemological weakness of the attempted match but left the problem unresolved.

The emergence of humanism, which is in so many respects the life of Petrarch (although the earlier precedents are important), partly was simply a turn toward other branches of ancient culture—poetry, oratory, moral philosophy. But it was also partly a response to the sense of a gap between the current doctrines and practices of Christianity, and the experience of urban life. Petrarch's criticism of contemporary Aristotelians (not Aristotle from whom he learned very much) was essentially moral and not intellectual. In fact it was to some extent, by implication, anti-intellectual. It was the failure of the university-trained professionals of his day, whether lawyers, physicians or theologians, to be aware of the crying moral problems he sensed in his contemporaries or to be aware of the irrelevance of their studies for these problems which they sometimes sought too easily to solve. All of this had to mean an attempted return to the actuality of feelings and experience, in the first place to one's own. There was never in Petrarch's mind or in those of his contemporary humanist friends the slightest doubt about the truth of the Christian revelation, nor could there have been. There was, on the other hand, the gravest doubt about the relevance of the intellectualisations of scholasticism, of whatever school, for the problem of how to lead a Christian life. Verbal profession was not to be confused with faith, and subtle understanding of the ways in which Aristotelian metaphysics might illuminate Christian theology contributed little to the ordinary Christian, even the moderately educated one.

Petrarch therefore imitated Augustine both in the poignancy of his own search for wholeness and serenity and in his use of his own experiences as a guide for his brothers. . . .

It was particularly the fact that Augustine was himself a distinguished, late antique humanist who found the fulfilment and the vitalisation of the confused and formal values of his humanism in his hard-won Christian faith that appealed to the Italian humanists. There is a curious reversal of historical directions here. Where Augustine gave new life to a tried and formalised rhetorical tradition with the fervor of the newly discovered Divine Word, the humanists turned to the classics for a freshness and beauty and human relevance that the highly organised and practice-oriented Christian culture of the late Middle Ages lacked. Facing in the opposite direction with respect to antiquity they found in Augustine a Christianity that was highly antique in form and in content but standing in variance and contrast with pagan antiquity. It permitted them to open up and explore the writings of the ancients without fear of the demonic influence of paganism or of the suspicions and criticisms of their contemporaries. Ancient literature and philosophy, following Augustine's example, could be discussed calmly and rationally, but seriously and intently in a Christian context. With his help, as well as that of Lactantius and to a lesser extent of Jerome, the humanists were able to realise that sense of intimate familiarity with the culture of the ancient world along with a sense of its distance and difference from their own that Seznec and Panofsky insist is what distinguishes the Renaissance from the medieval attitude towards antiquity.

Augustine, despite his lack of Greek and his lack of direct knowledge of Plato or, apparently, of Aristotle, was the most superb and just critic of the values of classical culture that the world has known. By turning Christian apologetics away from either denunciation or uncritical and unconscious absorption of classical philosophy and towards serious and thoughtful knowledge and discriminating evaluation of all aspects of ancient culture from a point of view that was Christian but willing to accept what was true and best in the ancients, Augustine established his place in the grand tradition of western thought and philosophy. And by this he made possible the continuation of the western tradition through the ecclesiastical theology and philosophy of the Middle Ages, providing a precedent for all the great medieval humanists and scholastics from John of Salisbury, through Thomas Aquinas, to William of Ockham.

The scholastics, however, sought to carry further that process of objectification of theology that Augustine himself had begun. But with the exception of the mystics and the conservatives, they turned away from his moral, psychological and spiritual emphasis in order to explore the relations of Christian doctrine to ancient conceptions of the cosmos, the physical realm, the problems of logic. . . . The scholastic attitude towards classical culture was consistent with the popular attitude towards the antique gods. It was a mixture of a lack of a sufficiently critical discrimination between the Christian and the pagan and too absolute a rejection.

But the problem of the relation between Christian truth and pagan science covered over a more fundamental question, that of the relationship between the Christian religion and the life of man in this world. Because the philosophers, poets and orators of antiquity approached human existence in a variety of ways, but without any prescribed religious dogma, the classical views of the world (both of the material world and of the human world) came to represent to medieval culture a variety of dangerously autonomous approaches to life without either the safeguards of Church doctrine or the aid of grace. Thus the problems of the relation of the Church to the world, and of Christianity to classical thought, blended with each other. The coming of Renaissance humanism presented the same problem in a new form—the relation of Christian teaching to ancient literature and moral philosophy, rather than to ancient cosmology, physics and logic as with the scholastics. But the problem of the relationship of the teachings and practices of the Church to the continually expanding secular history of mankind and secular learning, literature and science, remained and gave rise to new conceptions of human nature constructed out of some amalgam of Christian and classical traditions.

What were some of the features of this problem of the relations of religious and secular humanity, which was substantially more fundamental than that of the relationship of the two traditions and was always present behind it? Christianity was being challenged from the twelfth century onward by secular thought and by secular action. Christian truth rested on faith in the verity of the divine revelation through the Scriptures, on faith in the verity of the divine intervention into this world through the Incarnation and the Atonement, and in the verity of the salvation thereby offered to mankind from their miseries and sins and from their mortality. Ancient science, as the early fathers quickly pointed out, recognised at least the existence of divinity and some form of immortality for man. In moving, in the course of the Middle Ages, from an age, not only of faith but of daily expectation of the magical and the miraculous and the demonic to an age where men were increasingly solving their problems of material existence, building cities, expanding trade and commerce, the question inevitably came to the fore of how far Christian truth, as revealed, could be discovered by men themselves by whatever human means, by whatever arts or sciences they had invented. Thus the great impetus to logic and metaphysics of the twelfth and thirteenth centuries was motivated in great part by an increasing confidence in human roads to truth and insight, systematised first in medicine, law and theology. . . .

The relationship of humanism to scholasticism has remained a problematical one. After all the admirable and necessary work of classification that has come from Kristeller and other scholars the one thing that we can be sure about is that most of the humanists were likely to know the works of the thirteenth- and fourteenth-century scholastics by reputation only, though there is ground for doubting even this in the case of certain humanists. The humanists in attacking the scholastics were asserting the importance of their own disciplines of grammar, rhetoric, poetry and history—the *studia humanitatis*. More than that, in seeking a new division of the arts (replacing the older *trivium* and *quadrivium* as preliminary studies to theology, law or medicine and ending the elevation of dialectic and the down-grading of grammar, rhetoric and poetry in the Arts faculties of the universities) they were asserting the importance of form and style.

While it may be said that they frequently accused the university scholars of bad and barbaric style and incoherence of form, and while it certainly has been said often enough that the humanists cared only about the form and not about the content of thought, neither of these allegations leads to the conclusion that the humanists as a whole were not concerned with the content of thought. The point the humanists made about the form of scholastic thought was that it made the content incomprehensible and therefore incommunicable and useless—not that form alone mattered. However, a second charge, not made by all but by a significant number of the humanists, was that the content, in so far as they could or attempted to make it out, was dialectics and natural philosophy and therefore irrelevant to the moral and spiritual needs of mankind. It needs to be added that, however much individual humanists were committed to the vacuities of contentless form of which they have been accused, their principles were derived from those of ancient rhetoric, especially Cicero's. Resting their case on these, they insisted on the inseparability of rhetoric and philosophy, of form and content, and argued that form without content was nonsense and not even form.

The point, however, that now needs to be stressed is that the humanists as part of the rhetorical tradition, itself, were concerned with philosophy. They were not concerned with philosophy within the technical branches of the subject inside which medieval scholasticism and the modern academic discipline of philosophy insist it must confine its discussion. Perhaps, "ethics" and "aesthetics" are the only branches that the humanists would or could recognise as legitimate. They certainly were most familiar with dialectic, which they rightly regarded as the traditional rival of rhetoric and which they were disposed by the nature of their own interests to consider as at best irrelevant. However, as we shall see, some humanists such as Valla attempted to reform dialectics and give it moral and rhetorical relevances. Although they did not enter into formal discussions of epistemology and metaphysics, it is hard to see how they could have dispensed with the problems involved in these disciplines. As a matter of fact they ordinarily assumed without analysis a certain mode of knowing and an underlying structure of reality, and probably for this most of all they deserve the charge of not being philosophers. But they did have their positions with regard to the problems of epistemology and metaphysics (excluding, of course, the epistemological and metaphysical problems involved in natural philosophy, physics, medicine, etc., which they reviled, with a certain justification, as irrelevant).

It should not be forgotten that they could, and did, read Cicero's *Academica*, his *De natura deorum*, his *Disputationes Tusculanae*; they had available, and some (Petrarch and Salutati) read the medieval Latin translation of the *Phaedo*. Not to mention the other Latin Platonic texts.

. . . It was impossible for them not to be aware of at least the general nature of the problems of philosophy even though it might be said that they knew philosophy from the threshold, looking in the door, without ever entering the house. Nevertheless it is important to remind ourselves that they were never so isolated from the content and problems of philosophy (though to be sure more usually ancient philosophy) as recognition of their identification with the rhetorical tradition sometimes seems to imply.

The rhetorical tradition, moreover, from the time of Protagoras certainly was centrally concerned with moral philosophy and the philosophy of man. It excluded other branches of philosophy from its purview not on the basis of mere disinterest or neglect but in principle. Natural philosophy, first of all, seemed to deal with an underlying physical or natural structure of the external world, comprehended in Plato's account of Protagoras' myth as the gifts of Epimetheus and Prometheus. These were not unimportant in the life of man, but they were given a preliminary and subordinate place. The humanists' antagonism to medicine, consistent with this position, was not mere professional jealousy but a desire to give recognition to the greater importance of their own range of problems (involving the soul more than the body) within the hierarchy of values that they accepted. The rhetorical tradition always regarded as central the problems of human existence, both individual and social. Piety and justice were Protagoras' demands. Men arrived at workable agreements—conventions—for regulating their collective existence largely in accord with two factors, the moral condition of the individual which was itself a product of his education, and the public communication and decision-making mediated by language, persuasion, rhetoric, political debate, and the administration of justice.

In making the world of man, and not the physical world, central to their concerns, it is important to note that the Greek and the Latin rhetorical traditions were also in agreement with the Socratic position, at least as Plato illustrates it in the *Phaedo* by Socrates' famous repudiation of Anaxagoras. It is of importance to note that Cicero also makes Socrates and Plato responsible for turning philosophy towards the problems of man. Platonism, however, made a turn, which the rhetorical tradition could not entirely follow, towards the search for a metaphysical or "supernatural" basis for human justice, a basis that in its absoluteness and eternity could only be divine. Whether Plato ever was satisfied that he had adequately demonstrated the existence of the world of ideas and of divinity to himself or communicated it to others, the rhetorical tradition following Carneades and the Academics chose to remain in doubt. Certainly Plato's own great debates in his dialogues with the sophists are more positive about the appalling consequences of their relativism than they are convincing that Plato had succeeded in transcending the realm of sense knowledge. Two roads were left open, that followed by the ancient Neoplatonists, and that followed by the Middle Academy and Cicero. Cicero's probabilism always insisted, however, that although absolute proof was lacking, it was essential to assume the existence of God and the divine world, of providence and the immortality of souls.

The ingredients of a complex position towards philosophy were, therefore, present in Cicero and the rhetorical tradition. And the Italian humanists could not avoid the questions and the problems involved in it, even if they had wished. Philosophy, however, as it appeared in the context of the rhetorical tradition, and as we have already illustrated from Petrarch, met its test not in the abstractions of dialectic and epistemology, but in its effectiveness in moving mankind, individually and collectively, towards piety and justice. A moral pragmatism may have been inherent in the rhetorical tradition. But there had to be a superstructure determining the nature of piety and justice.

For Petrarch, as for humanists generally, this superstructure was provided by the Christian religion in which they implicitly believed. . . . The superstructure, though, could not remain simply *implicit,* however much the concreteness and individuality of the specific problems the humanist was called upon to face could be solved relativistically, or casuistically (that is, by taking into account all of the particular circumstances of time, place, the person, etc.). In trying to make the nature of ultimate transexperiential reality, which was fully accepted as the measure of the validity of the moral positions assumed in their writings, explicit and not implicit, the humanists had certain possibilities available to them from which they could draw in the traditions of classical moral philosophy with which they were very familiar. But so much of this was itself presented to them, particularly by Cicero, in a noncommittal, or eclectic way, that eclecticism was a wide-open temptation, as well as the kind of oscillation and shifting of position that characterised so many humanists and certainly as Heitmann has so abundantly shown, Petrarch.

Ultimately they had to come up against the question of how any of these positions related to Christian doctrine. Since Christian doctrine itself was complex and multifaceted, with many disagreements among its interpreters, this was not easy. The humanists ordinarily opted for a taking of position in the broadest of terms, avoiding what they called subtleties and disputation; perhaps it might even be called a predilection for vagueness or for an untroubled inconsistency. But all of this was motivated by the fact that on the level of human decision and action, individual wills and beliefs were involved, and the subtleties were of less importance than the broadest items of faith. Nevertheless, they could not, and there is evidence for some of them that they did not, avoid looking at the nature of the problem of knowledge, of the verification of truth, Christian truth.

Although for the rhetorician the problem of decision and action makes truth necessarily concrete rather than abstract, and this was certainly true for the Italian humanists who, convinced of the rightness of a certain view in one situation, could be equally convinced of the rightness of another view in a different situation; nevertheless, as far as religious truth was concerned, as Christians they could not stand on even the limited skepticism of the Academics, as they encountered it in Cicero. They could follow Cicero in supporting the notion of appropriateness—*to prepon*, or of the right thing, in the right place at the right time, *eukairia* from *kairos*, as Cicero expressed it. But when it came to faith they could not examine the epistemological base of this position, since it was one which denied the validity of general statements, allowing only probability, and Christian faith demanded the absolute acceptance of general statements. They could use academic probabilism against philosophy, but not in relation to faith. In its place, they utilised a kind of *ad hominem* reliance on the authority and prestige of their classical sources, and even more of their Christian sources, the Church fathers, and finally, in the Scriptures, the authority of the Word of God Himself. . . .

William J. Bouwsma

The Two Faces of Humanism: Stoicism and Augustinianism in Renaissance Thought

In "The Two Faces of Humanism," Bouwsma employs "ideal types" in the classic, Weberian sense. Stoicism and Augustinianism represent the conceptual limits or theoretical poles between which he conceives of humanism as oscillating. He derived the idea for these poles in part from reading Trinkaus, though the latter did not treat Stoicism and Augustinianism as ideal types but rather as intertwining strands of humanist thought. By separating these strands and arraying them antithetically, Bouwsma hoped to essay the general dimensions of a movement characterized principally by its diversity.

He begins by asserting that Kristeller's fundamental insight into the rhetorical nature of the humanist movement had the unintentional effect of obscuring the rich variety of humanism, whose adherents quarreled with themselves as much as with their scholastic contemporaries. The full historical significance of the movement becomes apparent only when we take this diversity of opinions into account. By opting to explore the content of humanist thought with reference to the contrasting poles of Stoicism and Augustinianism, Bouwsma breaks with the traditional view of a division in Renaissance thought between Aristotelianism and Platonism. This view ignores the rhetorical nature of a humanist movement that drew its inspiration less from Hellenic Greece than Hellenistic Rome, which bequeathed its heritage to the Middle Ages and the Renaissance through a predominantly Stoic Latin oratory and the subtle rhetoric of Augustine's mature theology. Although acknowledging that both Stoicism and Augustinianism are notoriously difficult to define, Bouwsma outlines their affinities and, more important, their fundamental conflict in our first selection below, where the contrast between these two positions makes their characteristics

From William J. Bouwsma, "The Two Faces of Humanism: Stoicism and Augustinianism in Renaissance Thought," in *Itinerarium Italicum: The Profile of the Italian Renaissance in the Mirror of Its European Transformations*, ed. Heiko A. Oberman with Thomas A. Brady, Jr. (Leiden: E. J. Brill, 1975).

emerge in high relief. Subsequent selections detail the Stoical and Augustinian elements of humanist thought, a topic that Bouwsma takes up after having briefly described their medieval heritage.

Bouwsma's exposition is crosscut by deep ironies, not the least of which is that much of humanism's worldliness draws support from Augustinianism, whereas much of its religious sentiment draws upon Stoicism. We should also recall Bouwsma's concluding observation that these two conflicting elements often reside within the same author, thus indicating that Stoicism and Augustinianism are not so much identifiable factions within the humanist movement as they are ideal types for exploring its complex nature. By implication, the real value of ideal types comes when one recognizes their limitations, for then they have truly served their function of providing a surer grasp of difficult material. (A great strength of this essay lies in its wealth of quotations from diverse humanist writings. Unfortunately, space considerations have forced us to focus on capturing the outline of Bouwsma's complex argument, at the expense of some illustrative detail.)

. . . The notion of the compatibility and even the affinity between Stoicism and [Augustinian] Christianity goes back to the yearning of early Christian converts for some bridge between the old world of thought and the new. Stoic elements in the expression (if not the thought) of the Apostle Paul tended to obscure their radical differences, and the apocryphal correspondence between Paul and Seneca confused the issue further. The affinities, indeed, might seem immediately impressive, as they did in the Renaissance. The Stoics were commendably pious; they spoke much about the gods and even about God, praising His wisdom, His power, and His love for mankind. Their emphasis on divine providence and its ultimate benevolence seemed a particular point of contact with Christianity, and the idea of a single providential order led in turn to an ostensibly Christian ethic of absolute obedience and acceptance of the divine will. The Stoics displayed a singular moral seriousness; and their emphasis on virtue, through their famous contrast between the things that are within and those that are not within human control, recognized its inwardness; they acknowledged the problem of sin and stressed man's moral responsibility. They preached the brotherhood of man as well as the universal fatherhood of God, and they had much to say about the immortality of the soul.

But at a deeper level Stoicism and Augustinian Christianity were in radical opposition. The issue between them, in its most direct terms, was the difference between the biblical understanding of creation, which makes both man and the physical universe separate from and utterly dependent on God, and the hellenistic principle of immanence, which makes the universe eternal, by one means or another deifies the natural order, and by seeing a spark of divinity in man tends to make him something more than a creature of God.

This fundamental difference has massive implications, and from it we may derive the major issues on which Stoicism and Augustinianism would be in potential opposition within Renaissance humanism. The anthropological differences between the two positions were of particular importance. The Stoic view of man attributed to him a divine spark or seed, identified with reason, which gave man access to the divine order of the universe, from which the existence, the nature, and the will of God could be known. Stoicism therefore pointed to natural theology; and since reason was seen as a universal human attribute, which meant that all men have some natural understanding of God, Stoic anthropology virtually required a religious syncretism. As the distinctive quality of man, reason also gave him his specifically human identity; a man was most fully human, best realized the ends of his existence, and became perfect through the absolute sovereignty of reason over the other dimensions of the human personality. Virtue consisted, accordingly, in following the dictates of reason, to which the rebellious body and its passions were to be reduced by the will. But the will was not perceived as an independent faculty; it was the faithful and mechanical servant of reason, and therefore Stoicism rested on the assumption that to know the good is to do the good. Through rational illumination and rational control man was capable of reaching perfection. The body presented problems, but these could be solved through a disciplined *apatheia*, a cultivated indifference to physical needs and impulses, to the affections, and to external conditions. But since only man's reason was divine, immortality was reserved for the soul. Conversely Stoicism had a typically hellenistic contempt for the body.

Augustinianism contradicted this view at every point. Seeing man in every part of his being as a creature of God, it could not regard his reason (however wonderful) as divine and thus naturally capable of knowing the will of God. Such knowledge was available to man only in the Scriptures, particular revelations from God himself, which spoke not to mankind as a general category but to the individual. And because neither reason nor any other human faculty was intrinsically superior to the rest, Augustinianism tended to replace the monarchy of reason in the human personality with a kind of corporate democracy. The primary organ in Augustinian anthropology is not so much that which is highest as that which is central; it is literally the heart (*cor*), whose quality determines the quality of the whole. And that this quality is not a function of rational enlightenment is seen as a matter of common experience. The will is not, after all, an obedient servant of the reason; it has energies and impulses of its own, and man is a far more mysterious animal than the philosophers are inclined to admit. Human wickedness thus presents a much more serious problem than the Stoics dream of, and the notion that man in his fallen condition can rely on his own powers to achieve virtue is utterly implausible. Nor, in any event, is there virtue in withdrawal from engagement with the nonrational and external dimensions of existence. The physical body and the emotional constitution of man were created by God along with man's intellectual powers, and their needs too have dignity and are at least equally worthy of satisfaction. For the same reason immortality cannot be limited to the soul; man must be saved, since God made him so, as a whole.

The contrasts are equally significant in respect to the position of man in society. Although the self-centeredness in the Stoic ideal of individual existence was often uneasily and joylessly combined with a Roman concern for civic duty, the Stoics generally left the impression that social existence was a distraction from the good life, which could be satisfactorily pursued only by withdrawal from the world of men. Despite his recognition of the basic equality of man, the Stoic was also persuaded that the good life based on the contemplation of eternal verities was possible only for a few select souls; he was therefore contemptuous of the vulgar crowd. By contrast the mature Augustine, though still yearning for a contemplative life, insisted unequivocally on the obligations of the individual to society, obligations at once of duty, prudence, and love; and at the same time the conception of the blessed life opened up by his less intellectual vision of man was not for the few but accessible to all.

Stoicism, again, had little use for history. Its conception of a rational and unchanging law of nature underlying all things led to a peculiarly rigid notion of cyclical recurrence that denied all significance to discrete events, which in any case belonged to the uncontrollable outer world irrelevant to the good life, just as it precluded the idea of a direction and goal for history. Its cultural values were not the products of particular experience in the world of time and matter but eternal, perennially valid, and so perennially recoverable. Thus its only remedy for present discontents was a nostalgic return to a better past. But Augustine vigorously rejected the eternal round of the ancients. He brooded over the mystery of time as a creature and vehicle of God's will and proclaimed that history was guided to its appointed end by God Himself and therefore, expressing His wisdom, must be fraught with a mysterious significance.

But underlying all these particular contrasts was a fundamental difference over the order of the universe. For the Stoics a single cosmic order, rational and divine, pervaded all things, at once static and, through a divine impulse to achieve perfection planted in everything, dynamic, its principles operative alike in physical nature, in human society, and in the human personality. The existence of this order determined all human and social development; and the end of man, either individually or collectively, could not be freely chosen but consisted in subjective acceptance and conformity to destiny. The perfection of that order meant that whatever is is right, however uncomfortable or tragic for mankind; at the heart of Stoicism is that familiar cosmic optimism which signifies, for the actual experience of men, the deepest pessimism. Against all this, Augustinianism, though by no means denying in principle the ultimate order of the universe, rejected its intelligibility and thus its coherence and its practical significance for man. The result was to free both man and society from their old bondage to cosmic principles, and to open up a secular vision of human existence and a wide range of pragmatic accommodations to the exigencies of life impossible in the Stoic religious universe. In this sense Augustinianism provided a charter for human freedom and a release for the diverse possibilities of human creativity. . . .

Stoicism addressed itself to the problems of modern Europe, as to those of later antiquity, by reaffirming the divine, harmonious, and intelligible order of nature and drawing appropriate conclusions, practical as well as theoretical. The Stoicism of the Renaissance, perhaps especially when it was least aware of its Stoic inspiration, was based, like ancient Stoicism, on natural philosophy and cosmology, a point of some importance in view of the common supposition that Renaissance thinkers only drew isolated, practical ethical precepts from Stoic sources. Valla's Epicurean (in this case made, perhaps deliberately, to sound like a Stoic) declared nature virtually identical with God. Vives from time to time elaborated on the meaning of this proposition. The universe, he wrote, was governed "by the divine intelligence which commands and forbids according to reason." Calvin, for all his concern to maintain the distinction between God and nature, drew on the same conception. . . .

And man is also a part of this rational order of nature. Montaigne found this humbling: "We are neither superior nor inferior to the rest. All that is under heaven, says the sage, is subject to one law and one fate. . . . Man must be forced and lined up within the barriers of this organization." Others saw in it some justification for glorifying man. "This is the order of nature," wrote Vives, "that wisdom be the rule of the whole, that all creatures obey man, that in man the body abides by the orders of the soul, and that the soul itself comply with the will of God." . . .

Implicit in these passages, and sometimes more than implicit, is the assumption that this divinely ordered universe is accessible to the human understanding, that man's perception of the rational order of the universe tells him a good deal about the nature and will of God, and that man's reason is thus the link between himself and God. This conception of nature leads us accordingly to the notion of man as essentially an intellectual being. . . .

On the other hand this elevation of reason was often likely to be accompanied by a denigration of other dimensions of the personality, especially the passions and the body with which they were regularly associated, which threatened to challenge the sovereignty of reason. From this standpoint the body and the rational soul could be seen as radically opposed. Petrarch claimed to have learned from his own body only "that man is a vile, wretched animal unless he redeems the ignobility of the body with the nobility of the soul." He saw his soul as imprisoned in and weighed down by the body, the one "an immortal gift, the other corruptible and destined to pass away." With Vives, attack on the body achieved an almost pathological intensity. But happily the rational soul, however threatened by the body and the affections, was in the end clearly superior to them. As Lipsius remarked, "For although the soul is infected and somewhat corrupted by the filth of the body and the contagion of sense, it nevertheless retains some vestiges of its origin and is not without certain bright sparks of the pure fiery nature from whence it came forth."

Reason, in any case, because of its access to the divine order of the universe, is a legitimate source of religious insight, a point exploited at some length by Calvin, who quoted Cicero that "there is no nation so barbarous, no race so savage that they have not a deep-seated conviction that there is a God." In sound Stoic fashion Calvin found the order of the heavens, but also the wonders of the human body, a natural witness to the greatness of God. "The natural order was," he declared, "that the frame of the universe should be the school in which we were to learn piety, and from it pass over to eternal life and perfect felicity." Because the religious insights from nature are the common possession of mankind, it must also be true that all peoples may be expected to reveal some knowledge of God; and this belief contributed heavily to the study of the classics. Petrarch, thinking of himself as following Augustine, was deeply impressed by Cicero's Stoic arguments for the providential order of the world, phrased, as he thought, "almost in a Catholic manner." Aeneas Sylvius maintained that Socrates had taught the Christian way of salvation and recommended "the poets and other authors of antiquity" because they were "saturated with the same faith" as the Fathers of the church. . . .

But rational knowledge was also a resource in a more practical sense. From an understanding of the general rationality of nature, man could discover the rational laws of his own nature and, by following them, variously perfect himself. . . . Erasmus made the point broadly: "All living things strive to develop according to their proper nature. What is the proper nature of man? Surely it is to live the life of reason, for reason is the peculiar prerogative of man. . . .

But clearly the formation men most required in a brutal and disorderly world was training in morality, and it was in this area that Stoic doctrine seemed most relevant to contemporary needs, most immediately prescriptive. The rational order of nature was to be the foundation for the orderly behavior of men; this was its practical function. Stoic moralists were attractive, then, because of their emphasis on the supreme value of virtue. . . .

This concern with virtue reflects also the persistence of the intellectual conception of man so closely bound up with the rational order of the Stoic universe. This is apparent in two ways. In the first place Stoic virtue is acquired through the intellect; it is a product of philosophy, absorbed from books. Thus Erasmus believed that even small children could absorb it through beginning their education by reading ancient fables. He particularly recommended the story of Circe, with its lesson "that men who will not yield to the guidance of reason, but follow the enticements of the senses, are no more than brute beasts." "Could a Stoic philosopher," he asked rhetorically, "preach a graver truth?" But in the second place, as this passage also suggests, the practice of this Stoic virtue depended on the sovereignty of reason and its powers of control over the disorderly impulses arising out of other aspects of the personality. . . . And in this emphasis on rational control we may perhaps discern an important clue to the attraction of Stoic ethical doctrine for the age of the Renaissance. It presented itself as an antidote for a terrible fear of the consequences of the loss of self-control. Montaigne suggested this in his ruminations over the perils of drunkenness, which may cause man to spill out the secrets on which his survival and dignity depend. "The worst state of man," Montaigne concluded, "is when he loses the knowledge and control of himself." And the ability of men to control their lower impulses with the help of philosophy gave some hope for a better and more orderly world. So it seemed to Aeneas Sylvius: "Respect towards women, affection for children and for home; pity for the distressed, justice towards all, self-control in anger, restraint in indulgence, forbearance in success, contentment, courage, duty—these are some of the virtues to which philosophy will lead you."

The Stoic model for the order of society, like its model for the order of the individual personality, was also derived from the order of the cosmos. An authentic and durable social order that would properly reflect the stability of the cosmos had thus to meet two basic requirements. It had to be a single order, and it had to be governed by reason. This meant in practice that the human world must be organized as a universal empire, and that it must be ruled by the wise, by men who are themselves fully rational and in touch with the rational principles of the cosmos.

Thus the Stoic type of humanist tended, from Petrarch in some moods to Lipsius in the waning Renaissance, to admire imperial Rome. The conquest of the Roman Empire, Petrarch once remarked, had been "actuated by perfect justice and good will as regards men," however defective it may have been in regard to God. . . .

But the sovereignty of reason in the cosmos also required that the world be governed by the wise. All political disorder, Erasmus argued, was the result of stupidity; hence, he declared, "You cannot be a prince if you are not a philosopher." Vives saw the ruler as simply a sage with public authority. There was some discrepancy between this ideal and political actuality, but it could be remedied; since it was rarely possible to elevate sages into kings, it was necessary to convert kings, by education, into sages. This was the aim of Erasmus's *Institutio principis Christiani,* and Rabelais presented Grangousier as a model philosopher-king. Properly educated, the ruler might be made to excel all other men in

LIBRARY

wisdom and therefore in virtue, and his central duty was then to instruct his subjects in virtue. But always, in this conception of kingship, the Stoicizing humanist kept in mind the ultimate source of wisdom and virtue. The philosophy of the prince, for Erasmus, was the kind that "frees the mind from the false opinions and the ignoble passions of the masses, and following the eternal pattern laid up in heaven points the way to good government." . . .

The idealism in this conception of government generally makes it appear singularly unsuited to the actualities of political life, but in at least one respect it helped to meet genuine practical needs. By its conception of a rational law of nature, it assisted in the rationalization of law and social relations. . . . It seems likely that the Stoic conception of a natural law governing all human intercourse and authenticating all particular laws gave some impetus, perhaps most powerful when the cosmic vibrations in the conception were least felt, to the systematic codification of the chaos of existing legislation, to the general rule of law, and to more equal justice. Yet we may sense something equivocal, however opportune, even here. This is apparent in the impersonal rationality in the Stoic idea of social virtue based on law, which corresponded to the increasing legalism and impersonality of the new urban scene. It tended to base social order not on the unreliable vagaries of personal ties, personal loyalties, and personal affection, but on abstract and general social relationships: in a word, on duty rather than on love. The social thought of Stoic humanism thus reflected and probably helped to promote the rationalization of society on which large-scale organization in the modern world depended. But is also made the human world a colder place.

On the other hand the Stoic conception of social improvement was diametrically opposed to the actual direction in which European society was moving. Its ideal, like Seneca's, was nostalgic. As the retrospective prefix in the familiar Renaissance vocabulary of amelioration attests — *reñascentium, reformatio, restoratio, restitutio, renovatio,* etc. — it could only look backward for a better world. Petrarch chose deliberately to live in spirit in the ancient past; one of the participants in an Erasmian colloquy deplored the disappearance of "that old time equality, abolished by modern tyranny," which he also associated with the Apostles; Castiglione thought men in antiquity "of greater worth than now." . . .

All of this suggests the lack of a sense of the positive significance of change in Stoic humanism. Since excellence was associated with the divine origins of all things, change could only mean deterioration; and improvement necessarily implied the recovery of what was essentially timeless. The static character of this ideal was reflected in its vision of the good society which, once it had achieved perfection, could not be permitted to change. So Erasmus hoped that the conflicting interests of human society might "achieve an eternal truce" in which proper authority and degrees of status would be respected by all. One of the essential duties of the Erasmian ruler is to resist all innovation. The central virtue in the Stoic ideal of society is thus peace, which is not simply the absence of war but ultimately dependent on the correspondence of social organization to the unchanging principles of universal order. . . .

One service performed by Stoic humanism was, then, to supply a foundation for personal and social order in the very nature of things. But this was only one, and perhaps not the major, dimension of its significance. For there was a crucial ambiguity in its moral thought, and indeed in its understanding of virtue, which pointed not to the improvement of the conditions of life but rather to acceptance of the necessary and irremovable discomforts of existence. If the rationality of the universe could be regarded as a resource for a better order, it could also be taken to imply that in some sense the structure of the universe is already perfect and so beyond improvement. From this standpoint Stoicism became a strategy by which, through a combination of enlightenment and disciplined accommodation, the individual could come to terms with the humanly pessimistic implications of a cosmic optimism. It was a strategy of protection for the isolated self in a thoroughly unsatisfactory world. Virtue, in this light, was the ultimate resource by which the ego could minimize its vulnerability to adversity. And this represented a very different kind of adaptation to the changing patterns of European life.

This application of Stoicism was based on the crucial Stoic distinction between those external elements of existence, generally identified with fortune, that are not absolutely within the control of the individual, and the inner world that belongs entirely to himself, the realms, respectively, of necessity and freedom. The inner world alone is the area in which the highest dimension of the personality, man's reason, can exercise total sovereignty, and therefore in which alone man can realize his highest potentialities and attain the ends of his existence; thus it is also the only realm in which he can hope to achieve total happiness. For this is where man discovers the laws governing the universe. As Salutati declared "They inhere in our minds as of nature. Thus we know them with such certainty that they cannot escape us and that it is not necessary to seek them among external facts. For, as you see, they inhabit our most intimate selves." . . .

The ideal had various implications, notable among them the definition of virtue as that self-sufficiency which, by freeing the individual from all dependence on things external to himself, makes him invulnerable to fortune and so supplies him with inner freedom, the only freedom to which man can aspire. . . . Virtue in this sense was the power to raise the mind above all the external accidents of existence in order to dwell securely in the realm of the eternal. It enabled man to identify himself subjectively with the divine order of the universe, and accordingly a special kind of numinous awe surrounded it, of a sort that could hardly adhere to the more practical virtues of social existence. So this species of virtue meant at once identification with higher and separation from lower things, especially from all those dimensions of existence that distracted or troubled the mind and threatened the self-sufficiency of the discrete individual. . . . Petrarch, who periodically longed for a Stoic repose, reproached Cicero for betraying his own best convictions by giving up the "peaceful ease" of his old age to return to public service. The Stoic impulse in Renaissance humanism favoring such contemplative withdrawal would find regular expression among later writers, from Salutati to Montaigne. . . .

A more positive dimension of this emphasis in Stoic humanism was its contribution to that inwardness which, with its genuine affinity to one aspect of Augustinianism, deepened consciences and provided one source for the moral sensitivity of the Catholic as well as the Protestant Reformation. Inwardness pointed to the role of conscience in the moral life, the inner voice which is concerned rather with motives than with outward acts and results. The young Calvin recognized this element in Stoicism. "Nothing is great for the Stoics," he wrote, "which is not also good and inwardly sound"; and he attacked *"monsters of men, dripping with inner vices*, yet putting forth the outward appearance and mask of uprightness." In his maturity he noted that men can discover some ideas of God within themselves and denounced the indolence of those who refused this inward search. Montaigne's habitual self-examination also owed much to Stoicism. "For many years now," he declared, "my thoughts have had no other aim but myself, I have studied and examined myself only, and if I study any other things, it is to apply them immediately to, or rather within myself." Only by looking within, rather than at his deeds, could he discover his "essence," for here resided his "virtue." The Stoic pursuit of truth within would also leave a fundamental mark on the thought of Descartes.

And from this source also came the remedy for the disagreeable agitation of mind resulting from the trials of modern life. The Stoic humanist recognized that perturbation of mind was a response to external stimuli; but he also saw that, since it was in the mind, it was potentially subject to rational control. . . . Philosophy, then, could quiet the wars of the self and induce a genuine and reliable tranquility of mind, as Pico argued. . . .

But it was also a regular and conscious feature of the Stoic prescription for human trouble that it was available only to the few; in practice Stoic humanism consistently rejected the implications of that vision of human brotherhood which had been one of the most genial features of ancient Stoicism. The aristocratic impulses in Renaissance society therefore found support in the powerful analogy between the order of the universe, the order of the human personality, and the social order, which suggested that society too must consist of both a higher rational principle and a lower, duller and less reliable component to which the higher force, personified by an elite, was in the nature of things superior. The blessedness to which the Stoic aspired was available only to a select few capable of the rational enlightenment and self-discipline of the wise; the masses were condemned to the external and turbulent life of the body, the passions, the senses. And one of the marks of the Stoic humanist was his constant, rather nervous concern to differentiate himself from the vulgar crowd and to reassure himself, somewhat in the manner at times discerned in the Protestant elect, of his spiritual superiority. . . .

Stoicism, then, had both attractions and weaknesses as the basis for accommodation to the conditions of Renaissance life, and these were not unrelated to one another. It identified the major problems of modern existence, often vividly and concretely, as the schoolmen did not. It reaffirmed in a new form a traditional vision of universal order which seemed an attractive prescription for the practical evils of a singularly disorderly society. It affirmed personal responsibility, its inwardness corresponded to the growing inwardness of later medieval piety, and it promised consolation for the tribulations of existence. But the structure of assumptions that enabled Stoic humanism to perform these services was not altogether adequate to the changing needs of a new society. Its conception of a universal order was singularly contradicted by the concrete world of familiar experience, and its idealism, however plausible in theory, ran the risk of seeming as irrelevant to life as the great systems of the schoolmen. Its intellectual vision of man was hardly adequate to a world in which men constantly encountered each other not as disembodied minds but as integral personalities whose bodies could not be ignored, whose passions were vividly and often positively as well as dangerously in evidence, and whose actions were profoundly unpredictable. The Stoic idea of freedom was too elevated to have much general application, and also severely limited by the large area of determinism in Stoic thought. And Stoicism appeared often to ignore or to reason away rather than to engage with and solve the practical problems of life; its disapproval of cities, of political particularity and individual eccentricity, of change, demonstrated the high-mindedness of its adherents, but it did not cause these awkward realities to go away. And it was scarcely helpful, especially since even the Stoic had no remedy for the misery of the overwhelming majority of mankind, to deny that suffering was real because it belonged to the lower world of appearances, or to direct the attention of wretched men from mutable to eternal things, or to insist that the world ought to be one and to be ruled by the wise. Like ancient Stoicism, therefore, the Stoic humanism of the Renaissance was ultimately hopeless. It is thus hardly surprising that, like the Stoicism of the hellenistic world, it was contested, within humanism itself, by another and very different vision of man, his potentialities, and his place in the universe. The great patron of this vision was Saint Augustine. . . .

. . . With Stoicism we must begin with the cosmos, and this in turn implies a certain view of man. But with Augustinianism we must begin with man, and from here we reach a certain view of the cosmos. In Augustinian humanism the nature and experience of man himself limit what can be known about the larger universes to which man belongs and how he can accommodate to them.

Thus Augustinian humanism saw man, not as a system of objectively distinguishable, discrete faculties reflecting ontological distinctions in the cosmos, but as a mysterious and organic unity. This conception, despite every tendency in his thought to the contrary, is repeatedly apparent in Petrarch, in the *Secretum* and elsewhere, and it explains Melanchthon's indifference to the value of distinguishing the various faculties of the human personality. One result was a marked retreat from the traditional sense of opposition between soul and body. . . . A corollary of this position is that the soul cannot be seen as a higher faculty in man, a spark of divinity which is intrinsically immune from sin and can only be corrupted from below. . . . It follows, therefore, that the distinctive quality of man cannot be his reason. Valla identified it with his immortality, Calvin with his capacity to know and worship God. It also follows that the abstract knowledge grasped by reason is not sufficient to make men virtuous and therefore blessed, a point made with considerable emphasis by Petrarch in praising oratory above philosophy; thus Aristotle suffered as a moralist in comparison with Cicero, whom Petrarch now exploited in his less Stoic mood. Since to know the good could no longer be identified with doing the good, it might also now be necessary to make a choice between knowledge and virtue, and the Augustinian humanist regularly came out on the side of virtue.

Despite their underlying belief in the integral unity of the personality, the Augustinian humanists accepted and argued in terms of the old vocabulary of the faculties; but the faculties they chose to emphasize implied a very different conception of the organization of man from that of the Stoics. They spoke above all of the will. Petrarch recognized clearly that Augustine's own conversion had been a function of his will rather than his intellect, and Calvin was similarly Augustinian in recognizing the crucial importance of the will in the economy of salvation. But the essential point in this conception of the will was its separation from and its elevation above reason. "It is safer," Petrarch declared, "to strive for a good and pious will than for a capable and clear intellect. . . . It is better to will the good than to know the truth." . . . One consequence was a new degree of freedom for the will, always severely restricted by the Stoic conception of the will as the automatic servant of reason. Salutati recognized this with particular clarity. Nothing, he wrote, could "even reach the intellect without the consent or command of the will," and once knowledge had penetrated the intellect, the will could freely follow or disregard it. Valla saw in the freedom of the will the only conception of the matter consistent with the evident reality of sin, which would be impossible, and man would be deprived of responsibility and moral dignity, if reason in fact ruled will.

The will, in this view, is seen to take its direction not from reason but from the affections, which are in turn not merely the disorderly impulses of the treacherous body but expressions of the energy and quality of the heart, that mysterious organ which is the center of the personality, the source of its unity and its ultimate worth. The affections, therefore, are intrinsically neither good nor evil but the essential resources of the personality; and since they make possible man's beatitude and glory as well as his depravity, they are, in Augustinian humanism, treated with particular respect. . . .

This sense of the power and positive value of the passions was frequently the basis of an explicit attack on the Stoic ideal of *apatheia*, a point on which Stoicism seemed peculiarly unconvincing. Salutati doubted that "any mortal ever attained to such perfection besides Christ." Brandolini denied that Stoic virtue could be truly divine because of its rejection of feeling, "for whoever lack affects necessarily lack virtues." Erasmus denounced Stoic apathy in the *Praise of Folly*, as did the young Calvin, citing Augustine; the older Calvin also attacked "the foolish description given by the ancient Stoics of 'the great-souled man'" and also denounced "new Stoics who count it depraved not only to groan and weep but also to be sad and care-ridden." We, he declared, citing Christ's tears, "have nothing to do with this iron-hearted philosophy."

This same vision of man relieved the body of its old responsibility for evil and dignified its needs. Calvin particularly emphasized the error of associating sin primarily with the body; this mistake tended to make men "easily forgive themselves the most shocking vices as no sins at all." . . .

At the same time the impulses of the body could be viewed more tolerantly. . . . Calvin argued that "God certainly did not intend that man should be slenderly and sparingly sustained; but rather . . . he promises a liberal abundance, which should leave nothing wanting to a sweet and pleasant life." He insisted on the legitimacy of pleasure, at least in moderation; severity on this score would lead to "the very dangerous error of fettering consciences more tightly than does the word of the Lord." Calvin was thinking of the monks, but the point applied equally to Stoic moralism. It applied especially to sex, so often the special worry of traditional moralists because of its association with the body. Civic humanism had long applauded the family as the source of new citizens, and Valla had suggested a positive view of sex because it gave pleasure. But the sense, among the Augustinian humanists, of the integrity of the personality also provided a deeper foundation for the value of the sexual bond. As Bucer declared, "There is no true marriage without a true assent of hearts between those who make the agreement," and marriage is accordingly "a contract not only of body and of goods but also of the soul." Calvin praised marriage, attributing disapproval of it to "immoderate affection for virginity." A higher estimate of the body and of sex led also to some perception of the dignity of women.

This better view of the body had even wider ramifications. It was related to Renaissance debate over the value of the active life, for the alleged inferiority of activity to contemplation assumed the inferiority to the mind of the body, which does the active business of the world. It also had deep theological significance, for it redirected attention from the immortality of the soul to the resurrection of the body; the more Augustinian humanist was likely to emphasize the central importance of the resurrection. Thus, although Petrarch often spoke of the soul, he had also learned "the hope of resurrection, and that this very body after death will be reassumed, indeed agile, shining, and inviolable, with much glory in the resurrection." Calvin saw with particular clarity (and here his relation to Pomponazzi is evident) that "the life of the soul without hope of resurrection will be a mere dream." And this Augustinian anthropology also posed the question of human freedom and man's need for grace in a new way. If it freed the will from obedience to reason, it perceived that this only meant the bondage of the will to the affections of the heart. And this meant that man can only be saved by grace, not by knowledge; for knowledge can at best reach only the mind, but grace alone can change the heart.

It thus precluded the natural theology towards which Stoic humanism tended; its theology regularly opposed the folly of the cross to the rational wisdom of the philosophers. . . . In reply to his own more Stoic vision of the order of the universe, Calvin insisted on the actual inability of men, as the vain and contradictory speculations of the philosophers clearly demonstrated, to discover religious truths from nature. Valla had argued that philosophy was the mother of heresy. The Augustinian humanist was clear that, however valuable they might be for other purposes, the classics, based on reason alone, were valueless for Christianity. There was, Petrarch suggested, a qualitative difference between knowledge and faith, which he saw as something like the difference between seeing and listening: the difference, that is to say, between learning by means of one's own natural powers and learning directly, and so with peculiar certainty, from God. Thus an Augustinian anthropology was fundamental to the new emphasis among humanists on the Bible, on the "school of the Gospel," which Budé contrasted with the Stoa as well as the Academy and the "subtle debates of the Peripatetics."

Ultimate truth, then, is mysterious, beyond rational comprehension, and therefore first planted in the heart by grace, not discovered by the mind. "It is not man's part to investigate the celestial mystery through his own powers," Petrarch declared after emphasizing the gulf between God the creator and man his creature; and Petrarch's sense of the incalculability of the world was carried by Salutati to a more general skepticism. "Every truth which is grasped by reason," Salutati wrote, "can be made doubtful by a contrary reason"; consequently man's rational knowledge cannot be absolute but, at best, is "a kind of reasonable uncertainty." . . . This skepticism is obviously fundamental to the humanist case for the superiority of rhetoric to philosophy; like Scripture, rhetoric recognized the weakness of reason and spoke to the heart.

The Augustinian humanist recognized a very different tendency in Stoicism and occasionally displayed some insight into the affinities of Stoicism with medieval intellectuality. Valla sometimes used "Stoicism" to represent philosophy in general, by which he meant both ancient and medieval philosophy; and Brandolini pointed to the rational (and for him specious) methodology which the Stoics shared with "almost all the philosophers and theologians of our time." Calvin noted the "Stoic paradoxes and scholastic subtleties" in Seneca. Here, then, is another area in which the tensions between Stoic and Augustinian humanism were threatening to break out into the open.

But all this was evidently the reflection of a more general insistence, within Augustinian humanism, on man's absolute dependence on his creator, which contrasted sharply with the Stoic tendency to emphasize man's sufficiency. This sense of human dependence is especially apparent in the Augustinian attitude to virtue, the supreme good of the Stoic. . . . [The] humanists did not deny the practical value of the alleged virtues of the pagans, but they insisted on distinguishing between the restraint of human nature and its purification, which only grace could accomplish. From this standpoint the Stoic ideal was shallow and therefore, in the end, unreliable. Christianity, as Melanchthon remarked, was not primarily concerned with virtue, and the pursuit of instruction on this topic in the Scriptures "is more philosophical than Christian."

In fact a deeper knowledge of the self revealed that, like his knowledge of God, man's virtue and happiness also come entirely from God. To realize this was the goal of self-knowledge. Such knowledge, Calvin declared, "will strip us of all confidence in our own ability, deprive us of all occasion for boasting, and lead us to submission"; and Petrarch's own spiritual biography may be understood as a prolonged search for this kind of knowledge. It taught man, for example, the precise opposite of Stoic wisdom. Against the Stoic notion that blessedness can be founded only on the things that are man's own, Petrarch argued directly that in fact the only things that are a man's own are his sins; thus "in what is in one's own power" there is chiefly "matter of shame and fear." There is an obvious connection between this interest in self-knowledge and the Pauline teaching on the moral law as the tutor of mankind, a conception again quite at odds with the Stoic notion of the function of law. If Petrarch's self-knowledge brought him to despair, he could take hope if only "the Almighty Pity put forth his strong right hand and guide my vessel rightly ere it be too late, and bring me to shore." God was the only source of his virtues (these are clearly not his own), of his blessedness, of his very existence. . . .

But there are, for the general development of European culture, even broader implications in the sense, within Augustinian humanism, of man's intellectual limitations. It pointed to the general secularization of modern life, for it implied the futility of searching for the principles of human order in the divine order of the cosmos, which lay beyond human comprehension. Man was accordingly now seen to inhabit not a single universal order governed throughout by uniform principles but a multiplicity of orders: for example, an earthly as well as a heavenly city, which might be seen to operate in quite different ways. On earth, unless God had chosen to reveal his will about its arrangements unequivocally in Scripture, man was left to the uncertain and shifting insights of a humbler kind of reason, to work out whatever arrangements best suited his needs. Hence a sort of earthy practicality was inherent in this way of looking at the human condition.

Indeed it is likely that the sharp Augustinian distinction between creation and Creator, since it denied the eternity of the universe, also promoted that secularization of the cosmos implicit in the Copernican revolution. If human order no longer depended on the intelligible order of the cosmos, the motive for discerning any such order was seriously weakened; conversely much of the resistance to Copernicanism stemmed from a concern, so strong in Stoic humanism, to protect a universal order that supplied mankind with general guidance for its earthly arrangements. Galileo relied heavily on Augustine to support his argument that the proper concern of religion is how one goes to heaven, not how heaven goes.

If Machiavelli is the most famous example of the secularizing tendency in the Renaissance, he also had predecessors among earlier humanists of an Augustinian tendency. But the secularism implicit in Augustinian humanism achieved its clearest articulation in figures connected with the Reformation, not because Protestantism originated the secular impulse, but because, since Stoic arguments had been a major resource to support the old order, they now required a more direct attack. Calvin distinguished with particular clarity between the heavenly and earthly realms and the kinds of knowledge appropriate to each. . . . He was emphatic about the separation between the two, whose correspondence had been so long cited in support of the ecclesiastical hierarchy. There was no basis, he declared, "to philosophize subtly over a comparison of the heavenly and earthly hierarchies," thus challenging not only the Neoplatonism of Dionysius but also the fundamental principles of Stoic world order. . . .

The pragmatic secularism to which Augustinian humanism pointed opposed the political idealism of Stoic humanism in all its dimensions: its belief in the universal principles needed to validate all government, its universalism, its insistence on the rule of the wise, its indifference to changing circumstance, its pacifism. Bruni gave concrete expression to the secularist mood in his own acceptance, without setting them in a larger framework of objective justification, of the common political values of Florence. "I confess that I am moved by what men think good," he wrote in his *Florentine Histories*: "to extend one's borders, to increase one's power, to extol the splendor and glory of the city, to look after its utility and security." Here is the Machiavellian principle that the affairs of this world should be based on the dynamic interplay of earthly interests whose sordid realities are honestly faced; in short, the eternal reason of the Stoics must, for the practical good of men on earth, give way to reason of state.

This signified that laws and institutions must be accommodated to the variety of the human condition, and thus the desirability of many states with various kinds of government. This, rather than a universal empire, was, for Calvin, what God had intended. . . . Augustinian humanism was thus closely related, as Stoic humanism was not, to the political realities of contemporary Europe.

In the same way Augustinian humanism attacked the spiritual elitism of the Stoic tradition, both in its loftier forms and in its application to government; and it was thus more sympathetic to those populist movements that found religious expression in the dignity of lay piety, political expression in the challenge of republicanism to despotism. For it was obvious that if rational insight into cosmic order could not supply the principles of either religious or political life, neither the church nor civil society could be governed by sages. This conviction had deep roots in Italian humanism. Charles Trinkaus has presented at least one group of humanists as lay theologians who were concerned to assert the religious competence of ordinary men by their emphasis on Christianity as a religion of grace accessible to all. Valla contrasted the exclusiveness of Stoicism with the popularity of Epicureanism, and he rested his case for eloquence against philosophy largely on the fact that it employed the language of ordinary men rather than the specialized vocabulary of an elite who "teach us by an exquisite sort of reasoning both to inquire and answer, which illiterates and rustics do better than philosophers." . . . Augustinian humanism denied any privileged position to a philosophically enlightened class. Calvin attacked the monks on the basis of the equality of all callings before God and broke with traditional humanist elitism by praising the manual as well as the liberal arts. For the church this tendency would culminate in the priesthood of all believers. Melanchthon minimized the specialized competence of the clergy, and Calvin insisted on the popular election of ministers "so as not to diminish any part of the common right and liberty of the church." For civil society this impulse meant the rejection of theocracy, and a fully secular government. "Just as Socrates, at the beginning of the *Republic,* sent poets out of the state," Melanchthon asserted, "so we would not eject the theologians from the state but we would remove them from the governing group of the commonwealth," a principle also applied in the Italian republics. Calvin's preference for a republic over other forms of government is well known. "This is the most desirable kind of liberty," he wrote, "that we should not be compelled to obey every person who may be tyrannically put over our heads, but which allows of election, so that no one should rule except he be approved of us." This position did not preclude social hierarchy, but it meant that differences in status among men could only be seen as an accident of history; they are not rooted in the order of the universe, and accordingly social structures can be modified as needs change.

So the willingness to accommodate human institutions to the varieties of circumstance also implied a willingness to acknowledge the significance of change in human affairs. "Now we know," Calvin declared, "that external order admits, and even requires, various changes according to the varying conditions of the times." The historicism of the Renaissance, to which recent scholarship has given much attention, was distinctly not a function of the Stoic tendencies in humanism, which could only view mutability with alarm, but rather of the Augustinian tradition, in which God's purposes were understood to work themselves out in time. Thus for Salutati God "foresaw all that was and will be in time entirely without time and from eternity, and not only did he infallibly foresee and wish that they occur in their time, but also that through contingency they should be produced and be." Contingency was no longer a threat to order but the fulfillment of a divine plan, and discrete events thus acquired meaning. This repudiation of Stoic stasis opened the way to the feeling for anachronism that we encounter not only in Valla's analysis of the Donation of Constantine and Guicciardini's attack on Machiavelli's rather Stoic application of the repetition of analogous situations but also in a more general relativism that left its mark on Calvin's understanding of church history and on his exegetical methods. He saw the rise of episcopacy, for example, as a practical response to the problem of dissension in the early church, an "arrangement introduced by human agreement to meet the needs of the times"; and he noted that there are "many passages of Scripture whose meaning depends on their [historical] context." For Calvin fallen man seems to confront God in history rather than in nature.

At the same time these tendencies in Augustinian humanism also suggest the repudiation of the Stoic vision of peace as the ideal toward which man naturally aspires. This too was an expression of the greater realism in the Augustinian tradition; it had no conflict in principle with the acceptance by Renaissance society of warfare as a normal activity of mankind. Within the Renaissance republic conflict had been institutionalized by constitutional provisions for checks and balances among competing social interests; the Stoic ideal, on the contrary, would have sought to eliminate conflict by submitting all interests to the adjudication of reason, settling for nothing less than final solutions to human problems. And the restlessness of human society was paralleled, in the vision of Augustinian humanism, by the inescapable restlessness of individual existence. The Augustinian conception of man as passion and will implied that he could only realize himself fully in activity, which inevitably meant that life must be fraught with conflict, an external struggle with other men, but also an inner struggle with destructive impulses in the self that can never be fully overcome. . . .

Yet, far less equivocally than Stoic humanism, the vision of Augustinian humanism was social; and, based on the affective life of the whole man, its conception of social existence was animated not by abstract duty but by love. . . . Stoic withdrawal was countered by Augustinian engagement, which offered not the austere satisfactions of Stoic contemplation but the warmer and more practical consolations of a love applied to the needs of suffering mankind. . . . Calvin, who was explicit that man is by nature a social animal, saw in the limitations of individual knowledge a device by which God sought to insure human community. "God," he wrote, "has never so blessed his servants that they each possessed full and perfect knowledge of every part of their subject. It is clear that his purpose in so limiting our knowledge was first that we should be kept humble, and also that we should continue to have dealings with our fellows." Because of the needs of social existence he early rejected Stoic contempt for reputation; conscience was by itself an insufficient guide for human conduct, he argued, because, strictly a private and individual faculty, it was likely, operating in a social void, to cut man off from his neighbor. For Calvin the struggles of the Christian life were above all required by loving service to the human community. Augustinian humanism sought to meet the crisis of community in the age of the Renaissance not by protecting the individual from destructive involvement with the social world but by full engagement, if possible out of love, in meeting its deepest and most desperate needs.

At least two general conclusions emerge from this contrast between Stoic and Augustinian humanism. The first comes out of the fact that we can illustrate either with examples drawn indiscriminately from anywhere in the entire period of our concern, and this suggests that the tension between them found no general resolution in the age of the Renaissance and Reformation. But it is equally striking that we have often cited the same figures on both sides. Neither pure Stoics nor pure Augustinians are easy to find among the humanists, though individual figures may tend more to one position than the other. Erasmus, for example, seems more Stoic than Augustinian; Valla appears more Augustinian than Stoic. A closer study of individuals may reveal more personal development, from one position to another, than it has been possible to show here. Petrarch, Erasmus, and Calvin may especially invite such treatment. But the general ambivalence of humanists makes clear the central importance for the movement of the tension between the two positions. It was literally in the hearts of the humanists themselves. At the same time this ambiguity also reveals that Stoicism and Augustinianism do not represent distinguishable factions within a larger movement but ideal polarities that help us to understand its significance as a whole. . . .

Margaret L. King

Book-Lined Cells: Women and Humanism in the Early Italian Renaissance

The world of humanism was an almost exclusively male world, as King's article, "Book-Lined Cells," makes painfully clear. Her purpose in exploring this aspect of humanism, however, is not simply to decry the inequity but to use it to illuminate the nature of the movement as experienced by women. She begins by showing that a small but surprising number of women were active in the movement during the fourteenth and fifteenth centuries. The numbers she cites for this period—three well-known figures, a dozen or so who could be easily named, perhaps another twenty who could be identified, and the likelihood of many nameless others—should be viewed in the context of a movement that, by the early fifteenth century, centered in each city on only a handful of men. Even as the movement gained in popularity in the course of the century, it never really appealed beyond the small circle associated with the ruling elite. So women, as King shows, had greater visibility than their absolute numbers would indicate.

From Margaret L. King, "Book-Lined Cells: Women and Humanism in the Early Italian Renaissance," in *Beyond Their Sex: Learned Women of the European Past*, ed. Patricia H. Labalme (New York: New York University Press, 1980).

Humanistically trained women showed tremendous promise in their youth, according to King, mastering with relative ease the difficulties of classical Greek and Latin. Yet this promise went largely unfulfilled, for most abandoned their studies when they married. The lack of opportunities for learned women no doubt accentuated this choice, but King maintains that even those who chose learning over marriage failed to meet expectations, and not just because they had little outlet for their talents.

In the selections below, King argues that learned women censored themselves, limiting their own achievements, because they had internalized the notion that they were the weaker sex, not only physically but morally. This attitude reflects a Judeo-Christian bias in Western culture, rooted in the story of Adam and Eve. But King goes farther and isolates a subtle disincentive to achievement that is more unique to the Renaissance. In their sometimes extravagant praise for their female counterparts, male humanists described them as, in King's term, "armed maidens." They had transcended not only the weakness of their sex but sex itself. They stood Athena-like, in cold, distant, solitary, intellectual perfection. And men—threatened and perplexed by the newly emergent figure of female learning—enthroned them in this way to isolate them. Of course, women did not withdraw from the world simply because men wanted them to, but humanist rhetoric conspired with the lack of opportunity and the omnipresent sense of inferiority to encourage women to retreat into their "book-lined cells."

. . . Remarkable people sometimes know they are remarkable. Laura Cereta did. She enjoyed her studies; she understood her talents; she delighted in describing to those who asked and to some who didn't how she had progressed to her present stage of knowledge. Gradually her talents emerged, she reported; as her mind acquired small particles of knowledge, she learned to supply words to adorn them; her mind yearned for studies even more challenging; as her understanding expanded, so did her diligence; she loved philosophy above all; she burned with desire for mathematics; she delved deeply into theology, and she found there knowledge not "shadowy and vaporous" but "perpetually secure and perfect." At birth she had been given the name Laura, who Petrarch had immortalized in his sonnets; now she labored in imitation of Petrarch to lend that name still grander eternity. Cereta was proud of her mind. She was unique.

Learned women more typically betray their fragile self-confidence. . . . Isotta Nogarola apologizes not only for being a woman with pretenses of learning but for being a woman at all, in a work which is, I believe, the most important written by a woman in the early Italian Renaissance: the *De pari aut impari Evae atque Adae peccato,* a dialogue on the relative responsibility of Adam and Eve for the fall of mankind from grace. Nogarola condemned Adam in this dialogue, but based her defense of Eve, paradoxically, on the weakness of female nature. Eve, who had been created imperfect, could not be held responsible for universal sin: "for where there is less sense and less constancy," Nogarola wrote, "there there is less sin; and this is the case with Eve, wherefore she sinned less." Eve's ignorance was natural and deliberately planted by God; but Adam had been created perfect and could be expected to behave perfectly: "When God created man, from the beginning he created him perfect, and the potencies of his soul he made perfect, and gave him a greater understanding and knowledge of truth, and also a greater profundity of wisdom." Nogarola's uncertainties about her role as a woman—put into question by her confrontation with the world of male learning—culminate here in the clear conviction that woman was in fact created inferior to man and that all women had to bear the burden of this first act of creation.

Nogarola gives voice in this dialogue and in her other works to a concern shared certainly to some degree by several and perhaps by all. Her success in the society of the learned was inhibited by her membership in the female sex. The acuity of her mind could be undermined by the frailty of her nature. Not surprisingly, learned women on occasion regretted having been born female and attempted to distance themselves from other women. Not surprisingly, other women despised them. . . .

Nogarola's literary ambitions had exposed her to the envy and hostility of her sex. Laura Cereta, too, was the object of fierce criticism by women. She responded with spirit, understanding both the envy that may have motivated the attacks and the self-destructiveness implicit in any attack on women by women: these women search out others who have risen above them by their genius and destroy them with poisonous envy, she wrote. . . .

Less pained than Nogarola by the attacks of other women, Cereta more easily defends herself and more aggressively turns on her enemies. She ruthlessly condemns empty women, who strive for no good but exist to adorn themselves and do not understand that their condition is one of servitude: these women of majestic pride, fantastic coiffures, outlandish ornament, and necks bound with gold or pearls bear the glittering symbols of their captivity to men who are proud enough to be free. For Nogarola, women's inferiority derived from the order of things, from a divine decree asserted at the hour of creation; for Cereta it is derived from women themselves, who lacked the will to be good, to be learned, to be free: "For knowledge is not given as a gift, but through study. . . . The free mind, not afraid of labor, presses on to attain the good."

Nogarola and Cereta clearly reveal their attitudes toward them- selves as women and as learned women; others speak less fully, but suf- ficiently to persuade us that the consciousness of womanhood in the quest for intellectual integrity was probably general. Being women, they were burdened. To succeed wholly, they would have had to cast off that burden — but it is a burden that cannot be cast off. Or they would have had to elevate the whole of their sex — but this they were powerless to do. The ambitions of the learned women of the Renaissance were thwarted *in part* because, being women, they were vanquished from within: by their own self-doubt, punctuated by moments of pride; and by their low evaluation of their sex, which undermined their confidence further and which was confirmed by the behavior of other women for whom the intellectual strivings of a few threatened their condition of comfortable servitude.

The learned women, conquered from within, capitulated and with- drew from battle. They withdrew from study altogether, into marriage, or into grief. They withdrew to convents and to good works and to silence. They withdrew from secular studies, where men excelled, and took up sacred studies, appropriate for women, and formed cloisters of their minds. They withdrew from friendships, from the life of their cities, from public view, to small corners of the world where they worked in solitude: to self-constructed prisons, lined with books — to book-lined cells, my symbol for the condition of the learned women of this age.

There, they fascinated men. Matteo Bosso recalled years later his after-school visits to Isotta Nogarola in her "libraria cella" — literally, her book-lined cell. Ludovico Foscarini was struck by the same image of that learned woman — by then committed to sacred study and religious exercises — in her solitude: "In my mind I see again your little cell [*cellulam tuam*] redolent of sanctity." Years earlier, Antonio Loschi had been inspired by a similar image of Maddalena Scrovegni: "Your virtues, your manner of life . . . so moved me, and a vision of your little cell [*sacellum*], that one place in your father's house which you had chosen and set aside for silence, for study, and for prayer, was so fixed in my soul that it first gave birth to this mediation within me." Women enclosed themselves in studious solitude, and men applauded. And women sought their approbation. When learned women withdrew from the public discourse of the learned, they may have been moved in part by the powerful spur of male opinion. They were defeated, I have suggested, from within—but the attitudes toward them held by male contemporaries were sharp probes that could penetrate deep within the hearts where that battle raged that ended in surrender.

Male humanists praised learned women extravagantly. . . . In an age when learning was prized, learning in women was prized as well—all the more because it was rare.

But such praise is treacherous. For the women who competed with learned men and who had the boldness to equal or exceed them were not in recognition of their excellence admitted to the company of men—yet they were excluded from the company of women. Like divine miracles, they were both wondrous and terrible; as prodigies, they had exceeded— and violated—nature. Male by intellect, female in body and in soul, their sexual identity was rendered ambiguous: they were, to borrow Nogarola's imagery, rejected by donkeys and oxen alike, expelled from either stable, abandoned, restless, and sleepless. Not quite male, not quite female, learned women belonged to a third and amorphous sex.

The ambiguous sexual identity of learned women was assumed from the early age of humanism. In dedicating his book *De claris mulieribus* (*Concerning Famous Women*) to Andrea Accaiuoli, Boccaccio declared that learned woman to have so far exceeded the rest of womankind that her sexual being had in fact been transformed by a miraculous divine act. . . . Her very greatness, Boccaccio reasons, in which she equals male greatness, suggests that Andrea was not so much a talented female as a woman transformed by the Creator himself and made—not a man— but a being of compound and indefinite sexuality.

Other men in the next century would, like Boccaccio, in the rhetoric of praise question and transform the sexual identity of intelligent women. Lauro Querini found that Isotta Nogarola had attained greatness by overcoming her biological nature. . . . Pietro Dabuson said of Cassandra Fedele that she was the "miracle" of the age; for a male soul had been born in one of female sex. Angelo Poliziano understood that Fedele had, by attaining deep learning, detached herself from her sex, abandoning symbolic objects associated with women in favor of those associated with men: instead of wool, books; instead of a needle, a pen; instead of white dyes to blanch the skin, black ink to stain the page in the process of poetic creation. . . . The learned women of the Renaissance, in the eyes of their male contemporaries and friends, ceased, in becoming learned, to be women.

Whatever they were—and shortly I shall sketch the image I believe was applied to them—they aroused fear and anger in male contemporaries, who then joined to constrain these brilliant creatures perceived as threats to the natural and social order. Perhaps the most brutal attack was an anonymous one upon Isotta Nogarola: she was accused of incest. . . .

Other women were the victims, not of overt hostility, but of kind persuasion: male friends urged them to retreat from full participation in intellectual life, offering advice perhaps as inimical to their progress as heated opposition. Leonardo Bruni, in outlining for the daughter of Battista Montefeltro a program of humane studies, cautioned against the study of rhetoric—the one discipline the knowledge of which would enable a woman to participate publicly in intellectual discourse: "To her [i.e., the woman student] neither the intricacies of debate nor the oratorical artifices of action and delivery are of the least practical use, if indeed they are not positively unbecoming. Rhetoric in all its forms . . . lies absolutely outside the province of woman."

Learned women, then, were sometimes attacked, and sometimes urged to achieve less than could be expected of their talents and their hopes. They were also urged to be chaste. Cassandra Fedele and Isotta Nogarola were praised for their chastity; the latter, clearly influenced by men who preferred that she, as a learned woman, maintain her chastity, voluntarily committed herself outside the boundaries of organized religious life to celibacy. Now, the social function of chastity in the Italian Renaissance is a complex problem that calls for serious exploration. I hesitate to generalize, but given that the theme of chastity in relation to the learned women is so prominent, I feel a tentative hypothesis is required. I would suggest that when learned women (or men, for that matter) themselves chose a celibate life, they did so at least in part because they sought psychic freedom; when, on the other hand, men urged chastity upon learned women, they did so at least in part to constrain them. These fearful creatures of a third sex threatened male dominance in both the intellectual and the social realm. Chaste, they were perhaps less awesome. And chastity suited the stony asexuality that they possessed, or that they were seen as possessing. Learning and chastity were indissolubly linked—for in undertaking the life of learning women repudiated a normal life of reproduction. *She* rejected a sexually active role for the sake of the intellectual life; *he* insisted on her asexuality because by means of intellect she had penetrated a male preserve. Chastity was at once expressive, I propose, of the learned woman's defiance of the established natural order and of the learned man's attempt to constrain her energies by making her mind the prison for her body. In the first case, chastity is a source of pride and independence; in the second, it is an instrument of repression.

The tension between these two facets of chastity in relation to the learned woman is evident in Antonio Loschi's poetic tribute to Maddalena Scrovegni. Scrovegni, widowed while still young, had returned to her father's house in Padua and undertaken a life of study there in a small *sacellum*, as I mentioned earlier. There Loschi, a young humanist, had conversed with her, and impressed by her learning and virtue, was inspired to write a poem, accompanied by a dedicatory letter and exposition, in her honor. Struck by the image of this learned woman in her book-lined cell, Loschi built for her, as he put it, "on poetic foundations," a grander edifice, in which she might sit and reign. He called this larger and worthier edifice the Temple of Chastity, and Scrovegni herself the personification of chastity. The temple was perched on a mountain; the mountain itself rose from a broad plain; the broad plain, an island, was bounded by sea; temple, mountain, plain, and sea were set in the frozen land of Scythia, the home of the Amazons. The temple was huge, white, immaculate, symbolic of virtue. Within the temple's deepest recess was a room—reminiscent of Scrovgeni's cell—on the walls of which were carved images in relief of ancient and mythological figures noted for their chastity. Like the mind itself, one of whose principal functions is memory, this cave contained images of the past—for it was in fact the analogue, not only of Scrovegni's studious cell, but of her mind as well, by both of which she was enclosed. There in the center she sat imperious on a crystal throne, surrounded by her handmaidens Modesty, Virginity, Frugality, and others. A powerful, monumental figure, she dominates the space around her—and yet she is dominated by it. She is queen within her own domain, but she is constrained: rigid on her throne, engulfed by the massive weight of temple walls, denied access to the realm of sensation and pleasure by the very guard who, defending her, repels the assaults of Venus and her son, isolated on an uncharted island in a remote and frigid land. Loschi's tribute to Scrovegni is ambivalent indeed: as it honors her for that virtue concomitant with knowledge, it confines her to a timeless and frozen desert.

The ambivalence discernible in Loschi's encomium of Scrovegni is characteristic, I believe, of male attitudes toward learned women. At the very moment that they praised learned women, learned men undermined them. They perceived such women as desexualized, or of distorted sexuality, as neither male nor female, but as members of a third sex; and these creatures of a third sex aroused in them fear and anger that provoked, sometimes hostile retaliation, and sometimes sweet persuasion to passive roles and to the ultimate passivity of chastity. For the phenomenon of the learned woman, whose learning destroyed the integrity of her sexual identity, they fashioned a fitting image: that of the armed maiden, a fusion of the icons of Athena, the chaste goddess of wisdom, and the Amazons, fierce warriors ruthless to men. Male admirers repeatedly likened learned women to the Amazon queens and to other female warriors of myth and history. . . . And behind these visions of female warriors lay the vision of Athena, martially armed, unnaturally born, coldly virginal, and though female, defined not by sex but by intellect. The chill refinement of the symbol of wisdom coalesced with the ferocity of the Amazons. These images from antiquity were invested with fresh meaning when they were jointly applied to the learned woman: they expressed the relation men perceived between wisdom in women and preternatural aggression. Learned women fascinated learned men, and men applauded, *of course*, their retreat to quiet studies apart from male society. There, in solitude, they were both magnificent and chained: fierce goddesses in book-lined cells. Thus confined, it is no wonder that they won no battles.

Let us not leave her there, but reflect for a last few brief moments on the achievement of the learned woman of the Renaissance. She received no degrees. She wrote no truly great works. She exerted no great influence on emerging trends in the history of ideas. She was probably unhappy. But she was perhaps the earliest figure of the type of the learned woman who is still with us. She was educated and excelled in the highest tradition of learning available to male contemporaries—not in needlework, not in graceful conversation, not in tinkling accomplishments, but in the languages and literature that were the vehicles of the most profound thoughts the age produced. And she exercised her knowledge publicly, at least at some point in her career—not in the cloister, not in hermitage, nor merely within the well-insulated walls of domesticity—but in the marketplace, for the learned to hear and to judge.

The achievement of the learned women of the Renaissance, I suggest in closing, was enormous, and has not wholly been surpassed. Certainly, many more women are educated now than were educated then; many more seek careers in the public realm; and many are successful in attaining positions of authority—success that no Renaissance woman I know of enjoyed. But the inward experience of today's learned women is perhaps no more tranquil than that of the women I have discussed. Many learned women still doubt themselves—more than men do. Many men still view learned women with hostility—and their hostility is still often blended with fascination. Many women still choose between marriage and learning; and many, many must adjust their expectations of love, of marriage, of motherhood in order to pursue an active intellectual life, or, in order to permit themselves the warmth of these relationships, must adjust their intellectual goals. Few women, in my experience, have *not* had to face these choices; few men, in my experience, have had to. This is perhaps the last barrier to the achievement of female equality in the society of the learned—and it is obstinate. What the learned women of the Italian Renaissance attained, we have attained, in greater quantity; but what they suffered we have not escaped. We have confined their demons in a Pandoran box, from which they erupt to haunt us: book-lined cells; armed maidens; the thwarting of ambitions.

III Humanism and Politics

Recall that in identifying the special character of the Renaissance, Burckhardt distinguished between the unique political situation in Italy and its development of the individual on the one hand, and the revival of antiquity and humanism on the other. He insisted that the former features defined the Renaissance, which in principle could have occurred without the latter. In practice, though, the two intertwined so closely as to be almost inseparable. And on this account, Burckhardt saw in the humanists some of the finest examples of untrammeled individuality, in which classical culture served the interests of a self-presentation free of traditional constraints. Although Burckhardt had a deep appreciation of the classical influences on modern culture, influences that received powerful impetus in the Renaissance, his view of humanism relegates the movement to secondary status in defining the Renaissance and essentially reduces its classicism to the level of personal and cultural adornment.

Hans Baron (1900–1988) challenged this assessment of humanism in *The Crisis of the Early Italian Renaissance* (1955; revised ed. 1966), which is the next most influential interpretation of the period after Burckhardt's. A strong supporter of the Weimar Republic, Baron left Germany with the rise of Hitler, first for Italy and then for the

United States, where he settled in Chicago as a research fellow at the Newberry Library and lecturer in history at the University of Chicago. While at the Newberry, Baron burnished the theory of "civic humanism" that he had been shaping since the 1920s and that took final form in his masterwork. According to this theory, humanism underwent a profound reorientation around 1402, when the Republic of Florence stood alone against the encroaching tyranny of the Visconti dukes in Milan. Giangaleazzo Visconti's death by plague on 3 September 1402 suddenly erased the threat that had been intensifying since the 1390s, as the Milanese progressively surrounded and isolated Florence, leaving her by 1402 the sole defender of republican liberty in Italy. Before 1402, the practice of humanism was largely an antiquarian matter detached from Florentine civic traditions. After the Florentine "victory" over Giangaleazzo, civic humanism emerged, in which classical scholarship served political purposes, especially the celebration of republican liberty.

For Baron, this reorientation stands as the defining moment of the Renaissance, from which its originality and significance derive. The republican values that inform modern liberal democracy flow directly from civic humanism, according to Baron. So too does the modern ideal of the active life, which supplanted the medieval ideal of contemplative withdrawal from the world. He even ascribes our modern conception of history to this momentous shift, which turned attention away from God's plan and focused it squarely on politics and the affairs of this world. And he shows how all this was accomplished through a reinvigorated classicism, through a clear distinction between the republican and imperial phases of Roman history that made Florence heir to the former—defender of republican liberty by birthright. Along with this realization came the expropriation of classical models, both Greek and Roman, for wholly civic purposes. Thus, according to Baron, classicism was rescued from mere antiquarianism and was made a permanent, meaningful part of our cultural heritage.

Although he was not alone in maintaining that the humanist movement passed through a civic phase—the Italian historian Eugenio Garin was making the same point at around the same time—Baron forged so forceful an argument that it has become known as the "Baron thesis." It at once commanded respect, especially for his redating of two important manuscripts by a leading Florentine humanist, Leonardo Bruni, showing that they immediately followed the crisis of 1402 and exemplified the ideological shift to civic humanism. But the thesis also evoked some initial skepticism, with critics wondering whether Baron had magnified the conflict between Florence and Milan into an epic struggle between liberty and tyranny, especially given his pronounced antifascism.

Not until Jerrold E. Seigel, however, did a critic attack Baron's thesis where it lived and breathed, in the redating and reinterpretation of Bruni's manuscripts. Seigel's 1966 article in the journal *Past and Present,* and Baron's 1967 response to it in the same journal, are complex examples of textual analysis, but their contentions turn on a general issue clearly laid out in Seigel's subsequent book, *Rhetoric and Philosophy in Renaissance Humanism* (1968). Put crudely, that issue concerns whether we should take humanists like Bruni at their word. Did they truly espouse a civic ideology, championing the active political life over and against the medieval withdrawal from the world? Or were they merely functioning as rhetoricians, adapting their oratory to their republican audience? In maintaining the latter view, Seigel adheres to Kristeller's interpretation of humanism as a phase in the history of rhetoric, and of humanist thought as chiefly reflecting the practice and profession of that art.

Other critics have revised Baron's interpretation of the nature and origin of civic humanism, ascribing the movement to economic and political developments in mid-fourteenth-century Florence, questioning the significance of events around 1402 in favor of events later in the decade, and showing how the leading civic humanists belonged to Florence's ruling oligarchy and thus reflected its narrow political interests. These critiques hinge on a detailed understanding of Florentine politics and society, but recently the Cambridge political philosopher Quentin Skinner has attempted a more basic criticism of the thesis, by viewing Florentine developments from the perspective of medieval Italian political thought in general. In his book *The Foundations of Modern Political Thought* (1978), Skinner traces the idea of republican liberty back to the rhetorical and philosophical traditions of the thirteenth century, when many cities had yet to succumb to the threat of tyranny and were considering the best ways to combat it. Thus, ideas that Baron had regarded as specific to fifteenth-century Florence were really (according to Skinner) the common property of medieval Italy, having been developed by the *dictatores* and scholastic philosophers. But Skinner was nonetheless forced to grant several points to Baron's defenders, namely, that the conflict between Florence and Milan may have inspired fifteenth-century humanists to revive the medieval ideal of republican liberty, and that these same humanists championed the active over the contemplative life.

After burning for nearly fifty years, the fire has by now largely gone out of these debates, leaving us for better or worse with the term *civic humanism* but with little clear idea about the relationship between humanism and politics. In his essay "Humanism and Political Theory" (1991) Anthony Grafton, professor of history at Princeton University, attempts to isolate what we can say with assurance about this relationship. His conclusions are less grandiose than Baron's and considerably more ironic. According to Grafton, the humanists created a new language for talking about family, city, and state as purely social and political entities. This language derived chiefly from the ancients and permeated the discourse not only of Florentine civic humanists but of court humanists in princely states. As implied by its broad diffusion, it represents less a political ideology than a style of speaking. Grafton maintains that this style brought certain ideas about citizenship and the state to the forefront, where they were discussed and debated by the humanists with such rhetorical skill that we still cannot pin down where they really stood.

Hans Baron

The Crisis of the Early Italian Renaissance

Our selections are drawn from the opening chapter and the epilogue of Baron's book, where he outlines the nature and significance of civic humanism. Recall his contention that this movement originated around 1402, during a confrontation between the Florentine republic and the duchy of Milan, a confrontation that Florence appeared on the verge of losing when Duke Giangaleazzo Visconti suddenly died. Our excerpts—coming from the beginning and the end of Baron's book—refer to this confrontation only obliquely, focusing instead on the cultural impact of these events.

In the body of the book, Baron presents an extensive, five-part proof of his thesis about the origins of civic humanism and its nature as the defining moment of the Italian Renaissance. The first part examines Florentine political and historical thought from the latter half of the fourteenth century through the crisis of 1402, showing that Florentine humanists underwent a revolutionary change in outlook by the early fifteenth century. They ceased to view politics from the medieval perspective of the struggle between papacy and empire, in which Florence had traditionally sided with the former; instead, they started to articulate a new vision of Florence as the defender of republican liberty against tyranny. Along with this vision came a new understanding of Roman history as more clearly divided into its republican and imperial phases. In the Middle Ages, Rome was identified with the state of the Caesars—an empire divinely sanctioned by the coming of Christ—for which her previous history was merely a little-studied prelude. Florentine civic humanists, however, rejected this traditional view by asserting the superiority of republic to empire. They regarded Florence as heir to the republican tradition because it was founded by free Romans before Caesar's overthrow of republican liberty.

The second part traces the genesis of this new outlook through the writings of the period, both humanist and nonhumanist alike. In addition to examining nascent civic humanism at the close of the fourteenth century, Baron also details the civic emphasis of nonhumanist writings at this

From Hans Baron, *The Crisis of the Early Italian Renaissance*, rev. ed. (Princeton, N.J.: Princeton University Press, 1966).

time, showing how these concerns were part of the intellectual atmosphere of Florence. The third part examines the life and work of the greatest Florentine humanist of his day, Leonardo Bruni, redating two of his earlier works to show how they follow the crisis of 1402 and reflect the new ideology of civic humanism. The fourth part shows how Bruni's civic ideology saved humanism from an antiquarian fate and turned it into a genuine cultural force, as manifested in vernacular humanist writings that celebrate modernity as well as antiquity. And the fifth part shows how the changes initiated around 1402 were reinforced by subsequent challenges to Florentine liberty, first from the kingdom of Naples and later from a reinvigorated duchy of Milan.

Ever since the humanists' own days, the transition from the fourteenth to the fifteenth century has been recognized as a time of big and decisive changes. In the realm of art, the break between the late Trecento schools, still half medieval, and the first Quattrocento generation of Brunelleschi, Donatello, and Masaccio is more radical than that between any other two generations in the course of the Renaissance. In the development of Renaissance thought, it is by humanists roughly coeval with Brunelleschi and Donatello—Niccoli, Bruni, and Poggio in Florence, and such men as Vergerio and Guarino in northern Italy—that Petrarch's Humanism and the mind of the Trecento were profoundly transformed; so profoundly indeed that, in the history of Humanism no less than in the history of art, the beginning of the new century coincides with the emergence of the full pattern of the Renaissance.

Students of the Renaissance, if asked to indicate the most conspicuous factor in the change, will point without hesitation to the new relationship of artists as well as humanists to antiquity. A new, almost dithyrambic worship of all things ancient pervaded the cultural atmosphere. Brunelleschi expended his small patrimony to pass some time studying, drawing, and measuring among the Roman ruins so that his art might become rooted in the world of the ancients. Niccoli, scion of a well-to-do Florentine merchant family, spent most of his fortune on ancient manuscripts and relics of classic art, until in the end he had to depend on Cosimo de' Medici's financial support. Only ancient authors were to be read and imitated—ancient authors in their genuine texts, unadulterated by the hands of medieval copyists; there was to be a break with the traditions founded by Dante and Petrarch in the Trecento. The time had come for the emergence of a brand of classicism characterized by a single-minded, even militant dedication to antiquity such as had been unknown to earlier centuries.

But classicism, however essential its part in the transformation, was not the only factor. No student of Renaissance art today will stress only the progress of classical imitation. We are accustomed to point out that the art of the Renaissance, in spite of its boundless enthusiasm for antiquity, became something vastly different from a mere return to classical forms and that many elements combined to produce a result which was as different from antiquity as it was from the Middle Ages. In reconstructing the development of culture and thought, it is also not enough to say that the revival of classical studies was merely a ferment in a much broader change. We must clearly define the other elements which acted in their own right, partly seconding and partly counter-acting and re-shaping the influence of antiquity until the results came to be much more than a crude preference for all things ancient.

Among those other elements, the most important was a new position assumed by the Florentine city-state republic.

During the greater part of the Trecento, Humanism had not been grounded in civic society, nor had it been closely associated with any particular one of the Italian communes. It is true that around 1300, in the days of Albertino Mussato of Padua, a beginning had been made toward a union of pre-Petrarchian Humanism with the civic world. At that time, a new type of civic culture inspired by ancient literature had been growing in the old city-republics of northern Italy, such as Padua, Vicenza, Verona, and Milan. But these beginnings had not gone very far when the independent life of the city-republics in northern Italy gave way to tyranny. In the advanced stages of its fourteenth-century development, Humanism was a literary movement some of whose exponents lacked all identification with any specific group of Italian society, while others began to be attached to tyranny. Humanism at that time was carried on chiefly by grammar-school teachers and the chancery officials of a multitude of secular and ecclesiastical princes, particularly in northern Italy, in Papal Avignon, and in the central-Italian territories of the Church. Petrarch, though Florentine by descent, had begun the essential training of his mind in Avignon. In the 1340s, he became spiritually an ally of Cola di Rienzo's republican revolt in Rome, and took part in it through political letters and manifestoes. In his later years, he was associated with several of the tyrant courts in northern Italy. There was in his native Florence, it is true, a circle of his admirers, led by Boccaccio, who slowly prepared the ground for the reception of Petrarch's aspirations among Florentine *literati* and clerics; but it was not to Florentine culture and politics that Humanism in Florence during and shortly after Petrarch's generation owed its direction of studies and its guiding values. Not until the last few decades of the Trecento, when Coluccio Salutati was the head of the Florentine chancery, and Filippo Villani, last of the three famous members of the family of Florentine chroniclers, wrote his book *On the Origin of the City of Florence and on Her Renowned Citizens*, did a gradual process of fusion begin between the humanistic and the civic outlook—whatever fusion there could be between the outlook of citizens who were required to conduct themselves as the members of a city-state republic, and the ideas of a movement still bearing the marks of scholarly aloofness and of the life at north-Italian tyrant courts.

Only a generation later, in the very first years of the Quattrocento, the cultural atmosphere had been transformed. From then on, through thirty years or more, Humanism and the development of Florentine culture were so closely united that for all practical purposes the history of Quattrocento Humanism begins in Florence. Not only did humanistic scholars all over Italy look to the new Athens on the Arno; the most significant effect for the future was that from Florence ideas and interests, such as could develop only in the society of a free city, spread through all Italy. This influence changed most of the ideas held by the humanists of the Trecento. There arose a new historical outlook, a new ethical attitude that opposed the scholars' withdrawal from social obligations, and a new literature, in Volgare as well as Latin, dealing with the family and civic life. Indeed, the more historical scholarship has explored the sociological setting of the early Renaissance, the more clearly has the significance of this Florentine civic component been recognized.

The histories of the Florentine Commonwealth from Leonardo Bruni onward, for instance, served as models of historiography outside Florence not only in so far as they introduced significant innovations of literary form and historical criticism; they also taught a new dynamic concept of history which had grown out of the Florentine experience of civic liberty and the independence of city-states. Within Florence itself, the historical ideas created by Florentine humanists survived to reach maturity in the days of Machiavelli, Guicciardini, and Giannotti—although by then Volgare had become the accepted language and the humanistic technique of presentation was considered obsolete. The link connecting the great Florentine historians of the early sixteenth century with the Florentine humanists of the early fifteenth was their common approach to history from the political experience of Florence.

Again, a civic hue, originally found in the Florentine group, characterizes the voluminous Quattrocento literature of humanistic dialogues and treatises on the *philosophia moralis*. It is not simply that in this literature secularism has gained the ascendency over asceticism; nor is it sufficient to say that classical models have been revived. The heart of the change since the early Quattrocento is that a revolt had taken place against the earlier philosophy of humanistic scholars who, compounding medieval ascetic ideals with stoic precepts, believed that the true sage ought to keep aloof from society and public duties. From the end of the Trecento onward, the ever-recurring themes in the humanistic philosophy of life were the superiority of the *vita activa* over "selfish" withdrawal into scholarship and contemplation, the praise of the family as the foundation of a sound society, and the argument that the perfect life is not that of the "sage" but that of the citizen who, in addition to his studies, consummates his *humanitas* by shouldering man's social duties and by serving his fellow-citizens in public office.

Once we are familiar with these early Quattrocento traits and the change in the role of Florence, we can no longer doubt that the cultural transformation from the end of the Trecento onward must have been accompanied by changes in the external setting. Like other cultural revolutions, this crisis must have included more than the unfolding of the intellectual and artistic elements prepared by preceding generations. There came a moment when new standards and new values arose and demanded their place—a place which the political and social framework of the Trecento had not allowed.

The period of transition about 1400, therefore, must have been marked not only by the rise of classicism, but also by a modification of the material frame in which the ideas of the Trecento had developed. This modification need not mean that the crisis had socio-economic causes. Although even in the economic field there may have been greater differences between the Trecento and the Quattrocento than are usually assumed, it is quite clear that since the late Trecento social and economic change was slow in the Italian Renaissance. Nothing in our sources suggests that the rapid transformation about 1400 was primarily rooted in this sector of life. No revolt with either social or economic overtones occurred in Florence between the 1370s and the Savonarolian revolution of the 1490s; and the unsuccessful rising in 1378 of the "Ciompi," the workers of the Florentine woolen industry, had left no traces that might have shaped the outlook and culture of the citizenry about 1400.

If fresh experience in the citizen's life was responsible for the rapidity and depth of cultural change in Florence, it must have been in the political arena—experience gained in the defense of civic freedom and the independence of the Florentine Republic. And, indeed, around 1400 great dislocations in the political interrelations of the Italian states came to a head and produced a violent upheaval that had long been in the making.

The Italy of the medieval communes had differed significantly from medieval Europe north of the Alps. It had not produced genuine feudalism. The hierarchy of feudal lords which began to develop in the early Middle Ages had been nipped in the bud, and the seigneurs of large landed estates had been forcibly transformed into city-dwellers and members of town society. But communal Italy had no more escaped local dismemberment than had the rest of medieval Europe. The many communes, each ruling over the neighboring countryside, were semi-autonomous and only affiliated with each other by the special bonds binding some of them to the Ghibelline group of princes and towns, others to the opposing camp of the Guelphs. Allegiance beyond the local sphere, therefore, was given only to the universal institutions of the Empire or the Church; in Italy no less than elsewhere, political and historical thought was either Ghibelline or Guelph and found its directives in the never-ceasing contests of Emperors and Popes for the leadership of the Christian world. In many parts of early fourteenth-century Italy, it is true, communal localism was gradually giving way to somewhat larger states under the rule of *signori*. But as long as these new political creations had neither reached stability nor established traditions, and as long as the radius of consolidation was as a rule still small, the longing of the age for pacification through the Emperor or Pope only increased. Although many new developments which were eventually to merge in a new political order of the Peninsula had already started, the impact of the new beginnings could not be strongly felt until some spectacular catastrophe broke the continuity of the inherited conditions.

In contrast to the still medieval atmosphere in the Trecento, Italy in the Quattrocento, as is well known, presents the first example of modern inter-state conditions: a system of sovereign region-states each of which had absorbed an abundance of local autonomies, created new loyalties, and replaced the allegiance to the Empire or the Church. One of these new political organisms was a north-Tuscan region-state under the rule of the Florentine Republic; and it was precisely in the years around 1400 that the final transition to a system of regional states took place during struggles which shook all of north and central Italy to the core.

There can be no doubt about the depth of the impression made by the wars that decided the political structure which the Peninsula was to have in the Renaissance. The issue was an alternative between two diametrically opposed ways into the future. One possible outcome would be a system of equal states including princedoms and republics—an equilibrium of forces making Renaissance Italy in some respects akin to the Greek pattern of independent city-states and, in other respects, a miniature prototype of the modern western family of nations. The other conceivable development was the emergence out of the competition of the surviving Italian states of a national monarchy comparable to those of England, France, and Spain, but unparalleled as a threat of despotic power since north and central Italy knew neither parliaments nor estates general nor any other of the counterpoises to unfettered absolutism that feudalism elsewhere in Europe had left as its legacy to the modern nation-states. Confronted with this tremendous decision, the same pioneering generation of the early Quattrocento that saw the triumph of classicism in all fields of culture experienced on the political plane a contest which, in significance and sweep, was not matched until the end of the Quattrocento when the transalpine European powers invaded the Peninsula.

In many regards, this political struggle was bound to counteract the direction in which the rise of classicism was drawing the intellectual life of Florence and Italy. While humanistic classicists among the Florentine citizens began to turn away contemptuously from the medieval and Trecento traditions of Florentine culture and to discard the old standards of the civic way of life, Florence was thrown into a fight for her existence which put these native traditions and civic ideals to the decisive test. . . .

. . . By engendering a new type of Humanism—*civic Humanism*—the transition about 1400 and in the early Quattrocento even transcended in significance the history of Florence and of Renaissance Italy. Civic Humanism, as it emerged from the challenge of the crisis, exhibited, as our analysis has shown, several diverse facets. There was the new philosophy of political engagement and active life, developed in opposition to ideals of scholarly withdrawal. There was the new historical interpretation of Rome and the *Imperium Romanum* from the vantage-point of contemporary political experience. And, finally, there was the fresh approach to a vernacular Humanism and a defense of the moderns against the ancients—the still inconsistent, but already unmistakable demand that in the present-day world, in dealing with one's own state, language, and literature, one should act as the ancients acted in dealing with *their* states, languages, and literatures. Obviously, these are not tendencies and attitudes that appeared accidentally at about the same time, within a few decades after Florence's political crisis. They represent complementary trends; they form a coherent pattern—inseparable elements of a type of Humanism not fully developed before the early Renaissance. What we learn from Florentine culture after 1400, therefore, is that we must not think of Humanism as an intellectual movement already basically complete in the Trecento, and merely adapting its outlook during the Quattrocento to the needs of diverse social and regional groups inside and outside Florence. We come much nearer to the truth when we think of Humanism as an organism, some vital parts of which did not develop until the Quattrocento. Humanism, as molded by the Florentine crisis, produced a pattern of conduct and thought which was not to remain limited to Florentine humanists. From that time on there would exist a kind of Humanism which endeavored to educate a man as a member of his society and state; a Humanism which refused to follow the medieval precedent of looking upon the Rome of the emperors as the divinely guided preparation for a Christian "Holy Empire" and the center of all interest in the ancient world; a Humanism which sought to learn from antiquity by looking upon it not melancholically as a golden age never again to be realized, but as an exemplary parallel to the present, encouraging the moderns to seek to rival antiquity in their vernacular languages and literatures and in many other fields. Whereas such an approach to the past and to the present had nowhere been found before 1400, it became inseparable from the growth of Humanism during the Renaissance.

This is not to say, of course, that all these characteristics—or, indeed, any—were to appear in every later humanist. We can easily find other types of basic humanistic attainments and approaches to the past and present. But Renaissance Humanism would by no means occupy the place in the growth of the modern world that is rightly attributed to it had those traits ever disappeared again after they had emerged from the early-Quattrocento crisis. They thoroughly shaped the aspirations of the later Italian Renaissance, outside as well as inside Florence, as everyone is aware who remembers the function of the new politico-historical thought and of vernacular Humanism in sixteenth-century Italy. They appeared in the transalpine countries, sometimes encouraged by the influence of Italian—and, especially Florentine—writings, and sometimes freshly re-created among humanists who served the rising western nation-states under conditions not so different from those which, during the early Italian Renaissance, had prevailed among humanists in the Florentine Republic. And although this type of a socially engaged, historically minded, and increasingly vernacular Humanism far from exhausts the rich variety of the humanistic movements of the Renaissance, in many respects it was the salt in the humanistic contribution to the rise of the modern world.

Whenever we want to visualize this contribution to modernity and its historical growth, we must revive the memory of what happened in Florence and among her citizens and humanists during the early Quattrocento. In this far-reaching impact, not only on Renaissance Italy, but on the entire course of Humanism, lies the ultimate significance of the developments whose history has here been traced.

Jerrold E. Seigel

Rhetoric and Philosophy in Renaissance Humanism

Our selections from *Rhetoric and Philosophy* are drawn from Seigel's final chapter, "The Intellectual and Social Setting of the Humanist Movement." Here he directly addresses the issue of civic humanism over which he and Baron had battled in the journal *Past and Present*. Rather than rehash that technical exchange, which concerned the arcana of dating Bruni's early writings, Seigel prefers to discuss the general attitude of the humanists

From Jerrold E. Seigel, *Rhetoric and Philosophy in Renaissance Humanism* (Princeton, N.J.: Princeton University Press, 1968).

toward civic life, an attitude that derives from their marriage of rhetoric and philosophy. His argument in these selections is somewhat compressed (summarizing key points in his book) and requires a bit of unpacking.

According to Seigel, the humanist movement in general paid homage to the Ciceronian ideal of the orator, combining eloquence and wisdom, rhetoric and philosophy. The orator's claim to philosophize resided in his ability to discuss any philosophical issue, not in his adherence to a particular school of thought. Indeed, he was if anything an Academic skeptic, believing that one could not know truth but only arbitrate between probabilities by setting them forth with equal conviction. Through his ability to speak eloquently on any side of a given question, the orator embodied the practice of wisdom, which in effect subordinated philosophy to rhetoric.

The marriage between the two was not only unequal but uneasy, with a manifest tension existing between philosophy and rhetoric in Cicero's thought. This tension played itself out in the opposition between his Stoical and Aristotelian (or Peripatetic) tendencies. In his more philosophical moods, Cicero preferred a Stoical morality that addressed human beings as they ought to be; in his more rhetorical moods, he took a Peripatetic stance better suited to the way people really were. But the facility with which he shifted stances reflects his predominantly rhetorical and skeptical footing.

Humanism revived this marriage and its inherent tension. To the extent that a humanist leaned toward one side or the other, according to Seigel, he favored either a Stoic withdrawal from the world or a Peripatetic engagement with it. And humanists not only differed from each other in this regard but also within themselves, depending on the issue under consideration. Humanist civic tendencies thus represent for Seigel not a political ideology but an aspect of the uneasy marriage between rhetoric and philosophy characteristic of the Ciceronian ideal of the orator. And as that ideal became more fully resurrected in the course of the fifteenth century, the tension within it diminished as the predominance of rhetoric over philosophy became more openly and frankly accepted.

. . . [I]n order to explain the popularity of humanism, or to show that the humanists expressed values implicit in the lives of less articulate men, we need not—and perhaps should not—limit our focus to those parts of their work in which the humanists specifically praised or served civic life. These aspects of humanist literature have been stressed by a number of recent scholars, who therefore speak of Quattrocento humanism as "civic humanism." The present writer has expressed elsewhere doubts about some of the interpretations of this school; these will not be repeated here. Here we shall attempt only to outline what seems to us a more balanced view of the attitude—expressed and implied—of the humanists toward civic life, and of the place they occupied in society. To do so within the general context of this book is appropriate because one important source of the humanists' civic attitudes was their belief that the best kind of learning required the combination of rhetoric and philosophy. It was as men who sought to be both orators and philosophers that the humanists discussed questions of civic participation and solitary withdrawal. In order to show how this was so, we must pause to recall some of the intellectual problems described in the earlier chapters of our study.

The attempt to combine rhetoric and philosophy always involved a basic ambivalence, one which can be discovered in Cicero and in all his successors. Cicero devoted much effort to the projected union of wisdom and eloquence, but at the same time he recognized deep-seated tensions between the two. Not only did he present some of the greatest Greek philosophers as unfriendly to oratory, he even suggested that philosophy itself was fundamentally—and perhaps even irreconcilably—hostile to rhetoric. Cicero insisted that the orator respect not only the linguistic standards of his community, but its moral standards as well. Philosophy, however, was free of such restrictions. Philosophy was among those arts in which "that is most excellent which is farthest removed from the understanding and mental capacity of the untrained." The philosophic enterprise caused men to turn their backs on the mundane necessities of everyday life; the orator's search for persuasive speech could not succeed if he did the same. Given this primary opposition between the two arts, how could any union be achieved?

In large part, Cicero's answer lay in the differences between various ancient philosophical schools. The school for which he felt the greatest sympathy was Academic skepticism, since its doctrines complemented and harmonized with the requirements of rhetoric. Both demanded of their followers a wide general culture, including a knowledge of diverse philosophical dogmas, but both also forbade a final commitment to the positive teachings of any philosophical school. The Academic skeptic, denying that any philosophical opinion could be accepted as true, at once trained his mind and supported his principles by arguing first for, and then against, various philosophical points of view. The orator, inspired by the traditional ideal of the combination of rhetoric and philosophy, also moved freely among the philosophic schools, demonstrating his ability to speak persuasively on every side of a question. Combining the roles of orator and skeptic, Cicero spoke at times on behalf of the moral philosophy of the Stoics, and at times for the Peripatetics.

While Cicero showed enthusiasm for both of these schools, he supported them on significantly different grounds. When he argued for the teaching of the Stoics he spoke of its superiority as a philosophical system per se: that is, of its perfect internal consistency, which resulted from its denial that any external circumstances could affect the happiness of the wise and virtuous man. In support of Peripatetic moral philosophy, however, Cicero adduced its greater relevance to actual human life—it admitted the moral importance of health and of external conditions—and therefore its suitability to the civic environment in which the orator lived. Stoicism was, Cicero admitted, the school of the "only true philosophers." Of all the dogmatic philosophical schools, however, it was Peripateticism that was most in harmony with oratory. Thus it was as orator that Cicero embraced Peripateticism, and as philosopher that he admired the Stoics. To support the two schools alternately was in a sense to try to combine rhetoric and philosophy. The perfect orator would be a Stoic in his most philosophical moments, a Peripatetic in his ordinary, common-sense moments, but fundamentally a skeptic at all times. In this way Cicero articulated a characteristically rhetorical point of view toward moral philosophy and the various ancient schools.

Petrarch rediscovered this rhetorical perspective on philosophy. He often spoke of the need to combine wisdom with eloquence, both to make philosophy active and to enroll rhetoric in the service of truth. Even more explicitly than Cicero, however, Petrarch acknowledged the fundamental contradiction within this ideal. The orator's commitment to the everyday world of the city made it impossible for him to share in the solitary philosophic quest for true self-knowledge, free from the confusions and errors of ordinary men. Thus Petrarch's attempt to join wisdom and eloquence, like Cicero's, had to overcome his own recognition of the basic opposition between the two. Following Cicero, Petrarch sought to overcome this antagonism between philosophy and oratory. This objective underlay his approach to the ancient philosophical schools.

As a Christian, Petrarch could not of course entirely share Cicero's enthusiasm for Academic skepticism, though he sometimes showed considerable sympathy for that school in matters which did not touch on faith. Yet in a sense he did not need to enlist skepticism as a philosophical support for oratory. Christianity itself provided firm reasons for believing that no ancient philosopher had been able to distinguish truth from mere opinion. Thus Petrarch (followed closely by Salutati) made free use of both Peripatetic and Stoic maxims in his letters and treatises, and defended both Stoic and Peripatetic points of view. For this reason, although Petrarch sometimes praised consistency, his writings are filled with contradictions. These contradictions should be understood within the context of Petrarch's Ciceronian style of thought. There is as much of Cicero as of Petrarch in the affirmation that "Just as my reason is often Stoic, so are my feelings always Peripatetic." The ethical stance of the Ciceronian orator is well summarized in Petrarch's statement: "You will act differently as a philosopher than you do as a man. No one is so given to wisdom that he does not, when he returns to the common human state, condescend also to public ways of acting."

The attitudes of Petrarch and other humanists toward civic life—its problems and its values—were in large part conditioned by this Ciceronian style of thought. Petrarch spoke sometimes in favor of the life of solitude and silent contemplation; this was to speak as a philosopher. At other times he stood for an acceptance of the city with its noisy activity, and praised the humanity of the moral values which the give and take of community life required; here he spoke as an orator. Petrarch's statements moved continually back and forth between these two positions, between the claims of an abstract wisdom and the moral standards of the everyday world. This alternation did not arise because Petrarch experienced any fundamental change of heart about the two opposed lives of civic action and philosophic contemplation, but rather grew out of his attempt to combine the lives of philosopher and orator. In Petrarch's vision rhetoric and philosophy both attracted and repelled each other, and humanist thought embodied this dialectic. One result was the simultaneous affirmation and rejection of civic life.

As we have seen, Salutati's position on these questions closely followed Petrarch's: he too vacillated between a Stoic and a Peripatetic point of view. Bruni departed somewhat from his predecessors in this respect. He seldom specifically shared Petrarch's sympathy for the Stoics, though he included them in his "conciliation of philosophers." His basic source for the study of ethics was Aristotle. His attitude toward philosophy was no less Ciceronian because of this, however. It was Peripateticism, after all, that Cicero had singled out in *De oratore* and *De finibus* as the philosophical school which best met the needs of the orator. In his own *Life of Aristotle*, Bruni emphasized both the harmony of the Philosopher's doctrines with everyday life and his interest in rhetoric. The difference between Bruni's philosophical posture and Petrarch's was therefore not fundamental; both men were inspired by the Ciceronian combination of philosophy with eloquence. Whereas Petrarch interpreted this goal in a way which sometimes led to a distrust of rhetoric, however, Bruni's procedures did not allow this. His vision of the ideal represented a more complete devotion to rhetoric, a more confident affirmation of the orator's own philosophical and ethical perspective. This was the meaning of his Aristotelianism, and of his slightly more consistent affirmation of civic life.

The close kinship between Bruni's position and that of Petrarch is clear in the attitude which Bruni adopted toward the active and contemplative lives. He wrote in his *Introduction to Moral Philosophy*: "Each life indeed has its own praise and commendation. The contemplative is surely more divine and more rare, the active however is more excellent by reason of its general usefulness." Strictly speaking, this placed the contemplative above the active, since divinity was the highest attribute Bruni could have applied to either. Yet Bruni's emphasis in his treatise belied this conclusion; it was the life of action and the active virtue of *prudentia* which drew forth his enthusiasm. The noblest ideal, Bruni wrote here and elsewhere, was a combination of the two lives. But he was able to regard each as praiseworthy in itself. He joined his praise of Dante's involvement in civic affairs to a commendation of Petrarch's solitude.

Thus Bruni's acceptance of civic life was not unqualified. His statements about wealth are an example of his varying attitudes toward the moral value of worldly success. Some recent writers have claimed great significance for Bruni's comments on wealth, and his apparent acceptance of riches as an aid to virtue. In some places he did praise wealth for the opportunity it afforded for the exercise of virtue, especially with regard to liberality and munificence, which by definition require large means. But this was not his only attitude. Writing to Cosimo de' Medici, Bruni cautioned that wealth was only an external good, not a good of the body or the soul. It therefore contributed to virtuous living even less than physical well-being did, and still less than wisdom. "To compare riches with wisdom is nothing else than to set the lowest grade of good against the highest." Bruni admitted that wealth created some possibilities of virtuous action, but he cautioned against pursuing it for its own sake.

As long as humanism remained loyal to the ideal of the combination—on professedly equal terms—of rhetoric and philosophy, the humanists' affirmation of civic life could not be unconditional. From a Ciceronian point of view, to admit the value of a strictly philosophical perspective was to set limits to the moral value of everyday life. Only when the application of philosophical standards to ethics was completely rejected, as it was by Lorenzo Valla, could humanism arrive at a stage of complete and uncritical acceptance of the morality of ordinary men. Valla frankly subordinated philosophy to rhetoric. The corollary of this position was the rejection of any philosophical morality which contradicted the standards of common sense. Refusing altogether to accept the independent value of philosophical standards, Valla could regard wealth much more positively than Bruni did. Writing in the *Elegantiae* about the word "happy" (*beatus*), he observed: "He is happy who abounds in all things which pertain to the use and ornament of life. Therefore we rightly call all the rich happy, as in Juvenal: 'the purse of the happy old woman.' And in Cicero: 'Let them be wealthy, let them be happy!' And in another place: 'Formerly when the Crotons prospered with all kinds of riches and when they were celebrated as the happiest people in Italy. . . .'" Here Valla implied that wealth had a much greater moral importance than Bruni ever attributed to it. Of all the humanists we have considered here, only Valla consistently affirmed the ethical values of the ordinary world. Only he openly and fully denied the value of philosophical contemplation separate from the active life.

This is certainly not to deny the importance of the contributions the other humanists made to the civic culture of their time. Even if they sometimes may have felt required by "philosophy" to temper their civic enthusiasm, at the moments when they gave free rein to their literary talents they celebrated civic life and its values in ways which were original, and which could not have been the product of any other form of contemporary culture. Bruni's *Panegyric on the City of Florence* and *History of Florence*, Salutati's chancery letters and *Invective against Antonio Loschi*, Petrarch's *De viris illustribus* and *Africa* — all these writings affirmed the life of action and civic participation with a depth of feeling and an enthusiasm unmistakably humanistic. To patricians seeking reassurance about the values implicit in their everyday activities — at least to those among them who could read Latin — these works must have spoken with genuine force. Giangaleazzo Visconti is said to have counted Salutati more valuable to the Florentines during their war against Milan than a troop of cavalry; no scholastic writer could match the service the humanists rendered to the city-state. In this regard, those who have emphasized the "civic" quality of humanist culture have cast light on important features of the humanist movement.

Important as it is to recognize the services which the humanists provided, however, it is also necessary to see that writings like Bruni's *Laudatio Florentinae Urbis* and the others mentioned above were examples of eloquence first of all, and that is was as rhetorical compositions that they contributed to civic sentiment. The humanists were willing and eager to place their pens at the service of the city-state, but they were conscious of the rhetorical nature of the declarations they made on such occasions. Bruni later excused some of his statements in the *Laudatio* on the grounds that the genre of panegyric "exalts many things above what is true." Bruni must have been aware of his exaggeration when he wrote that the fact that Florence was descended from Rome gave her the right to "the lordship of the world," and that in any war the city would be fighting only "for the defense or recovery of its own property." Given the rhetorical quality and purpose of such assertions, it is not surprising to find Bruni considerably detached from them in the following years, when he worked in the papal chancery at Rome, or to discover that Salutati could contradict his praises of civic life as easily as he could make them. For the humanists, eloquent affirmations of the virtue of a city-state and its citizens were not primarily expressions of personal feelings; they were the performance of a professional task. To say this is to repeat a view stated by several of the humanists themselves: that to affirm the values of civic life was to speak as an orator.

This same line of reasoning may also clarify the relationship between the humanists' often vacillating comments on civic life, and the apparent feelings of broader segments of Renaissance society toward it. If the success of preachers like San Bernardino (and, later, Savonarola) indicates that fifteenth-century men felt considerable uneasiness about the values embodied in their everyday activities, then it is doubtful that an ideology which merely affirmed civic values could have satisfied many of the humanists' contemporaries. One function of the noncivic or philosophical ideals retained by most of the humanists may have been to allow them—as in the case of Salutati or Bruni—to express those anxieties about civic life and doubts about the adequacy of a purely civic ideology which were more widely present among their contemporaries. If these speculations are not too wide of the mark, then it may be possible to understand something which otherwise remains puzzling: namely, the fact that it was Lorenzo Valla, a man much less at home in the civic society of his time than Bruni or Salutati, but more fully identified in his own eyes with the art of oratory, who produced the most insistent and extreme celebration of everyday life.

To understand the place of the humanists in the life of their time, therefore, one should regard them both under the general aspect of men of the fifteenth century, and under the specific aspect of intellectuals of a certain type. Their world view contained elements which were shared by other Renaissance men, as well as elements which were particularly and individually theirs. They participated in social and political life not simply as citizens, but rather as members of a distinguishable professional—and social—group. While their intellectual techniques contributed to both Renaissance education and politics, they were not the only intellectuals of the time, nor necessarily the most representative. These conclusions derive[. . .]from the identification of the humanists as professional orators seeking to model themselves on the Ciceronian ideal. It was as men of eloquence that they found a place in the society of their day.

Quentin Skinner

The Foundations of Modern Political Thought

The first part of Skinner's *Foundations of Modern Political Thought* gives an extended analysis of the ideal of liberty expounded in Italy by the medieval *dictatores* and scholastic philosophers. The second part, on the Italian Renaissance, begins with a chapter on "The Florentine Renaissance," from which our selections are taken. In this chapter, Skinner launches a direct, two-pronged attack on the Baron thesis. First, summarizing his previous conclusions, he argues that "so-called civic humanism" represents less the emergence of new ideas than the inheritance of old ones. Second, he argues

From Quentin Skinner, *The Foundations of Modern Political Thought*, 2 vols. (Cambridge: Cambridge University Press, 1978).

that Baron's civic emphasis obscures the continuities between fourteenth- and fifteenth-century humanism. In place of the Baron thesis, Skinner proposes that the humanist movement of the fourteenth and fifteenth centuries is best characterized by the progressive revival of the Ciceronian notion of the *vir virtutis*, the truly manly man, the offspring of the marriage of rhetoric and philosophy. Obviously, this argument owes much to Seigel, but Skinner also moves beyond Seigel's argument by showing how the ideal of the manly man underlies that of the orator and explains the increasing activism of the humanists. The distinctive contribution of humanism to Western thought lies in its conception of the *vir virtutis* as a creative social agent capable of shaping his own destiny.

. . . [T]here are two factors—both central to an understanding of Renaissance humanism—which must lead us to question Baron's account. The first is that, in treating the crisis of 1402 as "a catalyst in the emergence of new ideas," Baron has underestimated the extent to which the ideas involved were not in fact new at all, but were rather an inheritance from the City Republics of medieval Italy. The other problem is that, in emphasising the special qualities of "civic" humanism, Baron has also failed to appreciate the nature of the links between the Florentine writers of the early *quattrocento* and the wider movement of Petrarchan humanism which had already developed in the course of the fourteenth century. . . .

The first major difficulty with Baron's thesis about "civic humanism" can be expressed at its simplest by saying that it underestimates the extent to which the Florentine writers of the early *quattrocento* were following in the footsteps of the medieval *dictatores*. One important element of continuity between these two groups, as Kristeller in particular has emphasised, is that they generally received the same form of legal training, and subsequently went on to occupy very similar professional roles, acting either as teachers of rhetoric in the Italian universities or more usually as secretaries in the employment of cities or the Church. . . .

The most important similarities, however, between the medieval *dictatores* and the Florentine humanists of the early fifteenth century derive from the range of topics they chose to consider in their moral and political works. Like their predecessors, the humanists basically concerned themselves with the ideal of Republican liberty, concentrating their main attention on the question of how it comes to be jeopardised and how it can best be secured. . . .

The humanists begin by defining the concept of liberty in a traditional and well-established way. They habitually use the term to denote both independence and self-government—liberty in the sense of being free from external interference as well as in the sense of being free to take an active part in the running of the commonwealth. It is misleading of Hans Baron to describe this view as part of "a new ideology" which was "generated" in the course of "the long wars against tyranny" in the first half of the fifteenth century. The analysis the humanists give is in fact an extension of various themes which, as we have already seen, can be found in diplomatic negotiations, city chronicles and other forms of political propaganda dating back to least as far as the middle of the thirteenth century.

The first aspect of this traditional definition of "liberty" which the humanists adopt is the idea of preserving the integrity of the surviving City Republics against any further inroads by the *Signori*. . . .

The other traditional sense of "liberty" which the humanists continue to celebrate is the idea of maintaining a free constitution under which every citizen is able to enjoy an equal opportunity of involving himself actively in the business of government. Bruni sometimes refers to this as "the true liberty," and it is one of his proudest claims about the constitution of Florence that it does in fact serve to secure this value. . . .

The next and connected point at which the humanists continue to endorse the views of the earlier *dictatores* about the concept of political liberty is in the unequivocal preference they express for Republicanism over any other form of government. Hans Baron is again somewhat misleading in his treatment of this theme. He assumes that an enthusiastic adherence to "the Medieval idea of Imperial Monarchy" constituted one of the "traditional convictions" of Italian political theorists throughout the period before the start of the fifteenth century. He is thus led to speak of a complete "cleavage" between this background and "the new outlook" attained by the "civic humanists" of the early *quattrocento*, whose "criticism of Imperial monarchy" is said to place them in sharp contrast "to these features of the previous century." As we have seen, however, the repudiation of the Empire, together with the belief that a Republican form of government is the one best suited to the *Regnum Italicum*, can be found as early as Latini's political writings in the 1260s, as well as in Mussato's chronicles, Bartolus's commentaries and Ptolemy of Lucca's treatise on government in the first half of the next century. It would thus be more accurate to think in terms of the so-called "civic humanists" drawing on a considerable reservoir of anti-monarchical feeling in attempting once again to vindicate the special merits of Republicanism at the start of the fifteenth century. . . .

It is true, however, that in Bruni's commendation of Republican political life there is at least one original—and extremely influential—element. This is his view of the supposed connections between the freedom and the greatness of commonwealths. The special merit of a Republic, as he contends in his *Oration*, is that "the hope of rising to public honours, of building up a career by one's own efforts, is the same for everyone." . . . The closest possible connection is thus held to exist between the promotion of a competitive and *engagé* ethos amongst the citizens and the maintenance of a strong and effective commonwealth. This belief emerges most clearly at the end of Bruni's *Oration*, where he observes that "it is not at all surprising" that Florence "is so outstanding for its talents and industry," since "this hope of honour is in fact held out, and these energies are in fact released, amongst all the citizens of our city." . . .

While this account of the relationship between freedom and power is a novel one, it clearly arises out of two assumptions which we have already seen to be prominent in the writings of the medieval *dictatores*. The first is the claim that the promotion of a healthy and uncorrupt form of political life depends less on perfecting the machinery of government than on developing the energies and public spirit of the citizens. . . .

The other familiar assumption the humanists continue to accept is that a citizen's worth must be measured not by the length of his lineage or the extent of his wealth, but rather by his capacity to develop his talents, to achieve a proper sense of public spirit, and so to deploy his energies in the service of the community. Like their predecessors, the humanists incapsulate this value in the proposition that virtue constitutes the only true nobility. . . .

The final point at which the early *quattrocento* humanists may be said to build on earlier views about the concept of political liberty is in their historical philosophy, and especially in the preference they express for the freedom of the Roman Republic over the despotism of the later Empire. Here again Hans Baron speaks somewhat misleadingly when he repeatedly asserts that this "Republican interpretation of Roman history" constitutes one of the "novel elements in the historical thought of the

Renaissance." It is true that such an interpretation scarcely makes any appearance in the writings of the earlier *dictatores*—though even here Latini constitutes an important exception to the rule. We have already observed, however, that all the main elements of a Republican view of ancient Rome and its history can be found in the treatises of Remigio, Ptolemy, Bartolus and other scholastic writers of the early fourteenth century. The somewhat ironic truth—in view of their continual denigration of all scholastic thought—is that when Salutati, Bruni and their followers discuss the history of Rome, what they are basically doing is ratifying and extending this essentially scholastic interpretation of the facts. . . .

The only point at which Bruni and his followers may be said to extend the analysis offered by the earlier scholastic theorists is in the explanation they offer for the greatness of the Roman Republic and the decadence of the Empire. Bruni treats the history of Rome as the clearest evidence for his belief that a people is bound to achieve greatness as long as there is freedom to take part in the business of government, and bound to fall into corruption as soon as this liberty is taken away from them. . . .

So far we have examined the ways in which the themes of pre-humanist and scholastic political theory were taken up and developed by the so-called "civic humanists" at the start of the fifteenth century. Next we need to broaden our perspective and consider the links between these Florentine writers of the early *quattrocento* and the wider movement of humanism which had already arisen in the course of the fourteenth century.

We have already observed the beginnings, in early *trecento* Arezzo and Padua, of a literary movement that can properly be called "humanist"—a movement rooted in the teaching of rhetoric and increasingly devoted to the study and imitation of classical history, poetry and moral philosophy. We next need to note that, after the middle of the fourteenth century, this movement gathered momentum and confidence in two ways which in turn had a profound effect on the Florentine humanists of the early *quattrocento* period.

One important development took the form of a rapid growth of sheer information about the ancient world. The humanists began to institute systematic searches, especially in monastic libraries, for further writings by their favourite classical authors, looking in particular for additional texts by Cicero, whom they regarded (in Petrarch's phrase) as "the great genius" of antiquity. These treasure-hunts rapidly yielded a series of important discoveries. The full text of Cicero's *Familiar Letters* was recovered by Salutati from the Cathedral library at Milan in 1392. The histories of Tacitus and Thucydides, as well as a number of Plutarch's *Lives*, were rediscovered and made available for the first time in centuries. Bishop Landriani found a complete manuscript of Cicero's *Making of an Orator* in the library at Lodi in 1421. And Poggio Bracciolini made a series of spectacular discoveries in the northern monasteries which he visited while attending the Council of Constance between 1414 and 1418. Searching at St Gallen in 1416, he recovered a complete version of Quintilian's rhetoric for the first time since the ninth century. And two years later, evidently at Langres, he came upon the poems of Statius and Manilius, the philosophy of Lucretius, and several orations by Cicero previously thought to have been lost.

The most important development, however, was that in consequence of acquiring so many new texts, and so coming to recognise how far they had originally been written in—and for—a very different kind of society, the humanists gradually began to adopt a new attitude towards the ancient world. Hitherto the study of classical antiquity—which had ebbed and flowed throughout the Middle Ages—had failed to generate any feeling of radical discontinuity with the culture of Greece and Rome. A sense of belonging to essentially the same civilisation continued to persist, and nowhere more strongly than in Italy, where the legal code of Justinian was still effectively in force, the Latin language was in daily use on all formal as well as learned occasions, and most of the cities continued to inhabit the sites of ancient Roman settlements. As Panofsky has emphasised, the effect of this continuing sense of familiarity was that, in all the *rapprochements* with the classical tradition which took place throughout the Middle Ages, we never find any effort being made to approach the culture of the ancient world on its own terms. Instead we always encounter what Panofsky has called a "principle of disjunction"— a disjunction between the employment of classical forms and the insistence that they carry messages of contemporary significance. . . . A similar outlook, as we have already seen, also affected the medieval study of ancient rhetoric and philosophy. When the *dictatores* of the thirteenth century began to shift their attention away from the inculcation of rules, and called instead for a study of "the best authors," they fell upon the oratorical writings of Cicero with intense enthusiasm. But they never made any attempt to determine Cicero's own sense of the proper aims and purposes of rhetorical instruction. They merely fitted his oratorical texts into the existing framework of the traditional *Ars Dictaminis*.

Towards the end of the *trecento*, however, we come upon a completely changed attitude. As Panofsky sums it up, "the classical past was looked upon, for the first time, as a totality cut off from the present." A new sense of historical distance was achieved, as a result of which the civilisation of ancient Rome began to appear as a wholly separate culture, one which deserved—and indeed required—to be reconstructed and appreciated as far as possible on its own distinctive terms.

One striking symbol of this change can be seen in the new attitude adopted towards the physical remains of Imperial Rome. Throughout the Middle Ages there had been a trade in marble torn from the ancient buildings, some of which had found its way as far afield as Westminster Abbey and the Cathedral at Aachen. By the start of the fifteenth century, however, under the promptings of such writers as Flavio Biondo in his *Rome Restored,* such vandalism came to seem almost sacrilegious, and the archaeological investigation and preservation of the ancient city began to be undertaken for the first time. But the most important symptom of the new outlook was of course the development of a non-anachronistic classical style. This was first achieved in sculpture and architecture in early *quattrocento* Florence: Ghiberti and Donatello began to imitate the exact forms and techniques of ancient statuary, while Brunelleschi made a pilgrimage to Rome to measure the precise scale and proportions of the classical buildings, his intention being—as his contemporary biographer Antonio Manetti expressed it—to "renew and bring to light" a truly Roman instead of merely a Romanesque style. Within a generation a similar transformation had overtaken the art of painting: Mantegna began to introduce an exact classicism into his frescoes, and the same values were soon adopted and developed in Florence by Pollaiuolo, Botticelli and a long line of their pupils and followers.

The crucial point for the purposes of the present argument is that the same story can be told about the revolution engineered by the humanists in the study of ancient rhetoric and philosophy in the course of the fourteenth century. The hero of this story is Petrarch. He finally succeeded in overcoming the disjunction between the classical foundations of the *Ars Dictaminis* and the practical purposes it was mainly designed to serve. Rejecting all attempts to fit Cicero's writings into the pre-established traditions of instruction in the rhetorical arts, he sought to recover—in the genuinely historical spirit characteristic of the Renaissance—what Cicero himself had taken to be the special value of an education founded on a combination of rhetoric and philosophy. The outcome of this enquiry, as Seigel has phrased it, was that "Petrarch transformed Medieval Italian rhetoric by rediscovering its classical roots and scope, thus enabling practising rhetoricians to remake themselves in something like the Ciceronian image."

Petrarch first of all rediscovered Cicero's sense of the proper goals of education. As Cicero had stated his ideal in the *Tusculan Disputations*, the aim of education is not merely to produce a man with a certain range of technical skills, nor even a man capable of attaining all the virtues and "right-minded states." The ambition must rather be to cultivate "the single virtue" (*virtus*) which has been "found to outshine the rest." Cicero even maintains that "it is from the word for man (*vir*) that the word virtue (*virtus*) is derived." So he insists that this special quality of *virtus* is the one we must seek above all to acquire, not merely "if we wish to prove possessors of virtue" but also "if we wish to be men." The fundamental aim of all education is thus taken to be the development of the *vir virtutis*—the truly manly man, the person whose character can be summed up simply by saying (as Shakespeare makes Antony say of Brutus) "This was a man."

Petrarch also rediscovered the lofty place Cicero assigned to the study of rhetoric and philosophy in helping to shape the *vir virtutis* or man of true manliness. This theme is taken up in particular in *The Making of an Orator*, Cicero's longest and most important rhetorical work. The true *vir* must first of all be a man of wisdom. So Cicero makes the study of moral philosophy central to the training of his character. But he must also be capable of putting his wisdom to use, relating his philosophy to his life and fulfilling himself as a citizen rather than merely as a sage. According to Cicero, this means that rhetoric must be accorded a no less central place in his education. . . .

The key to interpreting the humanism of Petrarch and his successors lies in the fact that, as soon as they recovered this authentically classical perspective, they turned themselves into fervent advocates of the same Ciceronian ideals. The outcome was a transformation of existing views not merely about the proper aims and content of education, but also about the nature of man, the extent of his capacities and the proper goals of his life. It is this transformation which the rest of this chapter will attempt to analyse.

The first and fundamental move the humanists made was to spell out the sequence of assumptions underlying the Ciceronian concept of *virtus*: first that it is in fact possible for men to attain this highest kind of excellence; next that the right process of education is essential for the achievement of this goal; and finally that the contents of such an education must center on the linked study of rhetoric and ancient philosophy.

One immediate effect of adopting this classical scale of values was that the humanists arrived at a positively jubilant sense of the value of their own rhetorical studies. It now seemed to them unquestionable that rhetoric and philosophy must be regarded as the key cultural disciplines. They thus succeeded in bringing to birth a doctrine that was subsequently to prove almost embarrassingly long-lived: the doctrine that a classical education not only constitutes the only possible form of schooling for a gentleman, but also the best possible preparation for an entry into public life. . . .

A second effect of recovering the Ciceronian ideal of *virtus* was to give rise to a new sense amongst the humanists that the precise details of a young man's education—the question of what exactly he should be made to learn, and in what exact order of priorities—must be treated as matters of the highest importance. We find this belief reflected in the fact that, by the start of the fifteenth century, a number of humanists began to set up their own schools to ensure that the right subjects were properly taught. . . . Another sign of the same outlook was the emergence during this period of a distinctive new *genre* of moral and political thought—a *genre* of advice-books concerned not so much with supplying direct counsel to *podestà* and princes, but rather with offering guidance about the best form of education to be given to those who might subsequently find themselves discharging these important roles. . . .

A further effect of reviving the ideal of the *vir virtutis* was that it led the humanists to adopt a new and distinctive answer to the perennial question of what entitles a man to regard himself as truly well-educated. This involved them in rejecting a dichotomy central to the pedagogic theory and practice of the high Middle Ages. Hitherto it had generally been assumed that two different systems of education needed to be maintained, one suitable for gentlemen and the other for "clerks." . . . The ideal now being held out for imitation is that of the so-called "Renaissance man," the man who aims at nothing less than universal excellence. He is no longer allowed to think of himself as a specialist either in the arts of government or scholarship or war. He is only permitted to regard his education as completed when it is possible to say of him—as Ophelia says of Hamlet—that he has succeeded in combining "the courtier's, soldier's, scholar's eye, tongue, sword."

But by far the most important consequence of adopting the ideal of the *Uomo universale* was that it prompted the humanists to reject the entire Augustinian picture of human nature. St Augustine had explicitly laid it down in *The City of God* that the idea of pursuing *virtus*, or total human excellence, was based on a presumptuous and mistaken view of what a man can hope to achieve by his own efforts. . . .

One effect of this immensely influential argument was that, in all orthodox discussions about man's nature and capacities throughout the Middle Ages, the possibility of aspiring to the attainment of *virtus* ceased to be mentioned, just as the representation of the concept is wholly absent (so Panofsky assures us) from medieval art. It is of course accepted that a man of saintly disposition may be capable of attaining a number of individual virtues, and thus of avoiding most of the grosser forms of vice. It is always assumed, however, in line with St Paul's teachings in *Corinthians*, that *virtus generalis* is possessed by God alone and personified only by Christ. . . .

These values are deliberately reversed by Petrarch and his followers. We must be careful, however, not to confuse this return to a classical view of human nature with a reversion to paganism—a confusion which has often been held to run through Burckhardt's celebrated account of "the recovery of antiquity" in his *Civilization of the Renaissance*. There is no doubt that Petrarch was a fervently Christian writer, and bequeathed to the early *quattrocento* humanists an essentially Christian view of how the key concept of *virtus* should be analysed. . . .

It would be misleading, however, to conclude that Petrarch and his disciples were nothing more than orthodox Christian moralists. Although they fitted their accounts of the *vir virtutis* into a Christian framework, there is no doubt that their restoration of this classical ideal involved them in a sharp rejection of prevailing Augustinian assumptions about man's fallen nature. The force of this rejection can be seen as early as 1337, when Petrarch started to write the first version of his treatise *On Famous Men*. He devotes no attention at all to the customary medieval pantheon of worthies and saints. His heroes are entirely taken from the ancient world, and the reason he gives in almost every case for singling them out is that they are said to have succeeded in attaining true *virtus*. . . . The pervasive assumption throughout the lives is that true *virtus* can indeed be attained, and that any man worthy of the name must strive above all to attain it.

This anti-Augustinian view of man's nature and capacities recurs even more markedly amongst the humanists of early *quattrocento* Florence. They start by insisting that men do in fact have the power to attain the highest excellence. It is at this point that, by way of underlining this commitment, they invent one of the most characteristic *genres* of Renaissance moral thought—the *genre* devoted to extolling "the excellence and dignity of man." The most famous example is of course the oration on this theme composed by Pico della Mirandola in 1484. . . .

The next claim the Florentine writers stress is that, since men are capable of attaining such excellence, they have a duty to make the pursuit of *virtus* the main aim of their lives. Salutati announces this commitment as early as 1369, assuring a correspondent of that year that "others can glorify wealth, dignities and power," but "I always reserve my admiration for *virtus* itself." . . .

Finally, the humanists turn this view of man's capacities into an urgent patriotic plea. Having come to regard the Roman Republic as the greatest repository of *virtus* in the history of the world, they bewail the fact that the modern *Regnum Italicum* has fallen away so gravely from its pristine heights, and call upon their fellow-countrymen to restore the ancient glories of their native land. This demand—often expressed as a hope—is already central to Petrarch's discussion of *virtus*, and is beautifully embodied in his famous *canzone* "My Italy." . . .

To assert that men are capable of reaching the highest excellence is to imply that they must be capable of overcoming any obstacles to the attainment of this goal. The humanists willingly recognise that their view of human nature commits them to just such an optimistic analysis of man's freedom and powers, and in consequence go on to offer an exhilarating account of the *vir virtutis* as a creative social force, able to shape his own destiny and remake his social world to fit his own desires.

They begin by reverting to the classical belief that the human predicament is best envisaged as a struggle between man's will and fortune's wilfulness. The Romans had worshipped the goddess Fortuna as the daughter of Jupiter himself. They always conceded her a great power over human affairs, portraying her with a wheel on which the fates of men are kept turning by her sheer caprice. They insisted, however, that her sway is not inexorable, since she can always be wooed and even subdued by a man of true *virtus*. It was this classical apposition between *virtus* and *fortuna*—with the accompanying belief that fortune favours the brave—that the Renaissance moralists revived. . . .

The recovery of this classical dramatisation of the human condition again represents an almost Pelagian departure from the prevailing assumptions of Augustinian Christianity. St Augustine's definitive attack on Roman polytheism in Book IV of *The City of God* had actually focussed (after discussing Jupiter and the minor deities) on the twin goddesses of Virtus and Fortuna. He found two cardinal errors underlying the transformation of these forces into objects of worship. One was the fact that the deification of fortune involved denying the beneficent power of God's providence. St Augustine continually insists in his reply that it is by "divine providence" that "human kingdoms are set up," a process that can never happen "rashly or at random," since it is God himself, and "not Fortuna, the goddess of luck" whose will is involved. The other mistake is taken to lie in failing to appreciate that, since the whole world is in fact governed inexorably by God's providence, there can be no question of carving out one's own fate in the manner presupposed by the classical idea of a combat between *fortuna* and *virtus*. The truth is that, if men prove capable of achieving greatness, this is only because God has willed it: the power involved "is not a goddess, but the gift of God." . . .

. . . When we come to Petrarch and his successors, however, we encounter a deliberate attempt to reconstruct the classical image of man's predicament which Augustine had tried to obliterate. The humanists first of all revert to claiming that, where man's capacity for action is limited, the controlling factor at work is nothing more than the capricious power of fortune, not the inexorable force of providence. . . .

This sense of fortune's capricious tyranny sometimes induced in the humanists a mood of extreme pessimism. We encounter this tone above all in Poggio, and especially towards the end of his life, when he even wrote a treatise entitled *The Misery of the Human Condition*, bewailing "the license and power of fortune over human affairs." But the main effect of reverting to this classical picture of the human predicament was to generate amongst the humanists a new and exciting sense of man's ability to struggle against the tide of fortune, to channel and subdue its power, and in this way to become, at least to some extent, the master of his own fate.

One important reflection of this optimism can be seen in the novel and striking emphasis the humanists begin to place on the concept of the freedom of the will. This emerges most clearly in their treatises on the dignity of man. . . .

The same commitment is reflected in the confidence with which the humanists begin to deny that everything in the world is providentially ordained. This soon becomes evident in their approach to writing history. . . . The idea of equating Fortune with Providence and treating it as a lawlike force . . . begins to give way to a sense that Fortune amounts to little more than chance, and to a corresponding sense that human responsibility and choice play a far greater role in the flux of events than earlier historians had supposed. Soon afterwards the same outlook begins to appear in a number of humanist discussions of religious belief. . . .

The humanists summarise all these assumptions in the form of a doctrine which Garin has characterised as "the typical motif of the Renaissance": the claim that it is always open to men to exercise their *virtus* in such a way as to overcome the power of *Fortuna*. . . .

This emphasis on man's creative powers came to be one of the most influential as well as characteristic doctrines of Renaissance humanism. It first of all helped to foster a new interest in the individual personality. It came to seem possible for man to use his freedom to become the architect and the explorer of his own character. This in turn helps to explain the growing psychological complexity of much sixteenth-century literature, as well as the passion for introspection which was later to prompt Montaigne to devote the whole of his creative energies to the investigation of his own nature. The same outlook also helped to popularise a new view of man's relationship with his environment. The idea began to gain ground that man might be able to use his powers to bring about a transformation of the physical world. At one level this gave rise to the dramatic conception of the *magus*, the benign magician who employs his occult arts in order to uncover the secrets of nature. . . . At a more mundane level, the same emphasis on man's natural creativity gave rise to the no less influential doctrine of the moral significance of work. We are accustomed to think of this as a Puritan legacy, but it is arguable that part of the attraction of the Puritan glorification of labour at the end of the sixteenth century arose out of the fact that it resonated with a similar doctrine propagated by the Renaissance humanists over a century before. . . .

Having argued that it is possible to aspire to the highest excellence, the humanists conclude their account of the *vir virtutis* by explaining why it is also appropriate for men to devote their lives to the pursuit of this goal.

This leads them to describe the kinds of reward a man of true *virtus* should expect to receive from the full exercise of his noblest capacities. It is a remarkable measure of the extent to which men were by this time felt to possess God-like qualities that the humanists express this sense of what is due to a *vir virtutis* in precisely the same language later used in the Authorised Version of the Bible to describe what is due to God: in each case what is said to be owed to such unsurpassable excellence is the tribute of honour, glory and praise.

Once again this perspective involved a direct attack on the assumptions of Augustinian Christianity. St Augustine had roundly declared in *The City of God* that "the love of praise is a vice," that the quest for honour is "a pestilential notion" and that "there is no true virtue where virtue is subordinated to human glory." . . .

The moral and political writings of Petrarch and his successors again offer a completely contrasting point of view. As with the discussion of *virtus*, however, it is important not to confuse their classical perspective with a purely pagan outlook on life. They continue to insist on the fundamental Christian doctrine that the vices are to be avoided simply because they are evil, and the virtues pursued for no other reason than that they are good in themselves. As Alberti insists in *The Family*, we must learn to dismiss "ugly subterfuges" as "improper for a man," and to follow the pathway of virtue simply because it "has its own great reward" and hence "makes itself praised perforce."

Such saving clauses, however, to the effect that virtue constitutes its own reward scarcely amount to more than priggish asides. They do nothing to hinder the development of the full-blooded humanist belief that the appropriate goal for a man of *virtus*, and the fundamental reason for devoting oneself to a life of the highest excellence, is the hope of acquiring the greatest possible amount of honour, glory and worldly fame. . . . During the next generation this attitude was developed in the hands of Petrarch's followers into a full-scale ideology connecting the nature of man, the aims of education and the proper goals of human life. . . .

The swaggering figure of the Renaissance gentleman continued to be held up as an ideal, in spite of Machiavelli's scepticism, at least until the end of the sixteenth century. And a number of assumptions about his education have remained with us ever since. University students in the twentieth century are still described as pursuing "honours," and at the end of their course they are characteristically rewarded with glory, proceeding to their degrees *cum laude* or even *summa cum laude*. Apart from such quaint survivals, however, the ideology surrounding the *vir virtutis* was largely swept away, at least in northern Europe, by the middle of the seventeenth century. With his bristling code of honour and his continual thirst for glory, the typical hero of the Renaissance began to appear slightly comical in his wilful disregard for the natural instinct of self-preservation—and instinct stoutly defended by Falstaff in his famous denunciation of "honour" for urging men into battle without showing them how to "take away the grief of a wound." After this unashamed dismissal of the central ideal, it was not long before the entire structure of assumptions about virtue, honour and glory began to collapse—undermined by Rochefoucauld's ironic disbelief and Hobbes's rival theory about the universality of self-interest.

Anthony Grafton

Humanism and Political Theory

Grafton's essay begins with Justus Lipsius's (1547–1606) account of a lecture on Seneca he delivered at the University of Louvain, with the Hapsburg archduke and his wife in attendance. The royal auditors nodded most appreciatively as the humanistic scholar skillfully extracted modern political lessons from ancient wisdom. But were they really listening? And, more important, did Lipsius really think they were? Viewed in the context of these questions, Grafton finds the humanist contribution to political thought maddeningly elusive, as he demonstrates by tracing Lipsius's enterprise back to its Italian roots.

These roots were embedded in medieval soil, particularly that cultivated by the *dictatores* and early humanists. Grafton notes that when these two groups addressed political questions, they generally borrowed from Cicero and Seneca, in much the same manner as later humanists, although

From Anthony Grafton, "Humanism and Political Theory" in *The Cambridge History of Political Thought, 1450–1700*, ed. J. H. Burns (Cambridge: Cambridge University Press, 1991).

they made no effort to resurrect the civic ethos of ancient Rome. All this changed between 1390 and 1420, when humanism entered the service of the city-state. In this regard Grafton describes the rise of a republican ideology framed by the leading Florentine humanists, Coluccio Salutati (1331–1406) and Leonardo Bruni (1370–1444). By about 1420, humanism had contrived a civic ideology not only for republican but also for princely states, like Milan, Naples, and the Papacy, which acquired their own humanists to legitimate their political goals. As humanism increasingly found its role in justifying political power of whatever sort, Grafton argues, humanist education gained in popularity among the ruling elites, transforming their sensibilities.

"But," asks Grafton, "did this revolution in the canons of taste and the forms of public discourse also lead to revolutionary change in political thought?" Here he reviews the Baron thesis and sanctions many of its critics. He argues that Baron is guilty of overinterpreting Bruni; that "civic humanism" did not even gain the unqualified assent of Florence's ruling elite; that Baron's interpretation obscures the widespread belief in astrological influences on politics; and that medieval jurists, scholastics, and even mendicant friars had at least as much to say about practical political concerns as the humanists did.

In his concluding section, "The Topics of Humanist Political Discourse," Grafton rakes through the ashes of the Baron debate to find what can still be said about the relationship between humanism and politics, once one has subtracted the more extravagant claims for "civic humanism." We have excerpted this, the longest section of the essay, in its entirety because it takes us constructively beyond Baron, beyond the theory of civic humanism and back to the fundamentally rhetorical nature of the humanist enterprise, now viewed in a new, more ironic light.

. . . . What remains when all subtrahends are removed is still important. The humanists created a new language for talking about citizenship and the state. As specialists in discourse they made their way to prominence and power, offering in a language far more attractive and accessible than that of scholasticism a description of society as it is and prescriptions for what society should be that often fitted the needs of their time with supple elegance. This language, flexible, rich, and largely classical, was shared by civic humanists and monarchists, Florentines and Ferrarese. For the remainder of this essay we shall explore it, dividing its lexicon of concepts into three categories that the humanists themselves would have seen as legitimate. Humanist social and political language explicates the duties of the patrician towards household, city, and state. To deal with the household may seem to the twentieth-century reader a conflation of the personal and the political. Yet in fifteenth-century cities it seemed evident that the two forms of economic and administrative order were analogous and intimately related. Teachers of ethics like Ioannes Argyropoulos argued that they had to show from their texts that "man is born not for himself but for others as well, but not just any others, only those for whose care and rule he is responsible. These fall into two categories; some belong to the household, some to the state." Teachers of history like Ludovico Carbone promised to show their pupils how "to organise the family and administer the state." And all tended to assume in humble practice—whatever they might proclaim in lofty theory—that on these matters the classical philosophers had basically the same doctrines as our writers do.

First, then, the family. Here the humanists had much to say. They began by making classical materials available in a new way. Francesco Barbaro wrote an elaborate treatise *De re uxoria* in which he vulgarised the ideas and anecdotes of Plutarch about how to marry, raise children, and preserve a peaceful home. Leonardo Bruni retranslated the pseudo-Aristotelian treatise *Oeconomica*, "On Household Management," and used his knowledge of Greek history and customs to provide it with a commentary that made clear much that the scholastics had misunderstood—and even some points that the author himself (whom Bruni thought to be Aristotle) might have left obscure. Bruni was at pains to show that the text did not treat women, as it seemed at first to do, as domestic equipment on a par with cattle. He argued at length, in fact, that a wife had a status and rights guaranteed by laws which no husband could licitly violate. This work became a humanist bestseller; more than 200 manuscript copies of it survive, still bearing the marks left by owners who included clerics and laymen, scholars and merchants—a cross-section of the Italian elite. Others elaborated in treatises on education the doctrines on marriage and management of children that they had found in the witty, anecdotal essays of Plutarch and the systematic treatise of Quintilian.

So far as relations between husbands and wives, fathers and children were concerned, the humanists essentially fitted their classical sources to Italian realities. The major classical text on marriage, Plutarch's *Coniugalia Praecepta*, calls for husbands to remain on top, but does so in a moderate and qualified way. Plutarch insists that husbands accommodate themselves to their wives and not expect them to be constantly obsequious and complaisant in the style of courtesans. Barbaro, adapting Plutarch to an Italian world where husbands married young wives late in their own careers, speaks only to husbands and advises wives simply to be silent and obey. He twists Plutarch's anecdotes to support total subordination of women. In the same style, later treatises like Leon Battista Alberti's Italian dialogues *On the Family* offer a splendid male fantasy of docile young wives being ruled and instructed by powerful, mature husbands in everything from storage of food to sexual relations. If sometimes fanciful, though, these texts are far from insignificant. In a society that often seemed obsessed with the need to preserve the family against the aggression of rival families, the suspicions of state officials, and the high rate of infant mortality, they offered attractive and apparently effective advice that actually ratified the demographic realities of the time. But they did so at the double price of distorting classical sources and of ignoring many difficult modern situations, such as arose when a young and vigorous widow like Alessandra Scala came to control a family or a princess became the ruler of a state.

More ambitious—and probably far more influential—were the humanists' efforts to provide a moral rationale for the existence and power of the rich merchants and princes of their time to earn and spend their money without shame. They found in Aristotle above all justification for conspicuous expenditure: "But great expenditure is becoming to those who have suitable means to start with, secured by their own efforts or from ancestors or connections, and to people of high birth and reputation . . . For all these things bring with them greatness and prestige." They thus came to argue that wealth was not simply something "indifferent"—something that could be used for good or for ill—but that its possession could be the foundation of a virtue in its own right. "Magnificence," the proper expenditure of large sums, was a virtue peculiar to the rich; and the rich, in Florence and elsewhere, and their panegyrists rapidly appealed to these views as they dropped the traditional medieval habit of concealing wealth from tax officials and rivals and went in for display. Great families, in Florence above all, built themselves palaces that cut them off from the street-corner life of the city and loggias that offered in its place a private sociability for family and close friends. They became—most notoriously in the case of Cosimo de' Medici—patrons of architecture on the vast scale previously reserved for the church and secular rulers, and patrons of visual artists and dealers in fine clothing and antiquities as well. And they and those who designed for them, like Alberti, continually insisted that this new world of display was the conscious and virtuous exercise of magnificence in action. "Men of public spirit," Alberti wrote in the preface to his work on architecture, "approve and rejoice" at the sight of such activity.

As personal display came to seem desirable and virtuous, acquisitiveness too took on a newly laudable character. True, the humanists did not actually advance new economic doctrines to supplant those of the mendicants. But they did defend the activities of the merchant in a newly aggressive way, as vital to the exercise of virtue.

When the venerable Giannozzo in Alberti's *On the Family* insisted that his young relatives should examine their consciences nightly to determine if they had missed an appointment or an opportunity, failed to meet a commitment, or to act in good time, he spoke a language of innerworldly asceticism that the mendicants could not use—and that would have lacked any justification without the alternate ideologies of magnificence and civic service that Alberti espoused through other *personae*. In later bourgeois society "money is very ashamed of itself," as Lionel Trilling rightly pointed out. In fifteenth-century Italy the humanists devised a language in which money could speak without shame, if only as the sign and basis of a new idea of virtuous conduct. Humanist doctrines on the government of the household, in other words, were modern and attractive; and they helped to reshape the social and physical space in which the Italian elite lived.

Humanist doctrines about the nature and government of cities, like those on households, began from classical sources but were not confined to them. The humanists knew from Aristotle and his followers how to divide an urban population into ordinary people and patricians. They learned from Livy how the circumstances of a city's founding shape the character and virtues of its people. But they also learned from medieval intellectuals how to compile a powerful dossier in praise of the city to which they belonged, enumerating its saints and spectacles in overwhelming detail. And even their most classical descriptions of a city's virtues tend to enfold or reflect late medieval discussions of urban history and power.

Humanist texts on cities may at first seem somewhat bland to the uninitiated reader. Examples of epideictic rhetoric, oratory in praise (or blame) of a person or thing, they pile up the virtues and attributes of the cities they describe with little obvious regard for details or qualifications. Salutati defending Florence against Antonio Loschi and Bruni praising Florence both extol the city's climate, health, agriculture, trade, commerce, walls, and buildings—referring neither to the lowered scale of manufacturing and banking after the crash of the fourteenth century nor to the insalubrious conditions caused in Florence by some of her characteristic industries, like the tanning works and fullers' shops. Bruni explicates Florentine institutions as built around a central check, a *cautela*—the system of choosing members of the governing committees by lot from a large body of citizens that supposedly prevented the great families from controlling urban policies. Yet he wrote this at a time when one small group of families was in fact manipulating the city's policies towards war and expansion to serve their own economic interests, as well as opening up positions in the government to more citizens than before. Such rhetoric blurs the outlines of real cityscapes and institutions.

The classical and clerical sources of the humanists' language, moreover, did not offer them terms and tools for dealing with certain crucial features of Renaissance urban life. Florence, we know from several recent books, was less a single coherent city-state in the classical sense than a congeries of districts and guilds to which most citizens felt their primary loyalties—and from which they received such governmental interference as they met. But the classical language of social analysis of cities has little terminology for these intermediate bodies, and the works in praise of cities accordingly paid little attention to them. True, the Venetian humanists devised a more elaborate and novel language to deal with their city's unique constitution, its powerful doge, closed governing body, and remarkable social harmony. And reality slips through the rhetoric in Florence as well—as when Bruni, writing for his Greek friends at the Council of Ferrara-Florence, admitted that his city was now dominated by men of wealth and connected that fact with the replacement of the old civic militia by mercenary armies, who fought for money rather than sentiment. On the whole, however, it remained a language of praise.

Yet the humanists' civic discourse was novel in at least two vital ways. In the first place, they based cities' claims to antiquity and high origins on direct study of the ancient sources. Salutati's argument for Florence's Roman heritage, for example, rested on a passage in Sallust's history of Catiline in which he described discontented veterans of Sulla's army sent out to resist the inhabitants of Fiesole, turning rebellious after losing their property. Such arguments became more and more elaborate over time, as Bruni and others traced their cities back to Rome, to the Etruscans, and even—in the notorious case of Viterbo—to Isis and Osiris. And they often led to the bold invention of acts and documents where these were lacking, since, as Salutati had already admitted, the passage of time made urban origins tantalisingly obscure. Yet they had a powerful impact on political propaganda throughout Europe, and the invention of traditions about Trojan, Roman, or Greek origins that became a staple of Renaissance pageantry and propaganda had its origins in the Italy of the humanists.

In the second place, the humanists dwelt on the physical appearance of their cities with a new artistry and interest. They treated Florence under the Medici, Rome under Nicholas V, and Milan under the Sforza as cities rationally planned both to give aesthetic pleasure and to further economic activity and political power. Bruni, for example, emphasises in his *Praise of Florence* the city's ideal situation, splendid public buildings, clean and wide streets. The humanists in the papal curia did the same, ceasing to lament the decay of Roman inscriptions and buildings—and their misidentifications by past scholars—as papal architects rebuilt and population returned to the acres of sheep meadow within the old walls. These descriptions often misrepresented reality. They treated confused and over-built cities, with narrow streets and polluted rivers, as ideal and rational creations like the cities imagined in Antonio Filarete's treatise *Sforzinda* and Alberti's *On Architecture*. Yet in doing so they challenged rulers to build systematically and further the creation of rationally planned colonies—and a few such cities, like the fortress of Alessandria, were actually built. More importantly, perhaps, they helped to create the tradition of including detailed physical descriptions of public buildings, churches, hospitals, and open spaces in political writing—and of insisting on the effects of the built environment on its human inhabitants. These motifs became standard ones in the utopian writing of the sixteenth century, from Thomas More's *Utopia* to Tommaso Campanella's *City of the Sun*. To that extent the apparently unrealist epideictic orations of the humanists had a real impact—if not on most cities, at least on some of the most powerful and persistent western visions of what a good city should be. The image of the city as a rational, planned space, its buildings and quarters differentiated not by tradition and accretion but by logic and science, received its most powerful crystallisation in Leonardo's drawings. It is salutary to remember that these high Renaissance creations of one who called himself a "man without letters" have their roots in the political writing of the humanists.

The state, finally, *respublica* as opposed to *civitas*, called forth a great deal of discussion from the humanists. Writers about kingship, on the one hand, naturally directed their attention to relations between a court and all its subjects rather than the more limited political space of the city where a court was normally located. This they did partly because their rulers genuinely formed the heads of a wider political community, and—especially in Naples and Milan—found both special problems and special opportunities in the existence of lesser nobles and formerly independent cities in their domains. But they also did so because the tradition of writing on kingship that they inherited, stemming from Isocrates in classical Greece and brilliantly continued by John of Salisbury and many others in the middle ages, dictated this approach. An almost unvarying series of topics—including the proper relations between a king and his counsellors, the question of whether a king is above or below the law, and the king's moral duty to devote himself to the good of his subjects, avoiding excess taxes and unnecessary war—formed the staple of this genre in its Renaissance incarnation from Petrarch on. Modern readers know these topoi best from Machiavelli's inversions of them in *The Prince*, with its obsessive insistence on the role of fear and the vital importance of warfare. And for all the mordant injustice of his work, it must be admitted that the humanists of the fifteenth century added little of substance to the traditions that they drew upon.

Republican writers often addressed—but did not always have much of substance to say about—the increasingly large territorial states that surrounded Florence and Venice. In defending Florence against Antonio Loschi, Salutati tried to articulate an ideology that justified Florence's presence outside her own walls. Florence stood, he claimed, as the defender of *libertas*, not just at home but in the rest of north Italy; her territorial state was the necessary consequence of the need to defend republicanism against the aggression of the Visconti tyrant. This argument sounds pleasing now, but as Nicolai Rubinstein has shown, it would have evoked remarkably varied reactions around 1400 (and in fact did so from Salutati's literary opponent, Loschi). In Florentine political discourse *libertas* had a variety of meanings, including the republican constitution at home and freedom from interference from other powers. But it did not mean that formerly autonomous states that now came under Florentine rule would be granted autonomy in their own affairs. Pisa, captured in 1406 and made to serve as the base of the Florentine galley fleet, was occupied by a garrison and ruled by Florentine governors and tax collectors. Loschi did not fail to point out that *libertas* was more a cloak for self-interest than a programme for the political development of north Italy. In short, humanist political discourse did not offer an incisive analysis of the larger and larger political entities, centred on Milan, Florence, Venice, Rome, and Naples, that divided up the Italian political scene in the course of the fifteenth century, like monstrous paramecia seen on a microscope slide devouring smaller organisms.

What the humanists did offer, as usual, was a flexible and persuasive language of praise and justification for the states and rulers that they served. In this realm of epideictic discourse the humanist mastery of the ancient texts, with their rich resources of argument, anecdote, and metaphor, and the humanist command of rhetoric itself proved a decisive advantage. Any ruler and any subject could be provided with a terminology appropriate to the social and intellectual standing of both. Thus, as Alison Brown has shown, classical topoi could be deployed in praise of Cosimo de' Medici in at least three ways. A Greek humanist like Argyropoulos, appointed to a formal position in the Florentine *studio*, could draw on Plato's *Republic* to describe his master as the embodiment of the philosopher-king that Plato had thought could not exist except as an ideal. Members of established Florentine families like Donato Acciaiuoli could remain more reserved—and reveal less awareness of the political realities—by treating Cosimo as simply *primus inter pares*, a noble and beneficent citizen who had saved the state from chaos, held only a few offices, and devoted himself to the public good. And the admirers and beneficiaries of Cosimo's lavish patronage of the arts, drawing on the rich resources of Horace and Virgil, could compare Cosimo to Augustus and Maecenas, the great benefactors of the Augustan age whose most lasting material was the classical literary works they had supported.

Humanist epideictic proved remarkably supple and inventive. Some orators employed premises that seemed unexceptionally Roman and republican to praise absolute—and absolutely non-Roman—rulers. Thus Pier Paolo Vergerio, theorist of education and student of Cicero, insisted firmly on the preeminence of the active life in public service: "That man excels all others in character and way of life who devoted himself to the government of the state and to sharing in the labor for the common good." At one point he went even further, arguing like a good Florentine that "the best philosophy . . . dwells in cities and shuns solitude, strives both for its own advantage and for that of all," and denouncing Augustus as a tyrant. On the whole, however, the one string that he plucked in every context was the need for justice and the rule of law rather than violence. It comes as a surprise to learn from David Robey that he used these principles to build an edifice of praise for the Carrara of Padua, a family not known for their rigorous adherence to legal codes. And while one could argue—as Castiglione later would—that such idealised statements were a way of confronting the actions of a ruler with the values they violated, of teaching by indirection, the lasting impression one receives is of men deliberately setting out to conceal and divert attention from inconvenient realities. When Bartolomeo Fonzio set about praising Lorenzo de' Medici, a far less active patron than Cosimo (though a fine poet in his own right) and a more overt manipulator of Florentine government, he did so in the exalted term of Virgil's Fourth Eclogue; "You have at last resorted the rule of Saturn [the Golden Age] . . . The arts are restored, poets are prospering." Angelo Poliziano, similarly, finely conflated Virgil, Ovid, and others in a mock epic in which Lorenzo himself was made to learn not how to found a new race but how to love. These praises of Lorenzo had a clear political purpose despite their exalted sound. They distracted attention from the recent rise of the Medici and Lorenzo's personal lack of the military prowess which had distinguished princes in most traditional panegyrics (he himself confessed that he was not "a hard hitter" and won tournaments only because the judges wanted him to). And they did create a powerful image of Lorenzo as a patron of the arts—an image which persisted in histories of the Renaissance, despite his lack of means and low scale of real expenditure, into the twentieth century. Sometimes, indeed, the curtain-drawing seems painfully visible—as when Poliziano, writing the history of the conspiracy of the Pazzi against the Medici, modelled his work on Sallust's *Catiline* but completely omitted any counterpart to Sallust's social and political exposition of why conspiracy had taken place. To include such an explication was to call attention to the recency and illegitimacy of Medicean rule. Poliziano accordingly ignored social and political preconditions of revolt and instead included a stunningly vivid account of the rituals of inversion by which the Florentine crowd had humiliated the Pazzi alive and even dead.

In one area—and perhaps only in one city—humanist political discourse did transcend propaganda. In Venice, as Margaret King has recently shown, the fifteenth century saw the patriciate which dominated the Venetian economy and monopolised political life take a strong interest in humanistic scholarship. The Venetian elite, with its tradition of service to the state in a wide variety of positions at home and in the Venetian outposts (and eventually its growing empire in Italy) forged from partly classical ingredients and partly modern ones a new set of ideas. Ermolao Barbaro, for example, a great scholar and also a great state servant, wrote in classical Latin an account of the duties of the resident ambassadors of Venice, those officials of a new kind who made it possible for states to survive in the turmoil and continual rapid reversals of Italian politics. Here he articulated an ideal of absolute subservience, not to a single ruler but to the state as a whole, that had no counterpart in previous political discourse. Barbaro argued that the ambassador must place himself absolutely at the disposal of the home government, obeying its commands without hesitation or scruple, as a deliberate and dutiful sacrifice of that independence of action which a patrician normally cherished in other spheres. This call for absolute obedience to the political needs of the state, brief, cogent, and simple, resounds with reality and modernity just as powerfully as Bruni's admission of the role of money in Florentine affairs.

Specialists in discourse, the humanists did not articulate a new and compelling full-scale analysis of the new and dangerous political world that they inhabited. They praised, they blamed, they concealed; the classical themes and ideas they revived more often proved a template to be imposed on obdurate facts than a lens through which to inspect them more closely. And even when they obtained, translated, and discussed such powerful ancient works of political philosophy as Plato's *Republic* or of political reflection as Thucydides' history, they used them more as grab-bags of anecdote and edifying platitude than as models for comparably ambitious intellectual projects. These they left to the later writers of the age of the New Monarchies and after. Yet epideictic, though usually stereotyped and sometimes cloying, is far from insignificant. The humanists' idealisations of institutions and individuals took on a powerful life of their own, inspiring later thinkers and deceiving later historians. For that alone they deserve close scrutiny.

PART

IV Humanism
in Theory
and Practice

Like most curricula, humanism exhibits a marked discrepancy between its theoretical pronouncements and their practical implementation. In making this observation, we do not mean to impugn theory with practice but merely to gain a more balanced view of a movement that, by the very allure of its name, tends to foster great expectations. Kristeller's interpretation of humanism as a phase in the history of rhetoric has done much to bring our understanding of the movement back down to earth, but rhetoric itself has recently been shown to harbor unexpected conceptual depths. In Part IV we shall contrast the theory of *imitatio* (or "imitation") that lay at the heart of Renaissance rhetoric with its actual practice in humanist schools. This contrast will also highlight the controversy over whether humanist education actually achieved its aim of moral betterment or only served the interests of the status quo.

In *The Light in Troy: Imitation and Discovery in Renaissance Poetry* (1982), Thomas M. Greene—professor emeritus of English and comparative literature at Yale University—plumbs the conceptual depths of the theory of imitation, an exercise that would strike most modern readers as incongruous. We commonly regard imitation at best as unoriginal and at worst, in its unacknowledged form, as plagiarism. Many humanistic texts appear to us as boring pastiches of classical quotations, if not as instances of downright intellectual theft. Greene tries to take us beyond this modern sensibility, toward a conception of *imitatio* as embodying a theory of style, a philosophy of history, and conceptions of self. Through imitation, indeed, the best humanists defined themselves over and against their classical models, as they struggled with the newly perceived reality of a dead past. Greene's "light in Troy" comes from the fires of the sacked Homeric city—emblematic of the destruction of ancient culture—shining across the abyss of a "dark" age to illuminate, from behind, the path that the humanists must take.

This elegiac image notwithstanding, the practice of imitation in humanist schools could lead to intellectual sterility, as Greene notes. Anthony Grafton and Lisa Jardine (professor of history at the University of London) emphasize this aspect of the humanist program in their collaborative work, *From Humanism to the Humanities* (1986). In contrast to previous studies of the history of humanist education, which had relied on the theoretical statements of the humanists themselves or on the published statutes of humanist schools, Grafton and Jardine went to the archives and dug up actual student notes, compositions, and teachers' diaries, as well as plowing through the textbooks they used. This worm's eye view of the educational process reveals for Grafton and Jardine its fundamental drudgery, thus debunking the notion, popularized by the humanists themselves, that theirs was a progressive system designed to rear good citizens. In truth, Grafton and Jardine observe, it really served the needs of the ruling elite by creating intellectually docile servants of the state who could speak and write in a fashionable manner.

In his *Schooling in Renaissance Italy* (1989), Paul F. Grendler defends Renaissance education against the charges leveled by Grafton and Jardine, among others. Grendler, professor emeritus of history at the University of Toronto, allows that all educational systems reflect the societies they serve. In the case of Italian society in particular, mastery of classical Latin was highly prized, as was the knowledge of ancient civilization it unlocked, thus mitigating the monotony of rote learning that comes with the mastery of any language or skill. Further, Grendler argues, humanist education had tremendous moral content, especially apparent in the constantly reiterated ideal of the citizen-orator, the longevity of which indicates that students took the content seriously. Indeed, its rhetorical nature notwithstanding, humanist education imparted to students a core of moral and civic values, according to Grendler, providing them with a touchstone for life in the diverse social and political circumstances of Renaissance Italy.

Thomas M. Greene

The Light in Troy: Imitation and Discovery in Renaissance Poetry

Our selections from *The Light in Troy* are drawn from the third chapter, "Imitation and Anachronism," which begins by contrasting Dante and Petrarch. Whereas Dante felt himself part of a community of poets extending back to antiquity, Petrarch felt cut off from antiquity because he had a more highly refined sense of the differences between it and the Christian era. Our first selections describe how Petrarch's sense of historical distance created (at the very least) a twofold problem: how to bridge the gap between antiquity and modernity without undue anachronism, and how to write in the shadow of ancient grandeur. The humanists addressed this problem by means of a program of *imitatio*, the imitation of classical models. Greene details this program in the third and fourth sections of his chapter, from which come the bulk of our excerpts.

Greene describes four kinds of imitation: (1) the slavish following of a single model, (2) the eclectic borrowing from and allusion to several models, (3) the "heuristic" form of imitation that advertises the differences between text and model, and (4) the "dialectical" form of imitation that establishes a dynamic interplay between text and model. According to Greene, the last two forms are closely related, with authors exploiting the sense of historical anachronism—of the irremediable differences between past and present—to define themselves in relation to their models. In its most sophisticated forms,

From Thomas M. Greene, *The Light in Troy: Imitation and Discovery in Renaissance Poetry* (New Haven, Conn.: Yale University Press, 1982).

imitation thus embraces at one and the same time a theory of style, an attitude toward the past, and a sense of self.

. . . Petrarch precipitated his own personal creative crisis because he made a series of simultaneous discoveries that had been made only fragmentarily before him. It was he who first understood how radically classical antiquity differed from the Christian era; he also saw more clearly than his predecessors how the individual traits of a given society at a given moment form a distinctive constellation; he understood more clearly the philological meaning of anachronism. In view of his humanist piety and his literary ambition, these perceptions created a problem that he would bequeath to the generations that followed him: the problem of how to write with integrity under the shadow of a prestigious cultural alternative. To be a humanist after Petrarch was not simply to be an archaeologist but to feel an imitative/emulative pressure from a lost source.

In Italy the word after Petrarch is cast out of the maternal circle of *Latinitas*; it begins to betray its exile, its finitude, its relativity. The sense of privation, which was certainly present in medieval culture, became better informed and less resigned, became an incitement. History betrayed a rupture, whereas medieval historiography tended to stress continuities. . . . "Unlike the Humanists," wrote Franco Simone, "the men of the Middle Ages never lost the sense of continuity which they imagined passing from people to people, according to an idea of which the *translatio studii* is a mythical realization." It is this sense of continuity that accounts for the appeal of medieval anachronism: Apollo as bishop, Mars as knight, "Queen" Belisea (Catiline's wife) attending mass on Easter morning in the church of Fiesole. It is this which also accounts for the medieval attitude toward law as eternally given and untouchable, rather than the product of specific times, places, and men. Thus the sense of etiological itinerary was very weak. History before its ending knew no force of rupture, and this diachronic innocence explains in part the peculiar charm, security, and distinction of medieval literature.

In the literature of the Renaissance, intertextuality has to be analyzed as an interplay between stabilizing etiologies and a destabilizing perception of disjuncture. New etiological myths had to be produced which could contain the facts of loss and of anachronism, myths which could no longer assert the universal unity for which Dante fought and wrote. The Renaissance did produce such a myth or cluster of myths in its pervasive imagery of resurrection and rebirth, imagery still reflected in our period term. This was the etiological construct on the macrocosmic level of an entire civilization both in Italy and France, the means whereby the civilization incorporated the loss of antiquity into a myth that defined its own historical emergence. But this is a myth which can also be applied microcosmically at the level of the individual text, as a basis for interpretation and assessment. The characteristic risk of Renaissance imitation lay in the potential paralysis of its pieties, in a rhetoric so respectful of its subtexts that no vital emergence from the tradition could occur. The diachronic itinerary circles back to its starting point or peters out in a creative desert. But putting aside the reproductive hackwork, we see there is no question that imitative resurrection did act as a powerful creative principle in all realms of Renaissance civilization, so that the revivalist etiology can be invoked now as then without naiveté. . . .

Perhaps it should be stipulated first that each imitative literary work contains by definition what might be called a revivalist initiative, a gesture that signals the intent of reanimating an earlier text or texts situated on the far side of a rupture. For this purpose, maintaining a native contemporary convention does not truly count as imitation (although imitation itself could of course become conventional). The humanist text reaches across a cultural gap and takes the risk of anachronism. The reader then has the right to ask whether this initiative is completed and authenticated, whether the conflict of cultures and the potential conflict of attitude are put to use, whether something occurs within the imitation which truly renews. . . . The reader can ask, *should* ask, not whether anachronism has been suppressed but whether it has been controlled and employed. If it has not and no true renewal is carried out, then the revivalist initiative has to be seen as abortive or failed or in bad faith. But if the revivalist initiative has been made good, if the necromantic metaphor has been validated, then how is this validating process to be described? At this point, it would seem useful to distinguish four types of strategies of humanist imitation, each of which involves a distinct response to anachronism and each an implicit perspective on history. For the sake of economy, I shall illustrate each of them here chiefly from Petrarch's immense canon, Latin and vernacular. . . .

The simplest imitative strategy governs chiefly a few passages in the Latin poems that follow with religious fidelity their classical subtext. The longest of these is the dream of Scipio in books 1 and 2 of the *Africa,* an episode that visibly seeks to reproduce in epic verse a celebrated section of Cicero's *De re publica.* . . . The model or subtext is perceived as a fixed object on the far side of an abyss, beyond alteration and beyond criticism, a sacred original whose greatness can never be adequately reproduced despite the number of respectful reproductions.

Although this sacramental type of imitation corresponded to a new and appealing impulse, it could not in itself produce a large body of successful poetry, nor could it effect a genuine solution to the intertextual dilemma. Clearly it could not function transitively; it could not open a window in the prison house of culture nor could it deal satisfactorily with the newly perceived problem of anachronism. Rather it condemned the reproductive poet to a very elementary form of anachronism, since any reproduction must be made in a vocabulary that is unbecoming the original and whose violations remain out of artistic control. . . .

A second type of imitation appears in any number of Petrarch's Latin and vernacular poems alike, where quite simply allusions, echoes, phrases, and images from a large number of authors jostle each other indifferently. This eclectic mingling of heterogeneous allusions recurs repeatedly in the Italian poems throughout his entire career. The early sonnet that records the first vision of Laura (sonnet 3) brings together elements from the Christian gospels, the *dolce stil nuovo,* and Ovid's *Amores.* The "Triumph of Eternity," which he completed during the last year of his life, brings together allusions or echoes of Cicero, Horace, Saint Matthew, the *Apocalypse,* Saint Augustine, and Dante. Still other elements were conventional topoi that might or might not have recalled a familiar author but that had been reused over and over by many authors. This very simple type of imitation was termed *contaminatio* by Renaissance rhetoricians and it is by no means to be despised. Quite apart from Petrarch's sometimes brilliant manipulations, it would become the compositional principle of such a masterpiece as Poliziano's *Stanze per la Giostra.* We might call this type *eclectic* or *exploitative,* since it essentially treats all traditions as stockpiles to be drawn upon ostensibly at random. History becomes a vast container whose contents can be disarranged endlessly without suffering damage. The art of poetry finds its materials everywhere, materials bearing with them the aura of their original contexts, charged with an evocative power implanted by the poet or the convention from which they are taken. At its slackest, eclectic imitation falls back into mere anachronism and becomes indistinguishable from the ahistorical citations of the Middle Ages. But when it is employed with artistic intelligence, the imitative poet commands a vocabulary of a second and higher power, a second keyboard of richer harmonies, which however are combined with rhetorical skill rather than esemplastic vision. . . .

[I]f the technique of eclectic imitation produced a number of engaging poems, it could not adequately fulfill the transitive responsibilities of poetry as Petrarch himself had formulated them. It could not mediate effectively between a past and a future if the past was fragmented, jumbled, in effect dehistoricized. It could not deal at any profound level with the problem of anachronism; it could simply play with anachronism within a hospitable texture. It could reconcile within its own frame momentary conflicts of heterogeneous motifs; it could tolerate the counterpoint of the voices it brought together; but it could not find out the drama of that counterpoint at a deeper pitch of conflict. When that conflict is sounded, we are already dealing with another type of imitation. To choose a hugely remote example, *Paradise Lost* looks at first glance also to depend on an eclectic strategy of *contaminatio*. But in fact it establishes firmly a strong if sometimes complex relationship with each work and each tradition that it draws upon, according to each its own cultural weight and situation. It underscores rather than obscures the historicity of its sources, and so it permits a flood of imaginative energy to flow through it unimpeded. Conversely Poliziano's *Stanze* achieves a kind of exquisite quintessence of European poetry, but its alchemy leaves no room for mediatory passage and reaches rather an elegant stasis.

Insofar as Petrarch's poetry behaves like Milton's rather than Poliziano's, it can be said to follow a third imitative strategy, which could be termed *heuristic*. Heuristic imitations come to us advertising their derivation from the subtexts they carry with them, but having done that, they proceed to *distance themselves* from the subtexts and force us to recognize the poetic distance traversed. . . . [T]he informed reader notes the allusion but he notes simultaneously the gulf in the language, in sensibility, in cultural context, in world view, and in moral style. Each imitation embodies and dramatizes a passage of history, builds it into the poetic experience as a constitutive element. The imitation is able to act out this passage because the sensibility behind it is aware of itself as a cultural participant, aware of belonging to a cultural situation and helping to shape it. For Petrarch and for Renaissance humanism, a living culture is one which assumes historical responsibilities, one which remembers, preserves, resuscitates, and recreates; conversely a naïve culture betrays its transitive responsibilities if it fails to remember and preserve. It is through a diachronic structure, an acting out of passage, that the humanist poem demonstrates its own conscientious and creative memory.

Out of the indefinite number of texts stretching behind it in endless regression, the humanist poem singles out one text as its putative genesis and it defines itself through its rewriting, its "modernizing," its *aggiornamento* of that text. It sketches an incipient myth of origins but refuses to posit a "great Original" which has to be remembered liturgically, and its refusal takes the form of a simultaneous myth of modernity. The poem becomes a kind of *rite de passage* between a specified past and an emergent present. Thus it contrives to deal with that dilemma which Paul de Man attributes to all literature. "The writer," de Man says, "cannot renounce the claim to being modern but also cannot resign himself to his dependence on predecessors." It is precisely this dilemma which heuristic imitation quite consciously confronts and builds deliberately into the literary work. It points to a dependence which it then overcomes by a declaration of conditional independence. "Modernity," de Man writes, "invests its trust in the power of the present moment as an origin, but discovers that, in severing itself from the past, it has at the same time severed itself from the present." This discovery with its overtones of frustration and entrapment is skirted by the humanist ruse we have been studying, the double ruse of a myth of origin and a myth of modernist growth away from the origin. The term *myth* here does not of course mean necessarily deception, although it certainly means simplification. The passage of history will never be as simple as the *rite de passage* suggests. But by the reductive simplifications of its historical construct, the poem confronts the threat of history and asserts its own limited freedom from it. There is a term for the courage of the ancient or Renaissance artist who followed this strategy, who faced the threat of history and thereby found his artistic poise: the term is *classical*. The humanist poet is not a neurotic son crippled by a Freudian family romance, which is to say he is not in Harold Bloom's terms Romantic. He is rather like the son in a classical comedy who displaces his father at the moment of reconciliation.

Thus the imitative poem sketches, far more explicitly and plainly than most historically conscious texts, its own etiological derivation; it acts out its own coming into being. And since its subtext is by definition drawn from an alien culture, the imitative poem creates a bridge from one *mundus significans* to another. The passage of this rite moves not only from text to text but from an earlier semiotic matrix to a modern one. Thus the poem could be read as an attempt to heal that estrangement which humanism had constantly to face.

Imitation of this type is heuristic because it can come about only through a double process of discovery: on the one hand through a tentative and experimental groping for the subtext in its specificity and otherness, and on the other hand through a groping for the modern poet's own appropriate voice and idiom. It is this quest, superbly achieved, that lies behind Ben Jonson's *Discoveries*, so that the full meaning of that title has to be located in this richly double sense. A discovery in Seneca's Latin only fulfills itself when it issues in Jonson's crisp and civilized English. The modern voice distinguishes itself from the older voice, finds its own public accent, but it does so, can only do so, after sensitively apprehending that other accent in something like its particular timbre and personal force. Finding its own idiom the modern voice discovers that new experience which is the modern poem and measures its modernity through the *ballet of latencies* that poem sets in motion.

In the successful humanist text, heuristic play will tend to render its codes and conventions more flexible. If the constructing of diachronic fictions is to escape the charge of bad faith, of mystification, of a destructive myth of presence, then it has to lead toward more open forms; it has to prove that its myths are liberating. The text calls given codes into question by means of anachronistic juxtaposition and goes on to produce a fresher, more polysemous code. Ben Jonson, inviting a friend to supper, Englishes Martial in order to work over English, to thicken its texture and complicate its resonance. The text cannot simply leave us with two dead dialects. It has to create a miniature anachronistic crisis and then find a creative issue from the crisis. Imitation has to become something more than a pseudoarchaeology contrived as an illegitimate solace. If Renaissance literature is troubled by an anxiety of validation, then it finds its true validation in the discovery of more hospitable codes.

The modern work that results will always lie open to the charge of what in the realm of the visual arts Panofsky called "pseudomorphosis."

When a classical character had emerged from the Middle Ages in utterly non-classical disguise . . . and had been restored to its original appearance by the Renaissance, the final result often showed traces of this process. Some of the medieval garments or attributes would cling to the remodelled form, and thereby carry over a medieval element into the content of the new image.

This resulted in what I would like to call a "pseudomorphosis": Renaissance figures became invested with a meaning which, for all their classicizing appearance, had not been present in their classical prototypes, though it had frequently been foreshadowed in classical literature.

Most humanist poetry, by design or accident, deserves to be regarded in varying degrees as pseudomorphic; indeed, controlled pseudomorphosis tends to enrich a polyvocal *discordia concors*. What remains hard to know and discuss is the humanist poet's grasp of the classical text that initiated the creative process. We cannot expect that his reading approximate that of the text's original audience in order to produce a successful imitation. But we can expect that his response to his subtext recognize an organic complexity. There is no lack of impoverished imitations that act out a historical passage only hazily defined, imitations whose subtext is slackly and vaguely apprehended. One of Petrarch's most wooden sonnets— "Ponmi ove 'l sol . . ." (145)—appears to fail because he mistook the tone of his Horatian model. In this case, as in most of the *Bucolicum carmen*, misprision was fatal. The heuristic circle tended to be productive so long as historical intuition was assisted by an ear for moral style, even though at some point it involved a blind leap.

This blindness has to be faced. Heuristic imitation fails to escape fully a certain incompleteness of exchange. We meet it most visibly in the letters Petrarch addressed to his favorite ancient authors, letters that transcend whatever element of exhibitionism lay behind them and that are drenched in quixotic futility. The deep yearning for a *transaction*, a yearning that was by definition unquenchable, is best symbolized by the letter to Homer purporting to reply to a letter from that poet actually composed by a friend whom Petrarch had put up to it. The ancients whom he loved as friends maintained a marble or a bronze repose that could break hearts. The humanist poet attempted to establish his artistic identity by a process comparable to an infant's first grasp of self-consciousness as it sees itself the object of its mother's gaze. But in this case the attempt fails; the perceived object cannot recognize the subject. The subtext or its author cannot even appear to verify the interpretation that the imitative text presumes. The filial gesture of critical affection never truly reaches its destination. The humanist wanted to endow the ancient author with the "aura" evoked by Walter Benjamin: "The person we look at, or who feels he is being looked at, looks at us in turn. To perceive the aura of an object we look at means to invest it with the ability to look at us in return." This investment for the humanist could never definitively occur. Thus his dialogue with the past always remained finally constructed. The intercourse with the cultural other always came to a point where intuition had to replace historical consciousness. The pathos of this incomplete embrace never altogether faded from the humanist movement.

Heuristic imitation shades off into a fourth and last type, which is not altogether distinct from it but which can be described separately for the purposes of exposition. This type could be said to grow out of heuristic imitation in such a way as to respond to the radical incompleteness just analyzed. It also responds to that resistance or ambivalence toward imitation that was a necessary and congenital feature of humanism. Before any further consideration of imitative strategies, a glance at this resistance is indicated.

It would be surprising if there had been no hostility toward the pressure to imitate. Fortunately for the health of each national culture, there was a good deal. A late, vibrant letter of Petrarch contains a stirring exhortation to literary independence: "It is silly to trust only the ancients. The early discoverers were men too. If we should be discouraged by perceiving too many tracks of our predecessors, we should be ashamed. . . . And we should not be moved by that trite, vulgar saying that there is nothing new, and nothing new can be said." This is not truly inconsistent, but it illustrates the complexities of a mind not easily circumscribed. We shall meet in a later chapter what looks out of context like an even stronger manifesto from Poliziano ("Someone says 'You do not express Cicero.' What then? I am not Cicero. I think I express myself."), a gesture toward independence which, like Petrarch's, has to be studied within the context of an entire career. . . .

The humanism of the Renaissance as it evolved in Italy and spread through Europe assumed innumerable forms, produced manifold *mundi significantes*, gradually became estranged from its own origins. Yet it

remains possible to speak of humanism as a coherent movement because it continued to circle around this space. The whole enterprise
sustained conflicts between intuitions of intimacy and intuitions of
separation, between the belief in transmission and a despair of transmission, between the denial of estrangement and the acceptance of estrangement, between reverence for the *maiores* and rebellion against
them. Microcosmically the humanist text can be read as a reflection,
an instance of these conflicts.

In order to contain them, and in order to protect itself against its
failed quest for an exchange, the diachronic structure of the humanist
text had to be carried farther in a fourth imitative strategy. It had to ex-
pose the vulnerability of the subtext while exposing itself to the subtext's
potential aggression. It had to prove its historical courage and artistic
good faith by leaving room for a two-way current of mutual criticism
between authors and between eras. Thus we might say that Erasmus's
Praise of Folly makes an imitative gesture when it twice sketches its
own alleged literary genealogy, including the *Batrachomyomachia*,
Apuleius, and above all Lucian. The text then goes on to authenticate
that gesture by miming Lucian repeatedly while moving far away from
him. Then, in its concluding hymn to Christian folly, Erasmus introduces values totally incompatible with Lucian and ancient comedy.
The text makes a kind of implicit criticism of its subtexts, its authenticating models, but it also leaves itself open to criticism from the irreverent Lucianic spirit that it had begun by invoking. Thus *The Praise of
Folly* creates a kind of struggle between texts and between eras which
cannot easily be resolved. By exposing itself in this way to the destructive criticism of its acknowledged or alleged predecessors, by entering
into a conflict whose solution is withheld, the humanist text assumes
its full historicity and works to protect itself against its own pathos. In
Heideggerian terms, the text can fulfill itself only as a projection into
the future, an *Entwurf*, by acknowledging its *Geworfenheit*, its finite
and contingent temporality, its existence in a specific cultural situation
with its own particular and cultural vulnerabilities. This fourth type of
imitation might be called *dialectical. . . .*

. . . It is in this dialectical imitative strategy that the tensions or conflicts inherent in humanism rise closest to the surface of the text and
can be studied most usefully. And just as heuristic imitation involves a
passage from one semiotic universe to another, so dialectical imitation,

when it truly engages two eras or two civilizations at a profound level, involves a conflict between two *mundi significantes*. The text comes to terms most effectively with its own humanist problematics, its own incompleteness, by measuring its own signifying habits with those of the subtext. The text is the locus of a struggle between two rhetorical or semiotic systems that are vulnerable to one another and whose conflict cannot easily be resolved. In this dialectic, I think, one reaches the heart of the mystery of acculturation and perhaps its key. Anachronism becomes a dynamic source of artistic power.

One boundary of dialectical imitation is that complex form of assimilation we call parody. It is a moral style which Petrarch himself could not give us. His humanist piety was too devout and his makeup too humorless to permit any open gestures of ironic disrespect. But parody may well issue from creative imitation, and superior parody always engages its subtext in a dialectic of affectionate malice. Parody proper is intensely time-conscious and culture-conscious, and could be absorbed without strain by a poet with humanist training like Ariosto. The parodies of Dante in the *Orlando Furioso* are deliciously contrived without real damage to their subtexts, and the poem that contains them reveals a sensibility truly adult, skeptical, cosmopolitan, and disabused, but not incapable of respect for its predecessors. The same could be said of such different authors as Erasmus, Montaigne, Jonson, and Quevedo. In writers like these, the imitative modes nascent in Petrarch achieve their full development, and the literary text defines itself through its multiform, subtle range of sophisticated allusiveness.

The foregoing analysis of imitative strategies should not lead to the assumption that imitation cannot fail; it *can*, of course, and doubtless in more ways than it succeeds. It can fail if the original imitative gesture is made in bad faith, if the subtext is ornamental rather than constitutive, or if the subtext is misread so ineptly as to kill the possibility of a vital passage. It can fail if either subtext or surface text overwhelms the other by a disproportionate contrast of substance and value. The text can lapse into a misplaced scrupulosity of sacramental piety, or into a fruitless game of eclectic manipulation; or it can simply fail to produce an interesting model of history; it can fail to be heuristic. For each category of misfires examples could be found, but they do not in themselves invalidate their artistic genesis. The making of retrospective constructs represents an issue from the Hobson's choice of naïve synchronism and lonely diachronism, the unwillingness and the willingness to recognize historical solitude. The third choice permits a kind of issue, but it imposes its own responsibilities and introduces its own risks.

The movement from ritualistic repetition to improvisational imitation always involves of course a heightened vulnerability. Indeed, this movement might be seen as an extension of that original hardy secularizing step that is the writing down of records and events. "Documents," writes J. G. A. Pocock, "tend to secularize traditions."

> *They reduce them to a sequence of acts . . . taking place at distinguishable moments, in distinguishable circumstances, exercising and imposing distinguishable kinds and degrees of authority. They reduce time from a simple conceptualization of social continuity to that of an indefinite multiplicity of continuities, which — since in the last analysis they represent different ideas of action, authority and transmission — cannot be altogether consistent with one another.*

It was precisely this concrete specificity of history—"distinguishable moments" and "distinguishable circumstances"—that the new science of philology was designed to study, and it was disturbing to traditionalists like Frater Giovanni Dominici, as later to Savonarola, because it complicated the authority of the sacred text, shook its absolute status by calling attention to the specific circumstances of its production. "The traditionalists," writes Pocock, " . . . will always distrust the classicist, seeing in him the well-meaning author of a potentially radical doctrine." This radicality is present a fortiori in that humanist imitation which asserts a limited but authentic shaping power of the imagination over the passage of history. Beneath the superficial flow of fashion and convention, artistic success and failure, one can make out a certain element of courage in this swing away from ceremonial pattern. To imitate creatively is to assume the historicity of one's own particular place and moment and idiom, and thus to take on a kind of humility. . . .

Anthony Grafton and Lisa Jardine

From Humanism to the Humanities

The selections below are drawn from the first chapter of *From Humanism to the Humanities*, which contrasts the theory and practice of education in the school of Guarino of Verona, the most famous humanist teacher in fifteenth-century Italy. According to Grafton and Jardine, humanists like Guarino made extravagant claims for the moral and political utility of a rhetorical education that trained students to speak and write classical Latin. In theory, rhetorical training prepared students for an active life of civic engagement, and the acquisition of classical Latin style better enabled them to internalize the moral content of ancient writings. But in practice, Grafton and Jardine claim, the drudgery of learning classical Latin by rote precluded the possibility of attaining higher pedagogical ends. Instead, students acquired a cultural veneer in vogue among the elite and a habit of intellectual docility much prized by rulers. This interpretation of humanist education remains controversial, but we should bear in mind that Grafton and Jardine proposed it as a necessary corrective to the heretofore uncritical acceptance of the humanists' own educational propaganda.

Guarino Guarini of Verona (1374–1460) was the greatest teacher in a century of great teachers. He was also a preeminent example of a humanist whose level of cultivation and scholarship was unmatched since antiquity. Like Cicero he went to Greece to be educated—to Constantinople, the capital of the dying Byzantine empire. There he studied for some years with the most learned Greek scholar of the day, Manuel Chrysoloras. On his return to Italy in 1408 he taught first at Florence, then at Venice and Verona, and finally at Ferrara, where he established a school in 1429 at the request of the local ruling family, the Este. At Ferrara he taught the young Prince Leonello, and an ever-growing

From Anthony Grafton and Lisa Jardine, *From Humanism to the Humanities* (Cambridge, Mass.: Harvard University Press, 1986).

number of others, drawn at first from Ferrara, but eventually (as the reputation of his school grew) from a catchment area that ran from England to Hungary. His expanding school became the arts faculty of the new university of Ferrara. And it became the model for dozens of others that sprang up across Italy, whose masters looked back to Guarino as their inspiration—the modern equal of Theophrastus and Isocrates.

Guarino believed in education in its fullest sense—the classical *educatio*. A lengthy and arduous process, it involved the formation of character as well as the training of the mind. He saw as its ideal product not the professional scholar but the active man of affairs, who retains a solid and lasting interest in the literary studies of his youth. And he was at pains to remind any friend or alumnus who had passed through his hands that his literary, political and military triumphs were owed directly to the lessons he had learned in his Ferrara classroom. . . .

It does not follow, however, that we can simply assume that Guarino's classroom did provide the wherewithal for producing fine statesmen. Intellectual historians have long had an emotional vested interest in taking Guarino at his word on this matter. But it is curious nevertheless how readily generations of historians have seized on these prefatory boasts as proof of the success in the worldly arena of humanist teaching in the arts. What is in fact happening is that the *ideology* of Renaissance humanism is being taken over as part of a historical account of humanist achievement. But however persistently such ideal claims are made for a programme of study, its final achievement requires to be assessed independently of them.

One glance at the mass of surviving classroom material from the humanist schools of the fifteenth century must make it obvious that, whatever the principles on which it was based, the literary training it provided was a far cry from this sort of generalised grooming for life. Even a charismatic teacher presenting the information which survives in student notes and teachers' lecture notes would have been hard put to convert the dense accumulation of technical material into quintessential "humanity." Yet if we are to evaluate the impact of the humanist teaching curriculum on fifteenth-century "life and thought," it is to this body of taught humanism that we must turn.

The task before the student of humanism confronting the schoolbooks of the Ferrara classroom is a complex one. He has in front of him two *different* kinds of assessment which must be combined to produce any final judgment of the impact of humanistic studies. On the one hand there is the general claim that the goal of *educatio* is the inspiring and transforming initiation into mysteries which really does make a student a born-again "new man." On the other there is the immense task of the competent transmission of necessary literary skills. For the humanist teacher himself, what creates the bond between the two (practice and ideology) is the example of ancient Rome. There, according to the humanist, "culture" in the broad sense of a preparedness to deal wisely with civilised communal existence went hand in hand with a programme for passing on the skills of eloquence which had come down almost intact to the modern world. Revive the latter, the humanist argument went, and "new men" on the Roman model would inevitably follow. . . .

. . . [E]xtreme caution needs to be exercised when confronting Guarino's extravagant claims for a natural and self-evident relation between an education in the revived humanities and "preparation for life" as a mature citizen of integrity. There is no question of making serious headway in assessing the real achievements of humanistic education without probing the actual possibilities for linking Guarino's classroom teaching with the general claims he made for it as a propaedeutic for civilised living.

The question of what actually went on in Guarino's schoolroom to complement the elaborate claims to be found in his letters and orations can be answered with some precision. Detailed statements of his methods appear both in his own letters and in a general treatise produced by his son. Many of the schoolbooks he compiled and used survive. Taken together, these materials allow us to make detailed comparison between classroom practice and humanist theory concerning the merit and efficacy of an arts education. They reveal his curriculum as comprehensive and exacting. Like the Roman educators whom he took as his model (especially Quintilian) he expected his students to devote many years to the course: Leonello d'Este spent six years under Guarino's tuition, although he had only embarked on his studies at the age of twenty-two. On the whole Guarino preferred to have his students entrusted to him at an earlier age and for an even longer period.

The boys began with an "elementary" course in which they learned to read and pronounce Latin. Guarino had learned from Chrysoloras to take pronunciation seriously, and he insisted that it be studied and practised attentively as an essential aid to cultivated speech, close reading of texts (he instructed his students always to read aloud) and even good digestion. . . .

The second part of his course he called "grammatical," and (following Quintilian) he divided this into two parts. One, "methodical," covered the rules of grammar and syntax. The other, "historical," dealt with history, geography, mythology—all the facts needed to read and write classical Latin in an informed way.

The central text for the "methodical" part of grammar was Guarino's own manual, the *Regulae*. This defines the parts of speech, gives detailed instructions for the inflection of verbs and nouns and formulates the basic rules of Latin syntax. Like its medieval antecedents (on which it draws substantially) it crystallises these pieces of instruction into hundreds of mnemonic verses. . . . These verses were decidedly not merely ornamental; the student was expected to spend years committing them to memory, reciting them, being tested on them. . . . Memorisation, repetition, catechism—these are the activities on which Guarino's humane learning is firmly grounded. Written tests ensured that the student was not mechanically repeating sounds he did not understand, while oral practice gave him a fluency that would not necessarily have come from written drilling alone.

This rigorous grounding in the formal rules was only the first assault. As the pupil advanced he had to learn to write a "pure" Latin—that is, a Latin resembling as closely as possible that of the age of Cicero and Virgil. For this he needed a guide to proper usage, to using only such terms as the Romans had used and only in the senses in which they had used them. Guarino and his pupils compiled a series of such guides. At their most elementary (like the one by Bartolomeo Facio entitled "The Differences between Latin Words") they amounted to little more than a preventive against elementary solecisms: "This is the difference between a *fabula* and a *historia*: we call an invented narrative a *fabula* and a true one a *historia*." Equipped with such simple distinctions the pupil could at least avoid making a fool of himself on the public platform.

Guarino's aim, of course, was for his pupils to achieve more than this elementary level of security. He intended them to be in a position to use Latin discerningly, after the manner of the great ancient authors. Classical Latin vocabulary, like that of any sophisticated literary language, is highly complex. Any word has a broad range of more or less unexpected connotations; for, once a major author has used it in a particularly attractive extended sense, or made it part of an elegant metaphor, others will make a point of imitating him. The great Roman writers—the authors who formed the backbone of the curriculum—

pitched their works at a small and highly literate audience, trained to detect and enjoy such covert allusions. After several hundred years of Latin literature, the language was developed into a tissue of implicit allusion, glancing reference to metaphors and quotation from elsewhere in the canon, and similar plays on words. Renaissance humanists recognised quite early that this was a game the Romans had played—a game fostered by the habit of comparing Latin works with their Greek prototypes. The problem was to find a way of teaching the rules to students who could not immerse themselves in the classics as Petrarch might have done; how, in other words, to codify a practice which really depended on deep acquaintance with the entire canon of classical writing. For the aspiring Latinist whose native language was Italian, and whose knowledge of Latin was restricted (and coloured by church usage—a flexible but entirely non-classical idiom), the structure of the web of classical allusive usage was frustratingly hard to master.

Guarino devised an ingenious combination of pedagogical exercises in an attempt to overcome this problem. He amassed an elaborate corpus of linguistic information essential for an elegant Latin style, and he compressed it into a variety of readily retainable forms—on the one hand mnemonic verses packed with careful discriminations, on the other meticulous lexica dense with apposite quotation and citation.

The *Carmina differentialia* set out long mnemonic lists of homonyms, synonyms and words with other peculiar characteristics. . . . To complement this, Guarino's massive lexicon is a compilation of a much more detailed and sophisticated kind, which not only gives the common sense of Latin words, but explains their varying connotations and illustrates their usage with numerous quotations. . . . Neither of these forms of instruction was original to Guarino. The mnemonic verses had a good medieval precedent, while the large-scale lexicon was substantially a rearrangement of entries from the vast late-antique commentary on Virgil by Servius (fourth century AD). . . . The novelty, however, was the marriage of these two very different sorts of approach in Guarino's programme of instruction. For, to judge from the one surviving commentary on the *Carmina differentialia* (not in fact by Guarino himself, but by a later and lesser schoolmaster, Ludovico da Puppio), the *Carmina* were meant to serve not as a self-sufficient collection of mnemonic tags, but as an armature, to which the teacher could affix as much material as possible from other sources, and especially from such a lexicon as Guarino's own.

Ludovico tells us that his commentary rests on his teaching practice. His method was to explain the distinctions laid down in Guarino's verses, and then to amplify them, qualify them and take off from them into accounts of other related words, or even unrelated words for related things. He also managed to include a good deal of elementary historical and mythological information in his glosses, and once or twice he even enriched his teaching with relatively fresh material from recent works of text scholarship, such as Lorenzo Valla's *Elegantiae*. For the most part, however, his method is Guarino's, and his chief source is once again Servius. On the single line from the *Carmina*—*Hic Cancer cancri crescit aquis caelesteque signum* ("Here the Crab grows in the water and appears as a constellation in the heavens")—Ludovico goes on for more than a page. He lifts a complete list of signs of the Zodiac from Servius, with the months they were held to rule and the spheres of the planets that were assigned to their control. Only then does he pass on to Guarino's original level of simple lexical distinctions, and even so he finds it necessary to amplify and to explicate Guarino's already very simple Latin: "*Cancer cancri* and *cancer canceris* of the third declension and masculine, of a disease feared by all. *Crescit* means 'grows.' *Aquis* means 'in the water.'" One can imagine the cumulative impact of such lessons. The pupils were deluged with words, phrases and facts as they floated out of the teacher's memory, or out of Guarino's word lists. At the same time, the *Carmina* structured the mass of information, making it easy to retain, recall and put readily to use. By reciting (out loud or to himself) a section of the *Carmina*, the student would be induced to recall also much of the illustrative and supplementary matter that his teacher had provided. Such a system achieved what medieval grammar teaching had stopped short of: it turned out students whose grammar and usage were convincingly classical, who could read and write classical Latin with something like the native speaker's facility and sensitivity. The only wonder is that students were prepared to pay the high price in boredom and fatigue that entitled them to access to these mysteries.

Alongside this linguistic drilling, the student was expected to build up a large stock of pertinent factual information. The "historical" part of grammar comprised far more than history alone. It began with the study of the Roman historians, "so that the boys may adorn their speeches with examples relevant to every kind of virtue, to outstanding actions and sayings." But it also included the reading of poets whose graphic descriptions of everyday life were to be admired, and from whom "they will learn the names and locations of rivers, mountains, cities and countries." And it extended to the few Latins who had written on elementary scientific matters, such as astronomy and geography. In other words, this part of the course attempted to use classical literature as the basis for detailed anthropological and geographical knowledge of antiquity, as well as a modicum of science. All this would make it easier for the student to read and write classical Latin like a "native." . . .

In his general remarks on teaching methods Guarino's son Battista insists that this training must be supplemented by the student's independent reading. The student must study on his own the great encyclopaedic works of the empire: the *Attic Nights* of Aulus Gellius, the elder Pliny's *Natural History* and Augustine's *City of God.* Those with the stamina could also tackle Strabo's *Geography,* which Guarino translated and commented upon. These works were meant to fill out the grammatical programme, particularly in subjects like the history of ancient science and philosophy. But Battista entrusted this supporting reading to the energy of the individual student, stopping short of providing aids for the study of these massive and largely disorganised texts.

On a more realistic level, the pupil had to collaborate with his teachers in assembling and collating lexical and factual material as part of the constructive element in his training. Guarino knew that no one could become a real master of classical Latin on the basis of memorised, predigested rules. He instructed even his most exalted students to extend their working knowledge by compiling their own lexica and compendia in the course of their reading. Every pupil was expected to compile his own collection of specimens of interesting usage and edifying anecdotes, and to set them out systematically in indexed notebooks. . . .

The school exercise in which Guarino tested the pupil's "readiness" in the Latin language was the formal Latin essay on a set theme. Here was the opportunity for practical application of everything the student had learnt from his reading and recorded systematically in his notebooks. Like all the other parts of the course the theme was carefully regulated: Guarino provided his students with detailed instructions on both choice of subject matter and treatment. . . . The pupil is not expected to develop original or independent ideas; he is not to express his own emotions, or to treat the topic in a fresh or striking manner. Rather, he is to execute a stylised set-piece in a stylish way. Like the Roman student of formal declamation he must commit to memory a set of rhetorical *loci* (literally "places") where subject-matter may be classified according to the key kinds of topic needed to make a case ("virtue," "usefulness," "pleasure," "goodness" in the case above). These he must draw upon in his theme, not because he has thought the matter through and decided they are appropriate, but because they are proper *loci* for this sort of theme. He is to be a virtuoso at writing by numbers. He should know what *loci* are required for any category of theme, and then fill each of these out with the metaphors and anecdotes and fragments of ancient lore collected in his notebooks. . . .

The student's arduous training in grammar was followed by training in formal rhetoric. In theory this was a rounded education in philosophy as well as in expression: one that embraced Cicero's philosophical dialogues as well as his rhetorical works, and which went on to cover the Greek sources on which Cicero had drawn (the writings of Aristotle and Plato). At this stage the student was to make that life-giving contact with the ancient world, understood in all its historical vitality, that would enable him to be an active citizen in his own time. In short, Guarino's claims for his rhetorical training followed those made by Quintilian: it was to complete a full liberal education in the manner of the training assigned by antiquity to the rhetor.

In practice, as by now we might expect, Guarino's rhetoric course was considerably less ambitious than this. It seems to have centred on the *Rhetorica ad Herennium,* an anonymous work widely believed in the fifteenth century (though not ultimately by Guarino himself) to have been written by Cicero. . . . [E]ven in his advanced teaching, Guarino worked through his text slowly and meticulously, trying to discuss every phrase, almost every word, that presented a problem of interpretation or revealed a novel shade of meaning. . . . [H]is students tried to take down verbatim what he said. They failed. . . .

The notes convey an overwhelming preoccupation with a profusion of tiny details. They also make it clear that the rhetoric course cannot possibly have covered all the works that Guarino wished to include. To cover texts in the gruelling detail shown here, given an hour's lecturing per day per text, can hardly have taken less than an academic year for each book. Accordingly, even a student who spent several years attending Guarino's lectures on rhetoric would probably have studied only the equivalent of a few hundred modern pages of text *in all.* When we try to imagine what it felt like to be trained in rhetoric by Guarino we are faced with this mass of disparate information hung on a frame of one or two key texts. Plato and Aristotle can have been little more than names to most of those who listened to Guarino's dissection of philosophy into three parts.

The truth appears to be that the rhetoric course was simply a more elaborate introduction to the same sorts of material that had occupied the student of grammar: explanation of interesting words and constructions, very brief and sketchy discussions of historical points, bits of general information of the sort that a cultivated person should know and formal analysis of the rhetorical *loci* used by Cicero himself. There is little attention to Cicero's train of thought or line of argument—this is entirely lost in the scramble for detail.

Cicero's text becomes at once a scaffold to be decorated with all manner of general information, and a worked example of the very principles that the *Rhetorica ad Herennium* set out to instill, with a model formal *exordium* (introduction) constructed according to the set theme, and so on. It is as if the teacher had on his desk a beautiful completed jigsaw puzzle—the text. Instead of calling up his students to look at the puzzle, he takes it apart, piece by piece. He holds each piece up, and explains its significance carefully and at length. The students for their part busy themselves writing down each explanation before the piece in question vanishes into the box. And the vital question we have to ask ourselves is whether the accumulation of fragments which the student made his own could ever take shape as the whole from which they originated. . . .

The pupil learnt to read and write a classical Latin. He learnt it with a thoroughness that would be the envy of the modern classics teacher (and probably of the modern teacher of any of the European vernaculars). When he graduated, even the slowest of Guarino's pupils probably possessed the ability to pronounce and write in Latin, on issues ancient and modern, "like a native." That was the real achievement of the relentless, saturating instruction in the finer points of classical Latin grammar, usage, history, culture, geography and rhetoric. The modern teacher is likely to observe wistfully that he would dearly like his own classroom to be frequented by students who were *prepared to endure* such a training in the interests of true Latinity.

The price Guarino paid for his success in training Latinists of this calibre, however, was high in terms of his humanist ideals. The very nature of the meticulous, readily retainable, ready-to-recall instruction he devised precluded any kind of rich overview. To embark on generalised discussion of the intrinsic value of a classical education for character formation, or as a grooming for the public servant, would have been to distract the pupil from the task in hand. It would have required a different kind of attention from the pupil: something more intellectual and less disciplined than the regimented note-taking, rote-learning, repetition and imitation in which he was engaged.

Naturally Guarino did include some moral comment in the course of his lectures; it would have been hard to avoid doing so when his subject text was the *De senectute* or Persius' *Satires*. But these observations inevitably became absorbed into the pedagogical routine — something to be recorded between etymologies and paraphrases, rather than a coherent contribution to a fully articulated moral philosophy. . . .

At the same time "prospective employers," as we might term them, the patrons of Guarino's school, and the parents who sent their offspring in droves to sit at Guarino's feet, did apparently feel that he was providing a worthwhile and relevant training for future leaders and civic dignitaries. So, having pinpointed the discrepancy between the claims of humanists as educators to uphold the *dignitas hominis,* and the narrow cumbersomeness of classroom instruction, let us turn our attention to the *incidental* advantages of humanist pedagogy as actually practised.

In the first place, of course, humanist education was modish; it was in vogue with the élite. One ought not to underestimate the self-reinforcing quality of such preconceptions in the field of education. . . . [I]f an ability to quote Cicero is currently believed to be a mark of a much wider competence, then the ability to quote Cicero will go a long way towards satisfying an employer, even if this is the only skill the person has been taught.

But, beyond this, the actual classroom drill to which Guarino's pupils were subjected left its mark on them in ways that had a distinct and recognised value in Renaissance society. In the first place, the skills Guarino inculcated had an established practical value in fifteenth-century Italy. The ability to speak *extempore* on any subject in classical Latin, the ability to compose formal letters to order in the classical idiom, the ability to teach exactly as they had been taught, were all valuable assets. Equipped with them the student could serve as an ambassador, or secretary to a government department, or could become an advocate, a priest, or a professor of the *studia humanitatis* in his turn. In other words, although the programme was strictly literary and non-vocational, it nevertheless opened the way to a number of careers. . . .

Secondly, Guarino's schooling fostered the sort of personality traits that any Renaissance ruler found attractive: above all, obedience and docility. Much of the time in Guarino's classroom was spent (as we have seen) passively absorbing information, accumulating and classifying predigested and processed material. Active participation, like the formal disputation (or obligation debate) which had figured prominently in medieval training, played a comparatively small part in the programme; hence the insignificant place of dialectic or "active thinking" in the course. The consequences of this were much as they had been in late antiquity, or as they would be in the seventeenth and eighteenth centuries: students became accustomed to taking their orders and direction from an authority whose guiding principles were never revealed, much less questioned. Passivity had been a feature of monastic education, but then it had been future clerics who had been prepared for a life of obedience; in Guarino's school the pupils were laymen, often of high birth and destined for high office. Fluent and docile young noblemen were a commodity of which the oligarchs and tyrants of late fifteenth-century Italy could not fail to approve. . . .

Seen from this point of view, the general approval expressed for Guarino's kind of humanist instruction by the Italian establishment has more to do with its appropriateness as a commodity than with its intrinsic intellectual merits. As long as humanist schools turned out such suitable potential servants of the state, they were prepared to endorse the enthusiastic claims of humanist idealists for their literary studies as "a storehouse of recorded values," from which the individual acquired "a general fitness for a humane existence."

No doubt there will be some readers whose response to all this will be to exclaim: "Well, but what did you expect? It is inevitable that the elevated claims of all promoters of new educational programmes become more pedestrian when translated into classroom practice." And we would be bound to agree. But the reader must remember that this is *not* what the student of humanism is led to believe if he relies upon the most influential accounts of the impact of humanist pedagogy. There he finds passages like the following, manifestly conflating professional ideals with actual results:

> *Such was humanistic education: not as one has sometimes been led to believe, grammatical and rhetorical study as an end in itself, so much as the formation of a truly human consciousness, open in every direction, through historico-critical understanding of the cultural tradition. Litterae*

*(literature) are effectively the means of expanding our personality be-
yond the confines of the present instance, relating it to the paradigmatic
experience of man's history. . . . What matters is a moral preparation
based not on precepts, but on the effective mastery of a critical understanding of the human condition itself. What matters is to engage in dialogue with those who express archetypal humanity—that is, with the
true masters. Because in order to understand them, and in understanding them, that which is most elevated in us emerges.*

What we must now recognise is the inevitable *gap* between the beliefs
which such passages articulate about the saving, civilising qualities of
an arts education and the practical consequences for generations of students of pursuing the detailed curriculum to which the general pronouncements were affixed. . . .

We believe that the fact that individual gifted humanists succeeded
in making that mysterious transition from classroom aptitude to rich
familiarity with antique culture should serve to remind us of the mag-
nitude of their intellectual achievement. We have shown that while the
ruthless drilling of Guarino's classroom provided the foundation for
their prowess, it was by no means a *sufficient* condition for their success.
Guarino's pupils did include critical philologists like Fazio and Decem-
brio, and practising poets like Janus Pannonius, whose achievements
were naturally adduced by propagandists to support their contention that
a humanistic arts education was the ideal grooming for Renaissance civic
life. In our view these scattered achievements, diverse in kind and quality, are in fact evidence of the *problematic* nature of any attempt to show
a regular and causal link between routine competence and creative
achievement, let alone civic qualities of leadership and integrity.

In private letters to his alumni Guarino appears to endorse this
view. He urges his pupils to persevere with the studies to which he has
introduced them, to carry on reading and writing in expectation of the
enlightenment which he hopes will one day come to them. "Don't be
afraid, if at first you don't understand," he exhorts them. "Knock again,
and it will open for you." Even he could not claim to be sure quite how
or when in this process his students would be metamorphosed into his
erudite equals, and he was certainly aware that his instruction alone was
not sufficient to produce "new men"—even if he could only afford to
admit as much to those initiates who had progressed far enough in their
studies to deserve his confidence.

Paul F. Grendler

Schooling in Renaissance Italy

Grendler surveys the whole of Italian Renaissance education in one comprehensive volume. His subjects include not only the humanist (Latin) curriculum favored by the elite but also the vernacular curriculum favored by the merchant class, which was more concerned with the acquisition of practical business skills. He also shows how both curricula were shaped toward religious ends during the Catholic Reformation of the sixteenth century.

The selections below are drawn from the concluding chapter of his book, where Grendler briefly summarizes his findings. In particular, he tries to attain a more balanced view of the humanist curriculum than Grafton and Jardine, in part by comparing it with the vernacular curriculum and in part by weighing the inevitable drudgery of learning classical Latin against what he sees as the genuine moral content of humanist education.

Parents and communal councils organized the schools of the Italian Renaissance. After the collapse of church schools, parents in the fourteenth century provided for society's needs by paying numerous laymen and clerics to teach their sons as independent masters, either in small neighborhood schools of ten to thirty pupils or as household tutors. Communal councils, especially in smaller urban centers, also contracted with a master to teach a limited number of boys. A small number of towns supported communal masters through the university; that is, some teachers listed on university rolls taught children in different parts of the city. The structure of Italian schooling was set in the fourteenth century. It did not change for three centuries.

A close look at Venice in 1587 indicates the distribution of schools and pupils in a major city. Venice had a large number of independent

From Paul F. Grendler, *Schooling in Renaissance Italy: Literacy and Learning, 1300–1500* (Baltimore: Johns Hopkins University Press, 1989).

schools, a small number of communal Latin schools, and a few church schools to train future clerics. About 89 percent of the students attended independent schools, about 4 percent studied in communal Latin schools, and 7 percent church schools. About 47 percent of the students followed the Latin syllabus and 53 percent the vernacular curriculum. All but a handful of the pupils attending formal schools were boys, but some other boys and girls received a limited amount of informal schooling. Overall, probably 33 percent of the boys of school age and about 12 percent of the girls of school age acquired at least rudimentary literacy. Perhaps 23 percent of the inhabitants of Venice in 1587 were literate, a figure that may have been typical of an Italian Renaissance city.

The schools of Florence and Rome exhibited the same pattern as those in Venice, with minor variations. . . .

Although Renaissance schools were intended for upper- and middle-class boys and were staffed by men, female teachers and pupils played a small role. Female teachers appeared in limited numbers but in many places from the fourteenth century onward. They usually taught vernacular reading and writing to girls. Theorists recognized and approved of education for girls in order to make them more attractive and useful wives and mothers. But educational opportunity for girls depended heavily on class: the higher a girl's social position the greater the possibility that she would attend school. Girls usually studied with household tutors or as long-term boarders in convents. They also learned rudimentary vernacular literacy from catechism schools and from relatives. Although subject to some of the same disabilities as girls, working-class boys enjoyed greater opportunity to learn.

The humanists of the fifteenth century changed the Latin curriculum, a major academic revolution. They discarded the late medieval Latin curriculum of verse grammars and glossaries, morality poems, a handful of ancient poetical texts, and *ars dictaminis*. In its place they substituted grammar, rhetoric, poetry, and history based on Latin classical authors and texts just discovered or newly appreciated. Above all, they inserted the letters of Cicero as the Latin prose model. The early humanistic pedagogues Gasparino Barzizza, Guarino Guarini, and Vittorino da Feltre implemented the new curriculum among the sons of the powerful in northern Italy. Communal councils and parents responded by hiring schoolmasters trained in the new Latin humanistic curriculum. By about 1450 schools in a majority of northern and north-central Italian towns taught the *studia humanitatis*.

. . . All children, whether in Latin or vernacular schools, began by learning the alphabet, syllables, and words from a hornbook or primer consisting of a few Latin prayers. Children continued to use such hornbooks and primers through the nineteenth century. Learning to read at this level followed a pedagogy originating in ancient Greece and Rome. Teaching consisted of breaking the language down into its smallest parts (letters) and then reassembling it (syllable, word, phrase, and sentence) in an almost mechanical way.

Led by Valla, the humanistic pedagogues proclaimed their allegiance to grammar based on ancient usage. They dropped the medieval verse grammars in favor of new grammars, such as Guarino's *Regulae grammaticales*, and the ancient *Ars minor* of Donatus. But "*Donatus*" turned out to be a late medieval Italian composition that circulated under Donatus's name. Similarly, Guarino and other Renaissance grammarians retained a certain amount of medieval grammatical principles in their manuals and teaching. In time a Renaissance grammatical tradition combining old and new emerged. Classroom instruction consisted of patient memorization of discrete bits of grammar plus agreement exercises. Elementary Latin reading began with the *Disticha Catonis;* sixteenth-century teachers added Vives' *Colloquia.* Overall, grammar had a lower position in the *studia humanitatis* than in the medieval liberal arts because the Renaissance saw grammar as a preparatory study.

Renaissance Latin schools focused on secondary rhetoric (letter writing) rather than primary rhetoric (oratory). All teachers agreed that a good Latin style depended on imitating classical authors. But should students learn an eclectic style based on several authors or a unified style following a single model? Italians overwhelmingly chose to imitate a single prose model, Cicero, especially his *Epistulae ad familiares.* They admired his periodicity, use of dramatic contrast, and the content, which showed a Roman patrician conducting the affairs of state, family, friends, and self. Like medieval teachers of *dictamen,* the humanists taught rhetoric through imitation. But they loosened the structure and put a higher value on concreteness and human expression. Teachers also expected students to learn from the content: *verba* (words) led to *res* (knowledge of life). Hence, they required students to copy and memorize *sententiae* from Cicero's works.

The humanists gave poetry an independent position in the *studia humanitatis* which the medieval liberal arts had denied it. Humanists saw poetry as a model of good style and eloquent description; they defended ancient poets from the charge of corrupting youth. Teachers used the paraphrase-commentary, a comprehensive analysis ranging from synonyms to extended rhetorical explanation, to teach Vergil above all, but also Terence, Horace, and Ovid. History was a new subject not found in the medieval curriculum. Since no commentary tradition existed for ancient historians, the humanists created their own which emphasized geographical and historical information. They preferred Caesar, Sallust, and Valerius Maximus. Schools did not teach moral philosophy as a separate subject, but extracted moral lessons from most curriculum texts. Finally, Renaissance schools in Italy taught a limited amount of Greek and logic, the latter by means of both medieval and Renaissance texts. . . .

Renaissance Latin schooling has come under attack recently. One eminent scholar judges it to have been mentally rigid, full of tedium, and stifling to the imagination. It intended to "exalt authority, sanction imitation, and promote compliance." A very recent book levels the broader charge that Renaissance humanistic training failed to inculcate moral values and eloquence, and degenerated into grammatical drill lacking originality. It taught future civil servants to write "a stylized set-piece in a stylized way." Instead of producing the free, honorable, and eloquent citizen, Latin humanistic schools produced docile, obedient, upper-class servants of the state. The charges can be summarized under three headings: a concentration on tedium, the stifling of originality, and a failure to implant values.

The Latin humanistic curriculum lasted so far beyond the Renaissance that a twentieth-century perspective may underlie some of the criticism. But a curriculum and educational structure need satisfy only its own era. Viewing Renaissance schooling within the context of the Italian fourteenth, fifteenth, and sixteenth centuries makes it difficult to agree with the criticism.

Certainly Italian Renaissance Latin education required an enormous amount of grammatical drill and exercises. But whether students and teachers found it very tedious and oppressive is another matter. Learning to write and speak fluently a non-native language, especially one as complex as classical Latin, requires an enormous amount of drill and practice. Renaissance schoolboys put forth this effort because society valued these skills highly and rewarded those who mastered them.

And many Renaissance men loved Latin and the civilization that its mastery unlocked.

High motivation mitigates what outsiders see as drudgery. This point can be better understood through a modern analogy. Today learning Latin rouses few. But mastering a musical instrument or developing an athletic skill sufficiently well to perform at a high level of proficiency excites many. Both skills require an enormous amount of drill and practice that nonparticipants may judge tedious. But youthful musicians and athletes rarely complain. Most are so fascinated by the skill itself that they eagerly practice hours a day for years, just as Renaissance students studied Latin. Of course, learning musical or athletic skills today is a voluntary activity, whereas learning Latin was obligatory in the Renaissance. But the main point remains: much depends on the involvement and motivation of the learner, which outsiders may not comprehend. Proficiency in classical Latin during the Renaissance had much the same high visibility as proficiency in music and sports today, and earned many of the same rewards.

The charge that a humanistic education stifled originality is difficult to sustain. By any standard of judgment the Italian Renaissance was a period of great originality and genius. A Latin education did not throttle the creativity of a Pico, Machiavelli, or Galileo, but provided linguistic skills to serve it. What of the rest of Italian schoolboys, who may have had their potential originality stifled by immersion in Vergil, Cicero, and the rest? They met the standards of creativity decreed by their times. The Renaissance wanted them to exhibit their limited originality within the boundaries of classical expression, philosophy, science, and so on. The vast majority did so reasonably well.

The third objection is that Italian Renaissance Latin education failed to inculcate the values of the citizen-orator, partly because of a preoccupation with the minutiae of learning Vergil, Cicero, and others. Obviously, schools devoted a great deal of effort to the minutiae, particularly at the primary and secondary levels. But there seems no reason to doubt that teachers and theorists who asked students to compile notebooks of moral and civic *sententiae* tried to teach these values. And the reading, from the *Disticha Catonis* to Cicero's letters, was full of moral and social commonplaces. Vernacular school students read Guevara's *Vita di Marco Aurelio*, which offered more of the same. Renaissance education definitely included a great deal of moral and civic exhortation.

A S
LIBRARY
I B S

The second half of the sixteenth century added catechetical instruction. Did all this moralizing have any effect? In particular, did the schools produce men embodying the ideal of the citizen-orator, or servile courtiers who only mouthed the ideal?

The fact that Italian intellectuals and others clung to and repeated the values of the citizen-orator in the midst of the disasters of the Cinquecento argues that they took these commonplaces seriously, and that the values taught in humanistic schools had some impact. The historical circumstances had degenerated, to say the least. Several Italian states had lost their political independence to ultramontane "barbarians." Italian merchants no longer dominated European commerce. And the Italy of republican city-states was turning into an Old Regime society of *bravi*. That Italian intellectuals continued to voice the values of Ciceronian *humanitas* in the face of these circumstances testifies to their commitment.

But what of the intellectuals who lavished praise on the undeserving and thereby seemed to indicate that the values learned in school were only words? The answer is that Renaissance humanism had always had the capacity to adapt to different political ambiances without betraying its nucleus. Recent studies of Roman, Venetian, and Neapolitan humanism demonstrate this, and offer a more complete portrait of the humanistic movement than the earlier studies on Florence. Renaissance humanism remained faithful to its core, which was a combination of classically derived moral values and a critical approach to scholarship and life, in quite diverse political and social circumstances. Indeed, the humanistic rhetoric of praise for human and civic values showered on a blackguard of a prince or a rapacious city council was not completely hypocritical or worthless. Epideictic oratory sought to promote at least a generalized ideal of the upright society even when it could not be realized. Orators in all centuries do the same; they remind their listeners of values to be upheld.

Education always reflects the society it serves. Italian Renaissance schooling suggests several characteristics of the age.

Some common traits appeared across the educational spectrum. Despite different subject matter and a large social gap, Latin and vernacular schools shared a pedagogical approach. The subject matter, whether beginning reading, Latin grammar, advanced rhetoric, or abbaco, had to be divided into very small individual bits of knowledge.

Teachers and textbooks taught by breaking a skill down into its smallest components, drilling them intensively, and then assembling the bits to make the whole. It was pedagogy based on the belief that if the student learned the pieces thoroughly, he would grasp the whole. Teacher and pupil had to comprehend perfectly every step of the process; intuitive leaps of learning were distrusted. This same habit of mind can be found elsewhere in the Italian Renaissance, especially in legislation and procedural guides.

Renaissance schools sought to teach practical skills for different social roles. Latin schools taught the Latin that enabled students to go on to university studies and prepared them for careers in the civil service, the church, or the highest ranks of society, where a knowledge of Latin was expected. Vernacular schools taught the essential commercial skills of reading, writing, abbaco, and bookkeeping. The two streams prepared boys for different roles in a fairly rigid social order. Society's leaders learned Latin, those who would work at commerce or the trades learned vernacular skills. The two streams obviously reinforced existing social divisions. But they also facilitated a little upward mobility. Boys of modest circumstances fortunate enough to join the Latin stream almost automatically climbed a few rungs up the social ladder.

Both Latin and vernacular schools attempted to instill personal and social values based on classical and Christian sources and standards. They attempted to teach pupils how to behave honorably without losing any appreciable social or other benefit. One should do one's duty to family, *patria*, and God, without losing legitimate opportunity for personal advantage. If a choice had to be made, the texts exhorted the pupil to choose honor over gain. These values are found in both the Latin and vernacular texts, in Vergil's poetry and the *Fior di virtù*. Renaissance men mostly ignored contradictions between pagan classical and Christian moral and social values.

Renaissance education was secular. It inculcated civic morality for the ruling class and the professionals who served them. Humanistic and vernacular schools taught morality through classical examples. They did not stress Christian religious doctrine and practices until the advent of the Catholic Reformation. The church played no institutional role in Renaissance education until the late Renaissance. Indeed, most clergymen seem to have received the same education as laymen. This may help explain the nature of ecclesiastical life in the Renaissance, and why churchmen often behaved like laymen.

One cannot overestimate the importance of education in the Renaissance. The extraordinary political, social, economic, and even linguistic diversity—divisiveness would be the better term—threatened to pull the peninsula apart at any moment. But schooling united Italians and played a major role in creating the Renaissance. Humanistic pedagogues developed a new educational path very different from education in the rest of Europe in the early fifteenth century. Thereafter, Italy's elite of rulers, professionals, and humanists shared the language of classical Latin. They shared a common rhetoric. And they drew from the same storehouse of moral attitudes and life examples learned in school.

The humanistic curriculum unified the Renaissance, making it a cohesive cultural and historical epoch of great achievement. When humanistic education crossed the Alps, it created a similar cultural accord that endured beyond the shattering of religious unity. Jacob Burckhardt argued that individualism was the unifying force, the essence, of the Italian Renaissance and the modern world. He would have been better advised to look into the schoolroom for the spirit of the age.

Behind Renaissance education lay the optimistic presupposition that the world was susceptible to understanding and control. Through education the mind can be trained to understand, the will can be persuaded to choose good. With a few notable exceptions, Renaissance men believed that through learning people could improve themselves and their world. It may have been a utopian belief, but all education is based on belief in a civilized, rational universe.

Humanism and History

We have already seen in Part IV how the ideal of *imitatio* reflects a heightened awareness of the differences between past and present, between antiquity and modernity. This sense of anachronism is arguably the chief heritage of the humanist movement, for it points the way toward our modern historical view of the world and toward the modern practice of historical scholarship, both of which owe much to humanist philology. The philological impulse to resurrect classical texts in their linguistic purity was inherent in the ideal of *imitatio* from its very inception. And as the humanist movement spread, knowledge of the classical world deepened, revealing the unique historical circumstances surrounding the composition of ancient texts. Ironically, by the late sixteenth century, this development undermined the universality of classical models, for the sense of historical and cultural relativism born of humanist philology called into question both the possibility and the desirability of resurrecting classical culture.

The seminal article of Theodor E. Mommsen (1905–1958), "Petrarch's Conception of the 'Dark Ages'" (1942), remains a starting point for the study of the Renaissance attitude toward the past. Born into a renowned family of scholars (his grandfather of the same name was the greatest classical historian of the nineteenth century, and his uncle was the famous sociologist Max Weber), Mommsen left Germany for the United States when Hitler came to power. He taught at Johns Hopkins, Yale, and Princeton before finally accepting a position in medieval history at Cornell University. In his article, Mommsen argues that Petrarch originated the modern tripartite division of history into ancient, medieval, and modern periods. Although Petrarch himself distinguished only between antiquity and modernity (which he reviled as a degenerate age), he was spearheading a movement designed to revive classical culture. Implicit in this movement, according to Mommsen, was the notion of a modern cultural revival separated from the glories of antiquity by an intervening "dark age" that had lost the light of classical eloquence.

Myron P. Gilmore (1910–1978) taught for many years at Harvard University, with Hanna Gray and William Bouwsma numbering among his many students. He first published his classic essay, "The Renaissance Conception of the Lessons of History," in 1959 and later revised it for republication in 1963. In this piece Gilmore goes beyond Mommsen's observations about historical periodization to show how Petrarch first articulated an idea of anachronism by which the past had to be understood in its own terms. Further, he shows how the ensuing sense of historical and cultural relativism corroded the traditional conception of history as the *magistra vitae,* the teacher of life. According to this view, history was philosophy teaching by examples, providing vivid instances of moral and political instruction that struck home more effectively than general precepts. But the encroaching sense of relativism called the applicability of these lessons into question. In elaborating this point, Gilmore was one of the first American scholars to make reference to the philological study of Roman law in sixteenth-century France and the relativism it inspired.

Gilmore's insights into the effects of sixteenth-century French legal humanism represent the leading edge of a scholarly wave that crested in the next decade. During this period, several historians and political philosophers published important studies on the historiographical and philosophical impact of French legal humanism, which became generally known as the "French historical school" of law. The scholar most responsible for coining this phrase is Donald R. Kelley, professor of history at Rutgers University. His article "Guillaume Budé and the First Historical School of Law" (1967) describes the process by which law came to be viewed historically. Kelley traces this process back to Lorenzo Valla and the flowering of humanist philology in fifteenth-century Italy. According to Kelley, Valla established philology as a science based upon a historical methodology, and he thus stood in the vanguard of a revolution in historical thinking. Guillaume Budé subsequently applied Valla's methodology to the study of the text of Roman law, Justinian's *Corpus juris civilis,* showing that it constituted not universal law but the law of a past society. The legal relativism of Budé and his followers signals for Kelley the emergence of modern historicism, an attitude toward the past previously thought to have originated in late eighteenth- and early nineteenth-century Germany. Kelley thus pushes beyond Gilmore's observations to show that the breakdown of the conception of history as the *magistra vitae* gave rise in the sixteenth century to our modern historical view of the world.

The notion of the Renaissance origins of historicism remained unchallenged until Zachary S. Schiffman published his article "Renaissance Historicism Reconsidered" in 1984. This work reviews the scholarship of Kelley and others with the intent of showing that the humanist perception of relativism did not entail a historicist viewpoint. According to Schiffman, historicism attributes the uniqueness of historical entities to their development in time, whereas the humanist perception of uniqueness remained unaccompanied by an idea of historical development. Without such an idea, legal humanism engendered not modern historicism but what Schiffman calls "an individualizing view of the world" that treats each unique entity in isolation from the next.

The topic of humanism and history brings us full circle, back to Jacob Burckhardt, but with a twist. Recall yet one more time Burckhardt's fundamental insight into the development of the individual, which constitutes for him the defining characteristic of the Renaissance. We have already noted that Burckhardt's formulation embraces not only individual personalities but all kinds of historical entities, which came to be perceived in their uniqueness. Gilmore's idea of anachronism, Kelley's Renaissance historicism, Schiffman's individualizing view, not to mention Panofsky's reintegration of form and content in art—all these represent variations on the theme first introduced by Burckhardt. Yet for Burckhardt, the development of the individual remained distinct from the classical revival, which he regarded as an effect rather than a cause of the Renaissance. Not-withstanding the pervasiveness of classical culture, he insisted that the Renaissance could have occurred without the humanist revival of antiquity. As we can now see, however, twentieth-century schol-arship has progressively revealed a concept of individuality lying at the heart of the classical revival. Indeed, this concept is inherent in the very ideal of *imitatio* central to Renaissance rhetoric and the *studia humanitatis*. The humanist discovery of individuality—so dramatically evident in Petrarch's desire to leap across the Middle Ages and connect directly with antiquity—thus marks a starting point for the culture of the Renaissance. And the sixteenth-century sense of historical and cultural relativism, which led to the notion that antiquity was irretrievably dead and buried, marks an end point, beyond which Renaissance shades off into modernity.

Theodor E. Mommsen

Petrarch's Conception of the "Dark Ages"

Mommsen's famous essay begins by tracing the phrase "dark ages" back to Petrarch. He then isolates the period in Petrarch's career when this con-ception developed. Our selections are drawn from the concluding portion of the essay, where Mommsen discusses the implications of this concep-tion for Petrarch's idea of history.

Although Mommsen credibly traces the modern tripartite division of history into the ancient, medieval, and modern periods back to Petrarch and his followers, we should remember that the "middle age" was just that—a period between antiquity and modernity. In this sense, it had no legitimacy of its own for the humanists. It was simply an impediment to the revival of ancient culture, a gap to be bridged. Thus, even though Petrarch

From T. E. Mommsen, "Petrarch's Conception of the 'Dark Ages'," *Speculum* 17 (1942): 226–242.

directly inspired modern historical periodization, he did not share our modern conception of history, where antiquity gives way to the Middle Ages by a process of evolution, and where the medieval world in turn shapes the emerging modern one.

. . . Petrarch's conception of history, I think, cannot be better expressed than by the words which he wrote in the *Apologia contra cuiusdam anonymi Galli calumnias:* "What else, then, is all history, if not the praise of Rome?" This peculiar notion of history, very impressive in its Latin succinctness, was formulated by Petrarch only at the end of his life. But evidently he conceived of it much earlier, in the beginning of the 1340s, when he started work on the second version of *De viris illustribus.* When in his historical work Petrarch emphasized everything that was Roman and excluded everything that was outside Rome, he was entirely in accord with all his other writings; both in his letters and in his poetical works he confined himself to the same topic as in *De viris illustribus.*

This consistent restriction to subjects taken from Roman history makes it clear that Petrarch did not narrow down the scope of his historical studies for mere external reasons, but that he rather limited himself on principle. This limitation was based on a very definite judgement of value: the praise of Rome corresponded to the condemnation of the "barbarous" countries and peoples outside Rome. This point of view Petrarch expressed when in 1341 he drew a line of demarcation between "ancient" and "modern" history, and when later on he called the period stretching from the fall of the Roman Empire down to his own age a time of "darkness." In Petrarch's opinion that era was "dark" because it was worthless, not because it was little known. The sooner the period dropped from man's memory, the better. Therefore Petrarch, personally at least, was resolved to bury it in oblivion.

This notion, however, has an importance beyond its relation to the life and works of Petrarch. It offers not only a key to the understanding of Petrarch's personal standards of value, but it deserves attention as well in connection with the problem with which our discussion started, the problem of the humanist periodization of history.

As we have seen, Petrarch divided the course of history into two sharply separated periods and set as a dividing point between them either the time when Christianity became the state religion in the Roman Empire or the time when the Roman Empire began to "decline" under the rule of "barbarian," that is, non-Roman emperors. Medieval historiography was based on essentially different principles. Whereas after the modification of his original plan Petrarch concerned himself exclusively with the first period and concentrated upon the secular history of Rome "from Romulus to Titus," the mediaeval historians almost without exception wrote universal history, that is, in the words of Benedetto Croce, "a history of the universal, of the universal by excellence, which is history in labor with God and toward God." Even the most meager monastic chroniclers and annalists dealt usually with their particular monasteries within the framework of a history of the world from its creation to the present. In doing so they followed very definite schemes according to which universal history was divided up into the succession either of the four world-monarchies or of the six ages. . . . In these two schemes the beginnings of the last period coincided, since in the one it began with the foundation of the Roman Empire by Caesar or Augustus, in the other with the birth of Christ. "And thus," as Comparetti says, "history was divided into two distinct periods—a long period of error and darkness, and then a period of purification and truth, while midway between the two stood the Cross of Calvary."

Against this background we may now place Petrarch's division of history: he certainly drew an entirely different line of demarcation. Since he concerned himself exclusively with one particular state, Rome, he was not interested in the four world-monarchies. He started out from the very beginnings of Rome and showed her growth under the leadership of the great men of the republican period, whereas the mediaeval historians paid very little attention to the epoch preceding the foundation of the Empire. "The lamentable story of how things retrograded," Petrarch did not want to recount, and therefore he stopped precisely at the point where in his opinion the "decline" of the Empire began. The mediaeval historians, on the other hand, continued the history of the Empire straight through to their own time: in their opinion the *Imperium Romanum* still existed although the rule over it had been "transferred" from the Romans to other peoples.

By setting up the "decline of the Empire" as a dividing point and by passing over the traditional marks either of the foundation of the Empire or of the birth of Christ, Petrarch introduced a new chronological demarcation in history. This scheme has been distinguished from the older mediaeval or "Hellenistic" ones by the name "humanistic," for it formed the underlying principle of most of the historical works written

by Italian humanists. Its most manifest expression is found in the title of
Flavio Biondo's work *Decades historiarum ab inclinatione imperii*, a history of the period stretching from 410 to 1440. The origin of this new
chronological demarcation, therefore, has usually been dated hitherto
from the middle of the fifteenth century. But, since Petrarch consciously
confined his historical studies to the period *"usque ad declinationem
imperii,"* if we may say so, we are justified in stating that thereby he implicitly anticipated ideas of the fifteen-century Italian humanists.

This statement with regard to Petrarch's demarcation of "Antiquity"
raises another question. The humanists were to replace the older patterns with a division of history into three periods which, under the names
of "ancient," "mediaeval," and "modern" times, live to the present day. Is
it possible to connect Petrarch also with the origin of this division? I
think that the question can be answered in the affirmative. To be sure,
this threefold division we shall nowhere find expressed directly by
Petrarch. As we have seen, he speaks only of "ancient" and "modern" history. The use of the word "modern" in this connection cannot be interpreted otherwise than that Petrarch thought of his own time as still a part
of the period which had begun with the "decline" of the Empire. His
was an age of decadence: this idea Petrarch has expressed time and again
in his letters. The feeling of profound pessimism finds perhaps its most
impressive wording in an early letter where Petrarch says: "As conditions
are, I foresee worse things from day to day; but, although I can fear worse
things, I can scarcely imagine them." But like so many men of all ages,
Petrarch was a pessimist because he was an idealist at heart. In measuring the actual conditions of his time with the standards of his lofty ideals
he could not escape despair, a despair, however, which did not always
mean hopelessness. His "Golden Age," it is true, lay in the past but, on
occasion at least, he was able to visualize the possibility of its return in
the future. Thus, in a letter to Pope Urban V, he expresses his belief that
Christ desires the re-establishment of the papal court in Rome *"pro aurei
saeculi principio."* In similar, though less religious language Petrarch
phrases his passionate appeals to the Roman Tribune of the People, Cola
di Rienzo, and to the German Emperor Charles IV, urging them to take
over the legacy of Antiquity and to follow the models of the great men of
ancient Rome: by so doing they were to revive the grandeur of times past.
It was this same conviction which impelled Petrarch to pursue historical
studies. Since he believed that "Rome would rise up again if she but
began to know herself," he strove throughout his life and his work to

make his contemporaries conscious of the great traditions of the eternal city. In spite of his often expressed pessimism Petrarch evidently was convinced that there existed the chance of a spiritual rebirth which would put an end to the process of decline, and bring about the beginning of a "new time." This ardent hope of his for the future Petrarch voices nowhere more impressively than in the work which he himself considered as his greatest: at the very end of the *Africa* he addresses his own poem as follows: "My fate is to live amid varied and confusing storms. But for you perhaps, if as I hope and wish you will live long after me, there will follow a better age. This sleep of forgetfulness will not last for ever. When the darkness has been dispersed, our descendants can come again in the former pure radiance."

These verses of the *Africa* show clearly Petrarch's views on the periodization of history. He holds that there was an era of "pure radiance" in the past, Antiquity, and that there is an era of "darkness" succeeding this former period and lasting to the poet's own days. Thus, in Petrarch's opinion, there exists, for the time being, only a twofold division of history. But, since he hopes for the coming of "a better time," the conception of a third era is expressed, or at least implied, in his thoughts. This is illustrated most distinctly in one of his *Epistles*, in which he complains against Fate for having decreed his birth in such sad times, and in which he wishes that he had been born either earlier or much later; for he says, "there was a more fortunate age and probably there will be one again; in the middle, in our time, you see the confluence of wretches and ignominy." In these lines Petrarch plainly distinguishes between three eras: the fortunate ages of the past and, possibly, of the future; between them there is a "middle" time which has not yet come to an end. For the humanists of the fifteenth century periodization of history was to be much simpler. In their opinion the "new" era had actually come to light, because of the work of the great artists and poets of the fourteenth century, among them Petrarch himself. Thus, in their minds, there was no doubt about the reality of three periods: a "middle" period separated the Golden Age of Antiquity from a "modern" time of "renascence." It would be asking too much to expect Petrarch to proclaim himself explicitly the inaugurator of a new era, although occasionally he comes close to making such a claim. But implicitly he certainly paved the way to the idea which was to be set forth by the humanists of following generations. In this sense, then, our modern threefold division of history can be traced back to Petrarch. . . .

Myron P. Gilmore

The Renaissance Conception of the Lessons of History

A deep irony underlies Gilmore's "Renaissance Conception of the Lessons of History." The humanist curriculum showcased the ability of history to provide dramatic examples for one's rhetorical arguments, examples capable of moving one's audience toward action in the world. Humanism thus gave new life to the old Ciceronian commonplace about history as the *magistra vitae*, the teacher of life. Yet in the sixteenth century, this exemplar theory of history was undercut by the idea of anachronism that had accompanied the classical revival, for the growing awareness of the differences between past and present made the lessons of the past appear less and less relevant to the present.

. . . The concept of the Renaissance has given rise to much controversy and a voluminous literature. The metaphor was originally invoked to describe certain intellectual and artistic achievements first in Italy and subsequently in the rest of Europe in the period from the fourteenth to the seventeenth century but modern usage has popularized its application to the period as a whole. In spite of the vague and multiple meanings which the term has in consequence acquired, it has become deeply embedded in our historical vocabulary. In general it is applied with more precision to intellectual rather than to institutional history, using the term intellectual in its broadest sense, and this is the more justifiable because the great changes of the period were in the realm of the arts and the mind and not in political and economic life. The latter was far from static but, viewing the European scene as a whole, it cannot be said that the Renaissance saw transformations in institutions which

From Myron P. Gilmore, "The Renaissance Conception of the Lessons of History" in *Facets of the Renaissance*, ed. William H. Werkmeister (New York: Harper & Row, 1963).

matched in anything like the same degree those in the history of ideas. The intellectual revolution was profound, and was both cause and consequence of the enormous extension of knowledge and experience in time and space. Greek and Roman history and especially the latter came into ever clearer view and the increasing knowledge of classical civilization posed anew the problem of the relationship between classical and Christian values. The mass of information brought back to Europe by travellers and missionaries in the sixteenth century created an analogous problem on the relationship of contemporary non-Christian civilizations to that of western Europe. The exploration of antiquity preceded the exploration of Asia and the new world, and it is in fourteenth century Italy that we find the first consciously held new attitudes towards the classical past. In the elaboration of these attitudes as in so many other areas Petrarch was a figure of commanding importance and any description of the historical ideas of the Italian Renaissance must begin with a consideration of his thought.

In many of his works Petrarch reveals a preoccupation with time and the position of his own age in relation to the past and to the future. This is perhaps most dramatically apparent in the series of letters addressed to ancient authors in the last book of the *Familiares*. In these compositions Petrarch wrote to his favorite literary heroes in antiquity in the tone he would use in writing to his friends in his own age. It was an imaginative effort to cross the centuries which separated the classical authors from Petrarch but it was predicated on a real apprehension of the remoteness of the ancient world. The intensity of the longing together with the realization of the impossibility of its fulfilment created the conditions for these extraordinary communications.

In the letter to Livy Petrarch begins with the wish that he had been born in Livy's age or Livy in his. They would have been able to console each other. Petrarch bewails the destruction of the lost books and says that he resorts to reading Livy whenever he wishes to forget the conditions of Italy and the moral standards of his own time. "I am filled with bitter indignation," he writes, "against the mores of today when men value nothing except gold and silver and desire nothing except sensual pleasures." He is grateful to Livy for permitting him to forget the present evils and, as if closing a conversation which he had really had but which he can never have again, he concludes with the apostrophe: "Farewell forever, O matchless historian!" The letter is significantly dated, "Written in the land of the living, in that part of Italy and in that city in which I am now living and where you were once born and buried, in the vestibule of the temple of Justina Virge and in view of your very tombstone on the twenty-second of February and in the thirteen hundred and fiftieth year from the birth of him who you would have seen or of whose birth you would have heard, had you lived a little longer." Four of the other epistles in this group contain in their dating similar references to the pre-Christian era. The letter to Cicero is "written in the thirteen hundred and forty-fifth year of that God whom you never knew"; that to Seneca "in the thirteen hundred and fiftieth year from the birth of him whom your master preferred to persecute rather than profess."

These expressions show not only that Petrarch was acutely conscious of the distance which separated him from his admired classical authors but also that he realized psychologically at least something of what it meant to live before the Christian era. It does not matter that he was wrong in many of the details of his historical and architectural reconstructions—we now know for example that he was not looking at the actual tomb of Livy at Padua—but it is significant that these phrases in which he dates his letters and places his own position in time reveal the working of a historical imagination. Petrarch knew that Livy knew nothing of Christianity although he would have heard of it had he lived a little longer; he knew also that Quintilian had been employed by the emperor Domitian who persecuted the Christians. But with this knowledge he was able to imagine what these facts meant; he was able to some extent to place the lives and works of these authors in the context of their times; it is not too much to say that he had some conception of anachronism and that this conception underlay his understanding of the fact that no knowledge of Christianity could be attributed to Livy.

We are today so accustomed to applying the test of anachronism to our historical reconstructions that we take it for granted. . . . We know that if we are going to construct Colonial Williamsburg as it really was, the streets must be cobbled and the electric wires put under ground. It might indeed be said that in such extreme cases of stage-set reconstruction we commit anachronisms in reverse by requiring modern stores to encase themselves in Queen Anne or Georgian fronts. The very phrase "to commit an anachronism" is furthermore a reminder of the extent to which we think of the concept in pejorative terms. An anachronism is a bad thing. . . .

This over-developed modern consciousness is the product of a long evolution which may be said to have begun with Petrarch and those of his followers who shared his attitude towards the past. The conception of history which prevailed in the Middle Ages was one of a course of events extending from the creation in the past to the last judgment in the future. Within this unified Christian drama there was small scope for the realization of or interest in differences which divided one period from another, and consequently no conception of anachronism. In the history of art, Professor Panofsky has pointed out the divorce in the Middle Ages between classical form and classical content. Those who worked from literary sources represented ancient gods and goddesses or Greek and Trojan heroes in medieval costumes whereas the artists who had drawn on visual materials dressed Christian figures in classical drapery. Petrarch's attitude represents a decisive change from this medieval way of looking at the past. His letter to Livy does put Livy back into the Roman past in a way which is entirely different from the illustrator of the fourteenth-century French manuscript of Livy who represented the scenes of Roman history as if they were taking place in the France or Burgundy of his own day. The very idea of what is anachronistic, that is, something which is out of its own proper time, whether it is a detail of costume, an idea, an event, or a linguistic expression, rests on a sense of the differences that separate one historical epoch from another. This sense of difference between the present and various periods of the past was of course not as sharp as it later became; we are still far from the historicism of the nineteenth and twentieth centuries. In the drama and the arts anachronisms were not regarded as offensive until after the conquests of romanticism. Yet incomplete as it was, the Renaissance had some sense of the life and style of the past. The humanist followers of Petrarch used the argument from anachronism among others as a weapon of historical criticism. Conversely, the recovery of a sense of classical "style" made possible the imitation of ancient works of art and literature and we remember that Michelangelo's first sculpture was sold as a Roman marble and Alberti circulated a comedy which he had written as a newly found work of Latin literature. . . .

. . . The consciousness of the difference between his own time and republican Rome—the sense of historical perspective—was accompanied in Petrarch's thought by a re-evaluation of the traditional judgments on Roman history. The age about which Livy wrote in the Third Decade of his history, even the age in which Cicero had lived, appeared clearly to Petrarch's vision as in some important respects better than the present, and this in spite of the fact that it lacked the benefit of Christian revelation. In the letter to Livy as well as in many of his other works

Petrarch approaches the conception of a culturally "dark" or middle age lying between his own time and antiquity, a conception which has been so familiar a feature of the periodization of history from the Renaissance to the present time. . . .

. . . [T]he evils of Petrarch's own time were condemned by standards exhibited by the ancient Romans. Petrarch's appeal to the Roman past reflected the conviction that history, even pagan history, provided a basis for moral criticism. Insofar as the examples of virtue and vice furnished by the past could be imitated and actively realized in the present, history was philosophy teaching by example.

This conception is apparent . . . in Petrarch's . . . own historical compositions. His collection of biographies, *De viris illustribus*, was originally conceived to include epitomes of the lives of great men which Petrarch had found scattered through history books. In the version composed in the last years of his life at the request of the tyrant Francesco da Carrara, Petrarch dropped the pre-Roman lives in accordance with the preference expressed by the prince, who proposed to decorate a hall of his palace with the portraits of the subjects of Petrarch's biographies. His preference for the Romans again shows his sense of the division which separated classical and early Christian antiquity from the dark age that followed after. He had earlier expressed his reluctance to include any contemporary or recent figures in his collection of illustrious lives. In a letter to Agapito Colonna written in 1359 he says in answer to the charge that he did not include in his biographical collection any contemporary figures, "I did not wish to guide my pen so far and through such darkness." Even, however, when Petrarch did turn to this "darkness" for historical and biographical material, his purpose remained didactic. *Rerum memorandum libri* were composed to illustrate a traditional conception of virtue derived from Cicero. According to this tradition, prudence, one of the four cardinal virtues, was divided into three parts: the memory of things past, the consciousness of things present and the foreseeing of things to come. The individuals selected to illustrate these different aspects of prudence are divided into Roman, non-Roman and modern although the greater number by far is Roman and illustrates again Petrarch's belief in the superiority of Roman history as a source of moral examples.

In spite of the didactic purpose of Petrarch's formal historical and biographical work, it must not, however, be forgotten that there was another aspect of his historical interests which in the end was of far greater importance for European historiography. This is his appeal for a return to the sources, *ad fontes,* and his concern for what an ancient author had really said. In his Treatise *On His Own Ignorance* he condemns "the stupid Aristotelians, who day by day in every single word they speak do not cease to hammer into the heads of others Aristotle whom they know by name only." A great part of Petrarch's career was dedicated to his attempt to recover accurate texts of his beloved classical authors. If he was convinced that the history of Livy provided examples for the present, he was equally convinced that it was necessary to know precisely what Livy had said so far as this was possible after the destruction wrought by time and barbarians. We have only recently come to know through the researches of Professor Billanovich how much Petrarch contributed to the establishment of the text of Livy. Petrarch early copied one of the most important manuscripts of Livy, now known as the Harleian at Oxford and dedicated himself to the reconstruction of the best possible text. "The tradition of Livy during the Renaissance," says Professor Billanovich, "was for the most part the tradition which Petrarch himself had formed. By means of a fortunate comparison of texts, he corrected the books of the first *Decade;* which, although descended from a single archetype, had been transmitted through divergent channels. And he managed to obtained the fourth *Decade* when it had only just reached Avignon." Throughout his life Livy remained for Petrarch his favorite historian.

It may be pointed out that this effort to establish with the aid of grammar and philology what Livy or another ancient author had really written stopped a good deal short of what we understand by historical research. For Petrarch Livy *was* Roman history and there was no question of going behind his narrative to investigate what had actually happened through a process of comparing different documents and different kinds of evidence. Nevertheless the attempt to recover a correct text did involve coming into more direct contact with the character, personality, style and idiosyncrasies of the author—Livy was felt as a more real historical personage than had been the case in the middle ages. Furthermore, the comparison of two or more manuscripts was at least the beginning of criticism even if the scope was limited to the recovery of one narrative history rather than the reconstruction of a past through the testimony of many.

There may thus be distinguished in Petrarch's attitude towards history three different components. There is first the sense of historical distance, the consciousness of the differences between classical antiquity and the Christian era which followed with the dawning realization that this great gap in time and circumstances could be bridged by an effort of the imagination. Secondly, there is the conception that to the extent to which this past can be recovered, it provides moral lessons for a future generation. History is philosophy teaching by example in which the past, if correctly understood, informs and instructs the present. Thirdly, there is the basis for that correct understanding, that is, history as the intellectual conquest of what an ancient author had really said derived from a critical and philological study of the texts. Our modern habits of thought about history tend in general to make a sharp separation between these latter two components. Much that may be discovered by research is irrelevant to any "lessons" of history and conversely many moral and political "truths" cannot be supported by historical evidence or at any rate by historical evidence alone. In the minds of Petrarch and his immediate followers, however, there cannot be said to have been any sense of incompatibility between these two components of the historian's activity. For most of the characteristic thinkers of the Renaissance the cry for the return to the sources was accompanied by the conviction that the sources when recovered would be relevant to present concerns. Criticism and a program for moral and educational reform sustained each other, and until they began to be separated provided the basis of the hopes of the humanist publicists.

The intellectual impulse given by Petrarch to historical studies can be traced in succeeding generations. Editions and translations of ancient historians were produced in increasing numbers and many humanists wrote histories modelled on Livy. The study of history was elevated to an important and sometimes to a central place in the educational curriculum. The Florentine chancellor, Coluccio Salutati, one of Petrarch's great admirers, wrote in 1392, a letter to the Grand Master of the Order of St. John of Jerusalem praising him for his valuable collection of books. Among these he singled out for particular mention the histories and commended the Grand Master for having "cherished the historians whose duty it is to hand down to posterity the memory of things done so that the examples of kings, nations, and illustrious men can be either equalled or exceeded by imitating them. . . . The knowledge of things done warns princes, teaches people, and instructs individuals. . . . It is the most certain basis for the conduct of affairs. History teaches us the doctrines of philosophy. . . ."

The judgment of Salutati was confirmed by the formal treatises on education. Pier Paolo Vergerio, for example, whose *De ingenuis moribus* is of the beginning of the fifteenth century, declares in his discussion of the ideal curriculum: "We come now to the consideration of the various subjects which ought to be included under the name of liberal studies. Among these I accord the first place to history on the grounds both of its attractiveness and its utility, qualities which appeal equally to the scholar and the statesman. . . . History, then, gives us the concrete examples of the principles inculcated by philosophy. The one shows what men should do, the other what men have said and done in the past and what practical lessons men may draw therefrom for the present day." Such a text as this clearly reveals the consequences of Petrarch's approach to historical studies: there was no gulf between the study and the market place, no divorce between culture and politics. . . .

These views on history and particularly on Roman history as a source of moral example were adopted by educators. Most influential among those who founded new schools or reformed the traditional curricula was Vittorino da Feltre, the beloved schoolmaster of Mantua. . . .

In [his] school a great importance was accorded to the study of history and Livy remained always for Vittorino as he had been for Petrarch one of the most cherished authors. The pupils learned to read aloud and memorize passages from Livy and discussed the heroes of Roman history in the spirit in which Petrarch had collected his exemplary biographies. The results of this education can be followed in the later lives of two of his pupils, Giovanni Andrea Bussi, Bishop of Aleria, and Federigo da Montefeltro, Duke of Urbino.

The Bishop of Aleria in Corsica served four popes as acolyte, secretary and librarian, and although he was rewarded with two Corsican bishoprics, Alessio and Aleria, he never visited his sees. He enjoys the remarkable distinction of having collaborated with the first Roman printers Sweynheim and Pannartz at Subiaco and at Rome in the publishing of the *editiones principes* of a large number of Latin authors including Livy. In the preface to the Livy of 1469 he traces his first acquaintance with Livy to Vittorino's school and professes that he owes most of his knowledge of the text to Vittorino who had been the first to introduce him to Petrarch's work on Livy. . . . This famous edition appearing within five years of the centenary of the death of Petrarch is an eloquent testimony to the fruit of Petrarch's interest in the text of Livy. By an invention of which Petrarch could not even have dreamed his textual reconstruction which had descended to Vittorino and to Valla was now reproduced in a manner which would make it available to all readers and scholars.

The most famous pupil of Vittorino was Federigo da Montefeltro, Count and subsequently Duke of Urbino. . . . Although as a youth he had studied for only two years at Vittorino's school, he never forgot his master and in the study at the ducal palace where were enshrined portraits of the worthies of all ages there was included Berruguete's portrait of Vittorino with an inscription recording the gratitude of the duke. It was undoubtedly in Vittorino's school that he acquired the interest in reading Roman history which he always retained. Vespasiano, who greatly admired Federigo, included a brief life of him in his collections of lives of illustrious men. In this life he tells us that the Duke of Urbino observed a daily routine of public reading of Livy at mealtime. "When the duke had sat down the doors would be left open, so that all might enter, and he never ate except the hall were full, some one would always read to him; during Lent a spiritual work, and at other times the *Histories* of Livy, all in Latin." Thus we may see that the same teaching deriving ultimately from Petrarch had served as a stimulus for Andrea Bussi who edited the text of Livy and for Federigo da Montefeltro who reflected on the lessons to be derived from studying him. What the scholar elucidated the statesman applied. Nothing could testify more strongly to the strength of the conviction of the importance of historical studies and the relevance of the lessons of history.

When we reach the sixteenth century there is a break and it is signalized by Machiavelli. We know that Machiavelli was exposed during his early years to the traditional admiration for Livy. His father Bernardo tells in his *Libri di Ricordi* of the contract with the Florentine book binder for the binding of his copy of Livy and of the payment made by his "figliuolo Niccolo." In this copy Niccolo probably began his intensive reading in Livy, no doubt suspended during the time when he was employed as secretary of the Florentine chancery, but again resumed during his period of enforced leisure and culminating in the writing of the *Discourses* in 1516–1517. We are astonished, however, to find that Machiavelli writes at the beginning of the *Discourses* a condemnation of the way in which history had been taught. He considers that his predecessors have failed and begins by announcing the originality of his own approach. "I have decided," says Machiavelli, "to enter on a path which up to now has been trodden by no one, and if it brings me labor and difficulty it may bring me reward. . . ." He is astonished and grieved that examples from the history of antiquity are more admired than imitated. And the more so because in the study of the civil law or in medicine, "recourse is always had to those judgments or to those remedies which have been decreed or provided by the ancients, since the civil law is nothing else than the opinion of ancient jurisconsults, which opinions, when they are arranged in order, teach our present jurisconsults to judge." If the jurisconsults can be taught to judge according to a body of laws derived from the history of their profession, why cannot rulers be taught to rule? Machiavelli declares that he is convinced that this failure to profit by the example of the ancient world in the business of ruling men is due "not so much to the weakness to which the present religion has conducted the world nor to the evils that a proud indolence has brought on many Christian cities and provinces as to a lack of a true knowledge of history, through not extracting the sense of it when reading it and not savoring the knowledge that it has in itself."

Considering the number of appeals to the value of studying history which had been uttered by the humanist educators from the time of Petrarch to that of Machiavelli himself, this indictment appears the more curious. Surely Machiavelli knew that these educators had recommended the study of antiquity for its exemplary character and had pored over it in an effort "to extract the sense of it." The key to Machiavelli's condemnation, however, is to be found not in what the humanists professed but in what they had failed to accomplish. Looking at the political disorder which had come upon Florence and indeed upon all Italy since the French invasion of 1494, Machiavelli was above all impressed with the contrast between what was preached and what was practiced. He did not condemn a teacher like Vittorino or a ruler like Federigo because he had tried to make the study of history applicable to the present but because they had not succeeded. The easy confidence of an earlier generation that it was enough to find out what the lessons of history were and that they would be relevant to the present was beginning to crack. It is in this connection most significantly that Machiavelli appeals to the disciplines of jurisprudence and medicine as those which represent the successful use of antiquity.

Machiavelli, whose father was a lawyer, was impressed with the fact that in both medicine and the law the particular case was assimilated to a general rule, and this general rule had been tested by many authorities of classical antiquity. Those who had contemplated the course of history had indeed found examples of virtue and vice, wisdom and foolishness but these had never been reduced to a system; there existed no systematic body of knowledge which could be compared to that accumulated by the commentators on the civil law and this was the focal point of Machiavelli's criticism of the humanist tradition—a tradition from which he had himself started and upon which he had built but which he found wanting as he reflected on the failures of Italian political institutions to meet the shock of the northern invasions.

Machiavelli's appeal to the lawyers was founded on a recognition of their prestige and practical success. . . . In the Italian universities of the late Middle Ages and Renaissance the courses on the civil and canon law drew more students than did those on any other subject.

In citing the success of the profession of jurisprudence Machiavelli thus recognized a fact of the current social scene and the same was true to perhaps a lesser degree of the profession of medicine. Nevertheless his appeal to the lawyers contains an element of paradox. Machiavelli was pleading for both "history" and "system" but the very jurisconsults who most completely realized the ideal of a systematic body of knowledge, applicable to the present, were the least historical.

The greatest figure in the late medieval school of Italian jurisprudence had been Bartolus of Sassoferrato (1314–1357) whose authority was so great that his opinions were cited by rulers and by courts as if they had the authority of judicial decisions. Bartolus and his followers—the so-called Post-Glossators—were much more interested in the elaboration and application of a system of rules than they were in the achievement of any historical understanding of the growth of law or even of the existence of different periods in the history of institutions. For them the *Corpus* of Justinian was still *de jure* applicable to a Roman empire that had not ceased to exist. It was only necessary to take account of the *de facto* variations which made necessary subtle and elaborate adjustments in the universal rules to fit them to particular contemporary conditions. They did not feel that sense of distance either from the age of Justinian or from the classical jurists behind Justinian which we have seen dawning in the thought of Petrarch. In a word their thought may be said to have remained fundamentally medieval in its conception of the relationship between antiquity and the contemporary scene.

This school still dominated the teaching of law in the Italian universities in the sixteenth century. Ever since the time of Petrarch, however, its methods and conclusions had been under attack by the humanists. . . .

. . . Among these attacks the most incisive was that delivered against Bartolus by Lorenzo Valla in 1433. In that year the young humanist scholar, already a prodigy who dazzled his contemporaries, had been invited to a chair of rhetoric at the University of Pavia. . . . Valla one day encountered a group of law professors who were lavishing uncritical praise on the Bartolists. Someone in the company made the provocative remark that one small treatise of Bartolus, the *De insigniis et armis* was better than all the works of Cicero put together. Valla made an incredulous reply and then immediately sought out a friend from whom he borrowed a copy of the treatise of Bartolus which he read with a growing sense of indignation and amazement that anyone could have made such a comparison. He then sat down and directed a letter to his friend Sacco who, although on the law faculty, shared Valla's ideas on the value of humanist learning and on correct Latin. In this letter Valla expressed his condemnation of Bartolus' treatise in the strongest language. He began by bewailing the times in which anyone could have preferred a barbarous work of jurisprudence to the golden tongue of Cicero. He pointed out that even in the title of the Bartolist treatise there was an egregious error: "*insigniis*" should have been "*insignibus.*" He described Bartolus as an "ass," "idiot," and "madman," and found his work completely lacking in an understanding of Roman law and institutions. . . . The letter immediately created such hostility among the conservative faction in Pavia that Valla was forced to resign his chair and flee the city.

The humanists continued their attacks on the traditional teaching of the law throughout the fifteenth century and, impatient with the failure of the lawyers to reform, they began themselves to apply to the legal sources techniques of philological and historical criticism. Before the end of the century the great Angelo Poliziano had proposed a critical edition of the famous Florentine manuscript of the *Pandects*. And by the time when Machiavelli was beginning his *Discorsi*, Andrea Alciatus was already demonstrating that historical and literary evidence could be applied to the understanding of legal texts. . . .

Thus by the second decade of the sixteenth century there were already coming to be distinguished two schools of interpretation in legal studies. The first or traditional school afterwards known as the *mos italicus* emphasized the application to the present of rules derived from the analysis of the authoritative texts of antiquity. The second which came to be known as the *mos gallicus* (because widely adopted by the French legal scholars) devoted itself to the historical understanding of the classical law with all the resources that history and philology could supply, but without regard to the application of the results to the present. The aim of the former was systematic, that of the latter historical. When Machiavelli held up the example of jurisprudence to those humanists whom he accused of having failed in their teaching of history, he was in a sense taking a step backward. The *Discorsi* are in respect to their attitude towards history nearer Bartolus than they are to Machiavelli's contemporary, Alciatus. Although Machiavelli shared with the fifteenth century humanist tradition the interest in Roman history and the concentration on Livy, he did not believe that examples derived from understanding the text of Livy would produce lessons applicable to the present unless they were systematized. Although he started from the humanist interest in history as it had been initiated by Petrarch, he repudiated the confident humanist assumption that increased admiration and understanding of the text of Livy would automatically be followed by lessons which could be applied to the improvement of the individual and of society in his own time. This assumption which as we have seen had been held in the fifteenth century by such educators as Vittorino and such rulers as Federigo was perhaps first weakened by the growth, initiated by the humanist scholars themselves, of two schools of interpreting the legal tradition. It was, however, further undermined by Machiavelli's great appeal for the necessity for systematization from historical materials. What had begun in the early Renaissance as a conception of history that combined a real interest in the past with a belief in its relevance to the present was now in the process of being separated into what was to become the "merely historical" on the one hand and the materials of theoretical structures, political, social or constitutional, on the other. In the period after Machiavelli the consequences of that separation became clearer in the north than in Italy and it is perhaps most dramatically illustrated in France.

Jean Bodin published in 1566 the most philosophical book on the nature of historical thought written in the sixteenth century. At the beginning of this work he distinguished three kinds of history, divine, natural and human, which corresponded to three kinds of knowledge, faith, science and prudence. In the realm of human history, "which flows from the will of men which is ever variable," prudence may be acquired by a comparative study of civilizations with a view to eliciting the general rules of social behaviours which may be applied to recurring situations. Like Machiavelli before him, he wished to understand the true meaning of ancient history by finding in it examples which had a universal validity. Both of them might be described today as retrospective sociologists. The longest chapter in Bodin's book is devoted to the consideration of the foundations of states and of changes in their constitutions which Bodin considers to be the principal subject matter of history. In this endeavor he finds himself hindered by those who prefer to call themselves grammar-ians rather than jurisconsults. "We must not look for salvation," he says in a very interesting passage, "to those whom no one deigns to consult in matters of law, to those who prefer to consider themselves grammarians rather than jurisconsults, or to those . . . who expect from the power of words alone the safety of the establishment of justice, and the resolution of conflicts. This plague of grammar has in our day so inserted itself into all our disciplines that we have to endure under the guise of philoso-phers, orators, mathematicians and even theologians, petty grammarians who are barely out of school. Those who ought to have confined them-selves to cleaning the dirt and spots from ancient pictures so as to make the original painting appear, have taken a steel dagger and made such huge and indelible marks on all the books that the image of antiquity can hardly any longer be seen." How we seem to hear the voice of Machia-velli in the indictment of those "who expect from the power of words alone the safety of the state!" But Bodin's repudiation of a part of the hu-manist tradition goes farther. To condemn the study of grammar for hav-ing obscured the image of antiquity was to condemn what had been for the humanists the most important instrument for historical reconstruc-tion. The substance of the complaints against Bartolus of such critics as Petrarch and Valla had been that he did not know language and that this made it impossible for him to understand history. Now Bodin feels that it is the linguistic purists who have destroyed the vision of the past.

Bodin's argument was directed not only against his humanist prede-cessors but also against his contemporaries. Among them was one whose pre-eminence as a scholar of the law was unquestioned. Jacques Cujas particularly dedicated his scholarship to the restoration of juridical texts of the pre-Justinian period, and in this he followed faithfully the direc-tion in which Valla's work had pointed. His critical editions and learned commentaries include the discovery and study of interpolations in the text of Justinian's *Corpus* and his principal weapon was precisely that knowledge of grammar, that philology which Bodin had condemned. In the case of Cujas, however, the clearer the image of antiquity became, the less applicable to the modern world did it seem to be, and this was the point of Bodin's criticism. The story is told of Cujas that when his pupils came to him to ask what course they should follow in the terrible crises of the religious struggle, he replied, "*Nihil hoc ad edictum prae-toris.*" This had nothing to do with the edict of the praetor. By these words Cujas meant in the first place that religious problems ought not to be subject to civil legislation but secondly and more profoundly that it was his task to teach history and not to draw from it lessons for the present or the future. The image of antiquity had been recovered but at the same time it ceased to speak directly to the modern world. History was becoming academic. What it discovered might be archeologically true but it was irrelevant to the concerns of a later age. The opposition between Bodin and Cujas would have been incomprehensible to a Petrarch or a Valla. These humanists would not have understood Bodin's condemnation of grammar as a tool of historical understanding or Cujas' lack of interest in the application of the results of historical understanding. For about two hundred years—roughly the period between Petrarch and Erasmus—the humanist tradition just as it believed in the compatibility of classic and Christian was able to also combine a deeper historical knowledge of the classical past with an undiminished confidence in the relevance of the lessons of the past. But by the time Cujas gave his response to his students, this phase of the Renaissance was over.

Donald R. Kelley

Guillaume Budé and the First Historical School of Law

In the mid to late 1960s, Kelley published a series of articles that would form the core of his encyclopedic *Foundations of Modern Historical Scholarship* (1970), the most thorough treatment of the French historical school of law and its impact on late Renaissance historical thought. Although far more than the sum of its parts, this book makes several broad claims epitomized in one of its constituent pieces, "Guillaume Budé and the First Historical School of Law." Here, in particular, Kelley outlines the role of philology in

From Donald R. Kelley, "Guillaume Budé and the First Historical School of Law," *American Historical Review* 72 (1967): 807–834.

creating a historical revolution, and he traces how this revolution came about through the study of Roman law in sixteenth-century France.

According to Kelley, the philological study of Roman law gave rise to "historicism," the modern form of historical consciousness, fully 200 years before it is commonly believed to have originated, in late eighteenth-century Germany. Kelley begins by declaring that what the Germanic term *historicism* lacks in precision, it makes up for in utility: "It serves to designate the conceptual basis of the historian's quest, ill-defined as this may be, and, more important, it is a way of emphasizing the deep-rooted traditions of historical scholarship." He goes on to state that "historicism is a way of looking at the world that encompasses the principles of individuality, development, and relativism." In the body of the article, excerpted below, he argues that these principles are evident in the work of Lorenzo Valla (1406–1457), the first great Renaissance philologist, who in turn bequeathed them to Guillaume Budé (1468–1540) and his followers.

. . . There is no better place to begin an investigation of the roots of historicism than with the ideas of that *enfant terrible* of the Renaissance, Lorenzo Valla. . . . In his belligerent *Dialectical Disputations* Valla offered the first systematic humanist critique of the false school of philosophy that lived off the use and abuse of abstraction. What he did, in sum, was to reduce the three so-called "transcendentia" of Scholastic philosophy to a single category—thing (*res*)—and then reduce the ten "praedicamenta" to three—substance, action, and quality. In other words, having identified the world with concrete things, he went on—and this is the insidious part of his argument—to reduce man's understanding of the world to the "categories" of the grammarian, that is, to the principal parts of speech: the noun (substance), the verb (action), and the adjective or adverb (quality). . . . The conclusion was self-evident: it was the philologist (Valla would say the rhetorician) not the philosopher or the lawyer, the amateur not the professional, who was best fitted to investigate and to interpret the world of man's making. Valla's arguments constitute at once a declaration of independence for philology and an epistemological justification for the study of history.

Appropriately, the real key to Valla's thought was not his theory of knowledge; it was his feeling for language, especially his view of "style" . . . style in the sense not merely of a literary ideal but of the recognition of individual historical modes of expression. Here is one of the main links between philology and history. The method of the philologist was "historical" not only because it required the literal interpretation of texts (the *sensus historicus*) but because it meant reconstructing a departed way of thought and of life. Valla clearly understood that style, which after all was a public rather than a private creation, was closely bound up with law and religion, with art and literature. . . . From such stylistic judgments Valla drew those philological techniques which, illustrating in their own way the principles of individuality and of development, went into the making of modern historical method. This is shown not only in his notorious exposé of the Donation of Constantine and his emendations of Livy but, perhaps best of all, in his criticism of the New Testament and of Roman law. As one of the founding fathers of Biblical and of legal humanism, he was the intellectual ancestor both of Desiderius Erasmus and of Guillaume Budé, to name only the two most prominent sixteenth-century scholars.

Whether as an inspiration or as an irritant, Valla had an almost unparalleled influence. Representing (as Vittorio Rossi argued many years ago) the transition from humanism to historicism, he did more than anyone to bring about a "historical revolution." What he did, I would suggest, was to create a "paradigm" (in the sense that Thomas Kuhn applied this term to "scientific revolutions") for the cultural sciences. He established both an epistemology and a method for historical scholarship. Just as important, perhaps, he helped bring about a transformation of values that allowed philologists to follow their "trivial" calling without feeling inferior to the older professions. While it may be an exaggeration to regard Valla as the Copernicus of historical thought, he did come closer than any scholar to expressing the presumptions and methods of historical scholarship as it would be carried on for more than three centuries. Like Copernican astronomy, humanist philology became a "coherent tradition of scientific research," possessing a "consensus of scholarly values and techniques." As the founder of a tradition, of course, Valla could not be expected to do much more than set an example and advertise his product. The heavy work was in general carried on by his followers who, if they were less venturesome, were more learned, and if they did not care to examine the foundations of their disciple, were intensely devoted to the specific tasks of historical scholarship. These were the practitioners of "normal science" (in Kuhn's phrase) and included such men as Angelo Poliziano, Ermolao Barbaro, Pietro Crinito, Alessandro d'Alessandro, Erasmus, and Guillaume Budé. Although they were not quite discoverers, they were certainly pioneers in the territories claimed by the new science of philology. It is the work of such men that we must study in order to understand the beginnings of modern historical scholarship.

In the long and continuous tradition of humanist historicism . . . one of the recurrent themes has been the invigorating effects of legal and linguistic studies upon historical thought. Never wholly at ease with one another, historians and lawyers have nevertheless profited greatly from their mutual labors, in the sixteenth perhaps more than in the nineteenth century. One remarkable phenomenon in the history of scholarship is the lasting value of Renaissance studies in Roman law, perhaps unparalleled in any other field. . . . On the whole, however, historians have fallen behind the lawyers in their appreciation of legal scholarship. About the contributions of the nineteenth-century "historical school of law," of course, much has been said. . . . About the contributions of Renaissance philology, on the other hand, we know much less, and much of that is colored by nineteenth-century images of the Renaissance. The purpose of this paper is to suggest the significance of the sixteenth-century "historical school of law" for the philological investigation of the past and so to illuminate one of the more obscure phases of the history of historicism.

The real basis of the first historical school of law was Guillaume Budé's *Annotations on Twenty-four Books of the Pandects*. . . . [T]his work, published in 1508, did for Roman law what eight years later Erasmus' New Testament was to do for Biblical studies: it introduced a new method of historical criticism into one of the major professional domains in order to "reform" not only a university discipline but, by restoring ancient learning (*prisca doctrina*) in a neglected field, contemporary society in general.

Like Erasmus, his sometime friend and rival, Budé gave up plans for a professional career for reasons of personal taste. Turning his back on the practice of law as Erasmus had turned his on an ecclesiastical calling, Budé became a devout convert to the cause of "philology." For Budé's sake it is best not to pursue the inevitable parallel with Erasmus too far. . . .

In one respect, however, Budé was Erasmus' equal, if not his superior. In the field of Hellenic studies he could claim to be a pioneer . . . a man who almost singlehandedly brought the light of learning (*lampadem*) to France. . . . Budé's carefully cultivated image as the archhumanist of France rested upon three major books—the *Annotations*, the *De Asse*, and the *Commentaries on Greek*—and upon the alleged role he played in the establishment of the regius professorships of the classical languages, the institutional embodiment of philology that became the basis of the *Collège de France*. No one, it seems, did more than Budé to broadcast that "chorus of muses" whose strains Petrarch first heard. Thus in popular opinion Budé was installed, beside Erasmus and Vives, in the great "triumvirate" of sixteenth-century learning. Indeed J. J. Scaliger, the ultimate judge in such matters, called him "the greatest Greek in Europe."

For all his claims to originality, Budé did not deny the scholarly supremacy of Italy . . . nor his specific indebtedness to such Italian scholars as Valla and Poliziano. From these men he derived not only his approach to Roman law but, if only unconsciously, the assumptions of Renaissance historicism. For Budé it was an article of faith that words reflected reality (*verba rerum imagines*), that only a close study of language revealed the contours of the historical world; it was perhaps only natural that he should have turned, though without discarding his historical method, from textual criticism to lexicography. From Italian philology, too, Budé adopted the view that each age, as well as each national group, had its own cultural configuration, its characteristic "style," of which literature was the most sensitive indicator, and learned opinion (*consensus eruditorum*) the final judge. Budé was following ancient convention when he characterized particular ages (*Ciceronis aetas, Ulpiani tempus, seculum Accursiani*, and so forth) and when he distinguished between "classical" and "proletarian" writers, but he went beyond this in adding a sense of progressive stylistic change, even suggesting a periodization roughly equivalent to our ancient-medieval-modern convention (*antiqui, intermedii, recentiores*). A sense of history appears also in his discussion of national culture, hypostatized by such terms as "genius" (*genius* or *Minerva Franciae*). He plotted a life cycle beginning with childhood (*secula infantiae*), filled with superstition and poetry; then adolescence, characterized by learning and eloquence, that is, history and philology; finally a period of decline, arising from moral corruption and the vicissitudes of time (*inclinationes temporum*). And the key to these historical ideas, as well as to Budé's philological method, was the concept of style.

For Budé philology represented, in effect, a new world view. . . . To Budé as to Erasmus . . . philology was a real "science" based upon the *studia humanitatis*. It was a combination of grammar according to the famous definition of Poliziano and rhetoric according to the notorious views of Valla. In other words, philology involved the historical (that is, the literal) interpretation of texts in the light of the so-called "encyclopedia" of liberal arts; at the same time it depended upon eloquence, which "binds together this cycle of learning . . . like a living body," and without which (Budé added in Valla's words) "learning is blind, especially in civil law." As a literary ideal, philology stood above history—a possession of all the ages (*dicendi facultas ars sit omnium temporum et locorum*). In the sixteenth century, however, it had become rather a technique for resurrecting the past (*philologia olim ornatrix . . . hodie instauratrix et interpolatrix*). For Budé, then, philology was both a "cornucopia" of classical learning and a historical method.

About the study of history in a formal sense Budé had little to say beyond the tired *topoi* of humanist rhetoric, rehearsed all too often by Valla and others. . . . In Budé's view—"trivial" and "commonplace" in more than one sense—the function of history was didactic and commemorative (*exemplorum eventuumque memorabilium plena est historia*). What is more significant, Budé made a conscious connection between the truthfulness and accuracy of narrative history and the literalness (*sensus historicus*) of the grammatical method, celebrating both as the "faith of history" (*fides historiae*). This reinforces the view taken here that Budé conceived of history not as a literary genre but as an independent mode of thought. His purpose was not the fashioning of a narrative line but the investigation (*indagatio*) and restoration (*restitutio*) of ancient culture through philology.

Budé's most celebrated effort of reconstruction was probably his study of Roman coinage, a subject that had been the despair of such scholars as Flavio Biondo, Poliziano, and Barbaro. Budé did not limit himself merely to investigating the names and values of ancient moneys. He addressed himself to the larger question of the economic basis of the Roman Empire, comparing its wealth to that of modern Europe as well as of other ancient societies, discussing in detail such topics as usury, the beginning of coinage, and the incomes of the various professions (concluding, for example, that scholars were much better rewarded in ancient times). He had no doubt that the splendor of Rome depended largely upon the wealth and the ideas wrested from other peoples and that its political and cultural degeneration was closely tied to economic factors, such as the progressive devaluation of currency. This awareness of the economic foundations of civilization gave a dimension to Budé's view of antiquity that was lacking in his Italian forebears.

It was in the field of Roman law, however, that the quality of Budé's scholarship appears most clearly. Although civil law had long been one of the main preserves of Scholastic method, to humanists it was the

greatest monument of Roman civilization. As a locus of the most fundamental problems confronting the historian, moreover, it was an incomparable challenge to the historical imagination. Legal humanists had to
consider such questions as the extent of cultural influence, especially of
Greek philosophy; the effects of historical change, since Roman law was
a growth of centuries and showed signs both of social and stylistic variation; the possibility of "interpolations" and other textual alterations, since
Justinian's corpus was both fragmentary and corrupt; and finally the
value of legal sources and methods for the study of history. These problems obviously called for the talents not of a lawyer but of a philologist.

How did Roman law come to be looked at in this light? Once again
we must pay homage to Valla. Besides establishing the method of the historical school of law, Valla set down in unmistakable fashion the primary
themes of legal humanism. Of these the three most prominent were
"anti-Tribonianism," that is, the critique of the scholarship (as well as the
moral and religious failings) of the Byzantine editor of the *Digest*; "anti-
Bartolism," the bitter and often exaggerated attack upon the tangled
growth of Scholastic interpretation; and "juristic classicism," the judging
of the *Digest* in terms of such literary "authorities" as Cicero and Ulpian,
who provided a Latin standard (*norma latina*) for the detection of later
"depravities." On such grounds Valla made a number of emendations of
Roman law, especially in that favorite humanist target, the *Digest* title
"On the Meaning of Words." For the most part Valla's criticism was limited to rejecting senseless distinctions, deriding imaginary "etymologies"
(such as *testamentum* from "quod testatio mentis est"), and pointing out
inconsistencies (*antinomia*). Although lawyers took Valla's opinions to be
quibbling, Budé usually took them seriously.

More substantial was the textual criticism of Poliziano, who, though
he lacked Valla's philosophic acumen, had a superior knowledge of
Greek and, more important, access to the legendary Florentine codex,
indispensable to the study of the *Digest*. . . .

Budé took up just where these two philologists left off. He approached
the *Digest* not as a book of authority—which in Gallican France it could
not be anyway—but as a historical monument, an "image of antiquity"
(*effigies antiquitatis*). It was Valla's *Elegancies of the Latin Language*, he
tells us, "that led me to read the *Digest* more carefully, wherein I found
many things partly corrupted and partly mutilated, and so I turned my
attention to many words of good and ancient coinage, transformed by the

ignorance of the times into foreign usage." Budé regarded the *Digest* as a priceless but ill-preserved anthology of literature that showed in a striking fashion the destructive effects of time and a neglectful posterity. . . .

Like Petrarch, Budé wanted to return to the "fathers of jurisprudence," but in the case of the *Digest* this was easier said than done. The trouble had started with Justinian's editors, under the direction of Tribonian, who "in the manner of brutal surgeons cutting into living flesh," said Budé, "gave us a *Digest* not assembled but rather dissected." Many passages in one title, Budé pointed out, "were written by Greek authors and so left by Tribonian, as may be seen by the style, which is sordid and obscure compared to that of the classical jurists, and which was not so much translated as twisted from the Greek without knowledge of either language." "Nor," he remarked elsewhere, "is the skill greater in many laws of the Code, as the style bears witness." No less striking were the various contradictions (*antinomia*) in which Tribonian was "caught napping," such as the irreconcilable definitions of "veteran" and "novice" slaves, first noticed by Valla. It was not surprising that these contradictions occasioned much sophistry on the part of medieval commentators since, as Budé added, "many *antinomia* cannot be explained without knowing many things of which Accursius was ignorant." Budé looked upon these *antinomia* not as "dissonances" to be harmonized but as challenges to historical insight, and incidentally as evidence of the historical mutability of Roman law.

If Budé was critical of Tribonianism, he was outraged at Accursianism (*Accursianitas*). He adopted the bad manners and the bias of his Italian predecessors toward both the glossators (*Accursiani*) and the commentators (*Bartolisti*), who in his opinion were the essence of anti-intellectualism. . . . He denied these "barbarians" any claim to philosophy, "unless we call philosophers those who have mastered no philosophy, who are accustomed to forbid themselves and their pupils all those arts which show no immediate profit, and who thus have a minimal knowledge of all the authors." . . . Roman laws, Budé concluded, "were propagated by men ignorant of Latin, and so it is not surprising that they have been covered by many layers of errors, some permanent . . . , some correctable, unless one believes that the authority of Accursius is sacrosanct—which I, as a disciple of the ancient jurists and as a grammarian [literator], am not accustomed to do." In short, Roman law had become an intricate palimpsest that only the most skilled philologist could decipher.

And yet if Budé lamented the "degeneration of jurisprudence from its ancient purity," he pointed out repeatedly that the deficiencies of Scholasticism were after all "the fault of the times rather than of the men" . . . . Dealing with "so much law through such a variety of ages," Budé asked of Accursius, "could his judgment be perfect?" Thus, just as he admitted that his own achievements were owing, at least in part, to the excellence of his "golden age," so (like Valla) Budé had enough historical sense to recognize *Accursianitas* as a cultural rather than an individual failing. Commonplace as such an admission may seem, it indicates an important feature of Renaissance historicism: the replacing of a narrow and unhistorical classicism by an attitude of relativism.

The most concrete signs of Budé's historicism were displayed in his exegesis of the *Digest*. Instead of glossing over, he insisted upon the fundamental social changes reflected in Roman law, such as the decline of the Senate. "By the time of Ulpian," Budé remarked (apropos of the imperial formula, *princeps legibus solutus*), "nothing remained of that original public spirit [*prisca civilitas*], everything being ruled by the will of the prince." By appeal to history he was often able to correct Accursius, whose disregard of chronology led him to such misconceptions as confusing the Senate and the centumviral court. . . .

When history was silent, when manuscript authority was lacking, Budé resorted to a more precarious and yet a more characteristic technique: a kind of higher criticism based on his sense of style. Here again he was following a familiar humanist pattern, applying to the *Digest* those methods by which Valla had made his exposé of the Donation of Constantine. Suspicious as Budé was of the "divinations" of other authors, he did not himself hesitate to make conjectural emendations of passages that seemed to him "depraved" or "mutilated," and he played enthusiastically that humanist game, the hunt for interpolations. . . . Admittedly, Budé's conjectures were sometimes wide of the mark . . . and often more daring than later standards of scholarship would permit; nor has his work left much trace, at least ostensibly, in Mommsen's edition. The significant thing, however, is the method that Budé sanctioned and developed. . . .

One point where Budé departed significantly from the Italian tradition of philology was his adoption of a conscious comparative method. He despised modern jargon—he would have been horrified, for example, at being called a "humanist"—and yet he was fascinated with vulgar counterparts of ancient terms. He was disgusted with the Accursian practice of introducing barbarisms (such as *guerra* for *bellum*), and yet he almost compulsively made parallels between ancient institutions and those of modern France. . . .

For the most part, however, Budé was protected from the fallacies of classicism by his nominalist cast of mind and by his Gallican ideology. He borrowed Valla's philological tools, in short, without adopting his monolithic Romanism. He assumed that most institutions, ancient and modern, were unique, if not autochthonous. In his famous discussion of the Parlement of Paris, for example, he arrived at the conclusion that "it has everything in it that is in the Senate and the centumviral court, as far as power and jurisdiction are concerned," but that in spite of "accidental" resemblances, it was quite wrong to liken the French court to the Roman institutions. . . . Inevitably, Budé stood with the moderns in their age-old quarrel with the ancients. Besides rejecting the mindless mimesis of the rigid Ciceronians, he pointed out "unheard of" developments in military science (*res inauditas . . . ut machinas belli*) and in bookmaking (*l'invention des impressions, qui est l'instauration et perpetuation de l'antiquité*). According to the Italian formula, the moderns were emulators not imitators (*non imitatores . . . sed etiam aemuli*) of the ancients.

What is perhaps most significant about Budé's essays in comparative history is that he often took a greater interest in French institutions than in their ancient counterparts. The Roman praetor, for example, reminded him of the French chancellor, and he went on to trace this office from its "most ancient" (that is, twelfth-century) origins to modern times. Discussion of the word *libellus* led him to consider the French *arrêt* and the office of *maître des requêtes*, which he himself came to hold; while the Roman *scrinium* introduced the subject of the royal *trésor des chartes*, of which his family had long held the charge. He also considered one of the favorite topics of historians, the peers of France, which he compared to the Roman *patres* and patricians. In these monographic digressions Budé referred not only to his administrative experience but to historians (such as Paolo Emilio and the chroniclers of Saint-Denis) and to archival records (such as royal edicts and the unpublished journal of Pierre Barrière), especially in the *trésor des chartes*. All these "monuments" he treated with the same reverence and archaeological enthusiasm, and with the same philological acumen, as he did the *Digest* itself.

In this rather desultory fashion Budé began to apply the new science of philology to the vulgar and vernacular problems of medieval history. The result was not only to widen the range and to deepen the perspective of historical inquiry but, through the teachings of philology, to improve historical method. Budé's researches—his pioneering work on the history of French institutions and his restitution of the *Digest*—were fully recognized by later generations of historians and jurists, as was his view that, whatever aid might be derived from classical scholarship, modern society had to be interpreted in its own terms: the nature of any culture, ancient or modern, could be grasped neither through philosophic categories or even classical ideals, but only through an effort of philological learning and philological understanding. The relativism in Budé's point of view represents another important step in the rise of historicism.

If Budé was the Columbus of the historical exploration of Roman law, he was also, like that rather uncertain navigator, soon surpassed in his achievements. Yet Budé left not only a legend but a legacy of considerable proportions. Before his death in 1540 the methods and attitudes that he made famous had helped to create a new school of legal scholarship. . . . How had this come about?

Although Budé shared some of the blame, in fact the "French method of teaching law"—the *mos gallicus juris docendi*, as distinguished from the old-fashioned *mos italicus*—was none of his doing. A promoter, even a prophet he may have been; a teacher he was not. Indeed, despite the urging of friends throughout Europe, he never even completed his work on the *Digest*. Growing "a bit disgusted" with the subject and with secular learning in general, Budé decided to leave the task to a younger generation. One scholar in particular attracted his attention. "I perceive," Budé wrote to Andrea Alciato in 1521, "that you are capable of equaling and surpassing what I have begun in this century, the revelation of the corrupt and hidden meaning of the Pandects. . . . [If you have the necessary talents] I desire the glory of this task for you." Alciato, who had made his mark on the world of humanism just three years before with a somewhat ostentatious display of erudition, justified this choice. He did not, indeed, finish the job of "cleansing the Augean stables" of law (a job that is still going on). In the eyes of contemporaries, however, he did something quite as significant: he brought philology into the classroom, though perhaps not, as he himself boasted, for the first time in a thousand years. It is true that he did this at the urging of his students, who were probably attracted as much by the economy as by the elegance of the method, but this did not detract from his achievement. The story was told, and few disbelieved it, that in 1529 at the University of Bourges Alciato laid the foundations of humanist jurisprudence. For this reason as much as for his works, Alciato was installed, along with Budé and Zasius, in another of those sixteenth-century "triumvirates," this one of legal scholarship. At the end of his life Alciato himself modestly claimed a place between those "men of eternal fame," Budé and Erasmus. . . .

Where Alciato departed most radically from Budé's views was in his estimate of Valla, who though he may have been the "emperor of grammarians" was the despair of lawyers. It was Poliziano who "first restored the *Digest* to light, soon followed by others." Valla, on the other hand, he took as a scapegoat for all the literal- and literary-minded excesses of philology. . . . In general, Alciato was skeptical about Valla's uncompromising historicism, believing that a critic had to take into account the intention (*voluntas* or *mens*) as well as the words of an author. Like Erasmus he hoped to pass from the letter to the spirit of a text, ultimately, in fact, to the "spirit of the laws" (*mens legum*). It was an error, for Valla no less than for Accursius, to reduce things to present-day standards (*ad nostri temporis normam*). In this way, despite the polemical tone, Alciato helped to give maturity and further perspective to the philological method.

. . . Alciato's scholarly influence, resulting from only four years at Bourges, was . . . unprecedented. For the rest of the century the law faculty of this university, in spite of professional squabbles and bitter ideological conflict, was the home of the reformed jurisprudence. It was largely Alciato's intellectual progeny . . . that made up the historical school of law of the second half of the sixteenth century. Of Alciato's— and Budé's—French disciples, the most prominent were François le Douaren, François Baudouin, François Hotman, and Jacques Cujas. Together with a few other scholars they brought about a "golden age of Roman law," lasting roughly from 1550 (the year of Alciato's death and of the beginning of Le Douaren's dominance) to 1590 (the year of Cujas's and Hotman's deaths). . . .

The man who best illustrates what has been called the "historicization" of law was Baudouin. . . . [H]e took up that anti-Tribonianist theme that was coming to dominate legal humanism. In his *Justinian, or the New Law* he argued that in the translation "from the Roman forum to the Constantinopolitan palace" the Roman Empire "changed not only its seat but its form and face, having a different jurisdiction, different religion, different customs, and a different government." It was only natural that Justinian had "wanted to accommodate the Pandects to the usage of his age and of his courts," but the result was to leave modern scholars with a most difficult task: "determining what is old and what new . . . , for often what in a particular passage is said to be Ulpian's . . . is really Justinian's or Tribonian's." . . . In general, the subject of the book was anachronism or obsolescence: how to distinguish *jus antiquum* from *jus novum*, that is, sources that had only antiquarian interest (such as the Twelve Tables, which were "more fact than law") from those that had legal authority (such as the novels of Justinian). It was precisely this circumstance, that Roman law was a mélange of *de facto* and *de jure* texts, that led Baudouin to his major contribution to the study of history: his program for a permanent alliance between law and history.

Baudouin's *Institution of Universal History and Its Conjunction with Jurisprudence* was therefore more than a variation on that hackneyed humanist theme, the "art of history"; it was an original essay on legal humanism and its significance. Like Budé, Baudouin sang the praises of philology, and, like Alciato, he advocated a grammatical mode of interpretation that took into account the *voluntas* as well as the *verba* of the law. According to Baudouin, however, the real key to jurisprudence was history, by which one could determine both the original meaning and the chronological development of laws. Conversely, legal sources and procedures were valuable, though as yet hardly touched, auxiliaries to the study of history. Although each of these fields had been restored in Baudouin's time, as shown in the achievements of Alciato and Paolo Giovio, it still remained to unite the two. Such was the basis of Baudouin's ideal of "integral history," which he celebrated in much the same organistic terms as Budé had represented his "encyclopedia," likening it to "a body whose parts may not be separated." For Baudouin "universal history," deriving from Pomponius, Polybius, and Eusebius, involved more than geographical and temporal scope. It meant also the study of institutions instead of merely dynastic and military affairs (*arma cedant togae*); it required chronological order (*ordo temporum*), corresponding to the sequence of legislation; and it suggested the need for investigating barbarian customs as well as Roman law. Although Baudouin was not sure which was the senior partner in his alliance of law and history, he himself came to abandon legal for historical scholarship. For this reason, too, he seems to represent the culmination of legal humanism.

The most original feature of the historical school of law—and here the example of Budé rather than of Alciato was most effective—was the growing interest in medieval institutions, both ecclesiastical and feudal.

This is apparent from the work both of Baudouin, who from the beginning was concerned with customary law and with Church history, and of Le Douaren, who in the last decade of his life plunged into the study of canon and feudal law. This shift in interest, due partly to the pressures of the Reformation and the Council of Trent, was accompanied by a significant change in ideology: French jurists, while clinging to the ideals of philology, broadened its scope to include vernacular culture and came to throw off altogether that classicist bias which had infected even some of Budé's judgments. As Alciato himself had stipulated, "All peoples are accustomed to take their terms from their own rather than from a foreign idiom, and so they . . . err who are led to ascribe Latin roots to barbarous words," such as the Latin for "brothers" (*germani*) to the Germans. The point was that institutions and their terminology were indigenous and had to be understood by empirical study, not by classical analogy. This was the position, too, of Le Douaren. Rejecting the Ciceronian fallacy, he argued that new customs continually created new words; reversing the opinion of Budé, he defended the Germanic origin of feudal law on the grounds that *feudum* (a barbaric term which, legal convention notwithstanding, had no connection with the Latin *fides*) could be traced back no further than to the Lombards. This revisionist thesis had weaknesses of its own, but it served as a valuable corrective to the natural classicist bias of Renaissance scholarship.

During the religious wars the clash between the Romanist and Germanist points of view, so portentous for historical thought, was much intensified by the polemics of French Protestants, who tended to associate classicism (hence Roman law) with Jesuitism, ultramontanism, and other such Italianate excesses. This is illustrated, indeed almost caricatured, in the transformation of Hotman from a conventional humanist (in his *Jurisconsult* of 1559) into an aggressive Germanist (in his *Franco-Gallia* of 1573). The pivotal work of his career, however, was his *Anti-Tribonian*, written in 1567, when he was royal historiographer as well as professor of law at Bourges. Hotman's point of departure was the usual complaint about the condition of the *Digest*, in particular the existence of "tribonianisms" (*emblemata Triboniani*, he called them in his scholarly work), including the whole section "On the Origin of Law" attributed to Pomponius, and about the ineradicable differences between classical and Byzantine law. How much less relevant, Hotman argued, was Roman law to the French monarchy! This indeed was his primary message: that Roman law, with its rigid formulas and litigious tendencies, had little place in French law schools and less in French society. There is no doubt, moreover, that Hotman developed this thesis in the context of a broader conception of the relativity of legal systems. Under the influence perhaps of his own rootless existence, the feudist tradition, and the program of vernacular humanism, he suggested that it was ultimately impossible to transplant any custom or institution—or, for that matter, any language—from one social environment to another. This is the rationale not merely of Hotman's "Germanism" (which is after all only the function of his particular ideological position) but of his historicism. . . .

Yet in the final analysis the most positive contribution to historical scholarship was made by a man who hardly ever strayed from the confines of philology—unlike Hotman he was proud of the title "grammarian"—and who managed to avoid the *Kulturkampf* of Romanism and Germanism: Cujas, the greatest legal humanist of them all. . . . It was no accident that his disciples, especially Pierre and François Pithou, Antoine Loisel, Étienne Pasquier, Louis le Caron, Pierre Ayrault, and Papire Masson, were the leading figures in that antiquarian revival that occurred during the civil wars in France, thus fulfilling the demand made by Baudouin in 1561 for a synthesis of law and history. These men, lawyers by training but historians by method, classicist by taste but medievalists by persuasion, formed a kind of unofficial society of antiquaries devoted to the reconstruction of French culture and institutions in the critical spirit of philology. Although a number of traditional motives may be found in their work, their true point of departure was not formal historiography but legal humanism. . . .

. . . These men, doing for the French Middle Ages what had already been done for Roman antiquity, shared with legal humanists a fascination for the monuments as well as the methods of the new jurisprudence. They even retained Roman law as a historical standard, as a kind of compass in the wilderness of institutional history: witness the works in comparative law by Ayrault, Le Caron, Pasquier, and Loisel. Yet like their mentors, and on identical philological grounds, they regarded each society as unique. They assumed that the world of man's making was the product not of a universal logos but of a Tower of Babel, that human culture was irremediably pluralistic, radically unstable, and accessible only through concrete investigation of specific institutions and ideas. They assumed too, perhaps, though they did not quite say so, that they alone had the proper qualifications for explaining man's temporal nature.

In short, they were, within the limits of the original definition, historicists. They accepted the principle of individuality in the sense that, in nominalist fashion, they regarded language not only as a reflection of a particular culture but as a copy of reality in terms of that culture. If they believed in a suprahistorical world, they left it to the philosophers. They accepted the principle of development in the sense that they acknowledged—indeed tried to chart—the temporal changes to which every society was subject, especially in language and customs; for such (in the phrase of Cicero made famous by Montaigne) was the human condition. Finally, they accepted the principle of relativism in that they insisted upon the uniqueness, without denying the comparability, of individual cultures. Ultimately, it is the work of these men, alumni of the first historical school of law, that justifies the conclusion that legal humanism was one of the major steps in the rise of historicism.

Zachary S. Schiffman

Renaissance Historicism Reconsidered

Kelley was neither the first nor the only scholar to claim that the modern form of historical consciousness, "historicism," originated in the late Renaissance. This position drew support from several other historians and political philosophers, all writing around the same time and all studying humanist legal philology. Although some of them made less extensive claims for the modernity of the sixteenth-century historical revolution, others anticipated and seconded Kelley's views. Taken together, the work of these scholars has popularized the notion that historicism originated in the late Renaissance.

Schiffman's "Renaissance Historicism Reconsidered" challenges this interpretation. While not denying the importance of changes in sixteenth-century historical thinking, Schiffman maintains that the label *historicism*

From Zachary S. Schiffman, "Renaissance Historicism Reconsidered," *History and Theory* 24 (1985): 178–182.

distorts our understanding of these changes, making them appear more modern than they really were. He begins by distinguishing historical consciousness (a way of seeing the past and its relation to the present) from historical scholarship (a way of analyzing documents); although the two are related, they are not synonymous. According to Schiffman, proponents of sixteenth-century historicism have mistaken changes in historical scholarship for changes in historical consciousness. Furthermore, they have assumed that the philological awareness of mutations in language and law constitutes an idea of historical development. By contrast, Schiffman distinguishes between the modern idea of development (in which an entity is shaped by changing historical circumstances) and the Renaissance idea of unfolding (in which the shape of an entity is inherent in a seed or essence that remains untouched by events).

In the second half of his article, excerpted below, Schiffman examines some sixteenth-century figures commonly described as historicist. Although they have a highly refined sense of historical uniqueness, Schiffman argues that they did not understand this uniqueness as developing over time, in relation to ever-changing circumstances, but rather as unfolding in a predetermined way from a seed planted in the remote past. According to Schiffman, this attitude reveals an "individualizing" view of the world that by its very nature precluded the modern notion of historical development.

. . . An awareness of individuality is generally considered to be one of the defining characteristics of the Italian Renaissance. In the most famous chapter of his *Civilization of the Renaissance in Italy,* Jacob Burckhardt referred to the "discovery of the individual"; he meant that man recognized himself as a unique entity defined by his self-conscious mind, rather than by his status as a member of a social group. According to Burckhardt, this new conception of personality led man to appreciate the individual qualities of entities in the world around him. Erwin Panofsky later elaborated on this new view of the world when he described the reintegration of form and content which distinguished Renaissance art from that of preceding renascences. For example, Italian artists began to depict Virgil not as a medieval schoolman seated at his writing desk but as a classical poet clad in a toga and crowned with laurel. Myron Gilmore described how this appreciation of individuality manifested itself in a "sense of anachronism" which enabled Italian humanists to perceive what was appropriate to the ancient world as distinct from the modern one. Overriding this distinction between antiquity and modernity, however, was the elevation of ancient culture to the status of a norm to be emulated.

The primacy of ancient culture was challenged in the sixteenth century when French humanists began to assert the equality or superiority of their own culture to that of antiquity. This movement received additional impetus from the French civil wars, as scholars began to study the history of those indigenous customs, laws, and institutions on which France's future political stability could be based. Historical scholarship heightened the sense of individuality by demonstrating the relativity of laws and institutions, thereby undermining the notion of normative standards derived from antiquity.

François Hotman demonstrated a heightened sense of individuality in his *Francogallia*, which described the origins and history of the ancient constitution of France. According to Hotman, this constitution originated with the establishment of the Frankish kingdom in Gaul. The Franks combined monarchy, aristocracy, and democracy in a mixed constitution which gave primacy to a public council of notables charged with electing and, if necessary, deposing their kings. Hotman claimed that this traditional council continued to function throughout the Merovingian, Carolingian, and Capetian dynasties, assuming the form of the Estates General in the fourteenth and fifteenth centuries. He implied that when Louis XI undermined the Estates General in the late fifteenth century, he subverted the ancient constitution and hence laid the foundation for the civil strife of Hotman's own day. The *Francogallia* was thus not only an historical study of the ancient constitution of France but also a Huguenot polemic for the revival of the Estates General in the face of growing royal absolutism.

Given its double purpose, the *Francogallia* blends normative and historical thinking. Hotman extolled the mixed constitution as the most perfect form of government, citing the authority of ancient philosophers and the examples of noteworthy states. At the same time, however, he provided an historical account of the French constitution in particular. To the extent that he was engaged in an historical enterprise, he conceived of this constitution as an individuality, an entity unique by virtue of its own special origins and history. Yet he did not understand this individuality as developing through time; rather, he conceived of it as having been established in the very remote past and continuing until the fifteenth century. The ancient constitution endured until Louis XI corrupted it, thereby causing the kingdom to deviate from its preestablished norm.

Although Hotman genuinely believed in his theory of an ancient constitution, he subordinated historical scholarship to the requirements of Huguenot polemics. Perhaps a more objective scholar would have been more sensitive to the uniqueness of French institutions and thus more inclined to understand them in terms of their development. In his *Recherches de la France*, Estienne Pasquier applied the highest scholarly standards of his day to a study of French culture. He described the *Recherches* as his "gift" to "*ma France.*" Like Hotman he desired to affirm those traditional institutions which could stabilize the kingdom in a time of upheaval, but unlike Hotman he subordinated politics to scholarship.

Pasquier conceived of himself as having "broken the ice" for a new kind of scholarly project. Whereas the chroniclers of France had merely recounted the succession of events in the kingdom, he undertook to describe the distinctive nature of French culture. This undertaking was concerned more with institutions than events. He prefaced Book Two of the *Recherches*, about the chief political institutions of the kingdom, with a chapter on whether Fortune or *Conseil* had contributed more to the welfare of the kingdom. Although Fortune had undoubtedly favored the realm by providing her with good kings and captains at crucial moments in her history, he concluded that sound administration (*la police & bonne conduicte de nos Roys*) had nonetheless made an equal contribution to her welfare. In effect he was distinguishing here between the flux of events, born of God's incomprehensible will, and the continuity of institutions, born of man's rational calculation. The uniqueness of French culture was the sum of her own distinctive institutions, customs, literature, and language; and each of the man-made entities could only be understood relative to its own origin and history.

Despite his extreme relativism, however, Pasquier conceived of these entities not as developing through time but as unfolding into their predetermined forms. For example, his search for the origins of Parlement was guided by his conception of the modern institution which, after the decline of the Estates General, had assumed importance in Pasquier's own day as the chief restraint on royal absolutism. He traced this modern role of Parlement back to its origins in "a form of annual Parlement" established by the Merovingian Mayors of the Palace, and he even suggested that it was foreshadowed by the assemblies of the ancient Gauls. He described how the early "Parlements," which varied "according to the diversity of the seasons," steadily increased in importance under the Carolingians and Capetians until they were finally regularized in the fourteenth century.

Because he interpreted its past in terms of its present, Pasquier conceived of this institution as unfolding rather than developing. Indeed, according to one author, the *Recherches* provides not so much a history of parlement as a "spurious genealogy." Although Pasquier's political bias as a parlementarian may have led him to exaggerate the antiquity of this particular institution, his "genealogical" approach to historical entities in general is evident throughout the *Recherches*. In Book Seven, for example, he recounted the "origin, antiquity, and progress" of French poetry by isolating its defining characteristics, which he then traced back to their origins and forward through their mutations.

Pasquier used historical entities like Parlement and poetry to define France as an individuality distinct from Rome. In the *Recherches*, he loosely organized these entities to provide an almost analytical view of France. Book One describes the origins of France, Book Two her chief political institutions, Book Three her distinctive religious traditions, Book Four her customs and laws, Books Five and Six her exemplary historical figures, Book Seven her poetry, Book Eight her language, and Book Nine her learning. Despite the analytical appearance of the work, however, Pasquier's topics do not build on each other to present a systematic description of France. The order of parts could be reversed without changing the whole. Pasquier conceived of France as an individuality not by virtue of its development but rather by virtue of the individuality of its component parts, each of which he treated separately.

The *Recherches* is a hybrid work, partly historical and partly antiquarian. Could a more fully historical treatment of France have revealed the development of its individuality? La Popelinière outlined his plan for a "new history" of France in the *Dessein de l'histoire nouvelle des François*. Like Pasquier, La Popelinière disdained the chroniclers of France, maintaining that histories should not only recount diplomatic and military events but also describe customs and institutions. Yet unlike Pasquier, La Popelinière was a practicing historian who wanted to subordinate the description of institutions to the narrative of history.

He divided his proposed history into three parts: pre-Roman Gaul, Roman Gaul, and the kingdom of France from the Merovingians to the present. Part one would detail the religion of the ancient Gauls (its priests and rituals), the nobility (its composition, privileges, and lifestyle), the judicial apparatus (its judges and other officials), the lesser

social orders (merchants, artisans, and commoners)—"in brief, everything notable about so little known a state." Part two would follow the
same pattern but in even greater detail, examining the changes introduced by the Romans in society, religion, administration, justice, military discipline, finances, and business. Part three would describe the
history of the French monarchy in terms of topics—religion, nobility,
administration, and so forth—which were even more detailed than
either of the two preceding parts of the proposed work. The progressively increasing detail of the outline reflects the increasing availability
of documents as La Popelinière moved chronologically from ancient
Gaul to modern France. But as the detail of the outline increased, its
coherence decreased, until it resembled little more than a collection of
topics divided into a multitude of discrete subtopics.

The tendency for the awareness of individuality to grow exponen-
tially, already implicit in the structure of the *Recherches*, has become
explicit here. What La Popelinière expressed in his outline was not
simply an antiquarian impulse to collect information about the past but,
more importantly, an unbridled fascination with the individuality of historical entities, which resolved itself into a fascination with the individuality of their separate parts. La Popelinière himself epitomized this
frame of mind when he likened the writing of a new history of France
to the raising of a building. His proposed history has an architectonic
quality about it, as if it were divided into floors, each of which was further subdivided into apartments, and then into rooms. Yet this structure
was held together not by cement but by its own mass, which increased
geometrically with the addition of each new stage. No one ever constructed a history according to this blueprint, for it surely would have
collapsed under its own weight.

The proponents of the argument that historicism originated in sixteenth-
century France have tried to explain why it supposedly disappeared in
the seventeenth century, to be rediscovered over a century later. According to one interpretation, "historical criticism" as practiced by men like
Pasquier became associated with "libertinism," which was anathema in
the age of Louis XIV. According to another interpretation, the budding
"science" of history languished in the shadow of Cartesianism. But when
this "historicism" is seen for what it really was—a flowering of the idea
of individuality—it is not surprising that Pasquier and La Popelinière had
no successors in the seventeenth century. Their individualizing view of

the world was conceptually sterile. They conceived of historical entities as divided into separate parts which, in turn, were further subdivided into discrete pieces. This conception enabled them to describe entities in great detail, but not to understand them.

An understanding of historical entities emerged only in the late eighteenth century, when people began to explain them in terms of their development. This juncture of the ideas of individuality and development could not have been effected 200 years earlier, because the initial focus on the idea of individuality had precluded an awareness of development. When they viewed an historical entity, thinkers like Hotman, Pasquier, and La Popelinière perceived what the scholastics had termed its "haecceity," or "thisness," the essential quality which characterized it as an individuality. They could not even conceive of an entity as developing in relationship to its circumstances, for such a notion would have obliterated the very "thisness" which defined the entity. Instead, they conceived of it as unfolding from its germ or essence, a conception which enabled them to perceive its "thisness" despite its historical mutations.

The rise of historical scholarship in sixteenth-century France heightened the awareness of individuality. On the one hand, this awareness assumed a form which was incompatible with the idea of development and hence inhibited the emergence of historicism. On the other, it helped prepare the way for historicism by broadening the historical horizon to include all human creations. The idea of individuality both encouraged the expansion and restricted the range of historical consciousness in the French Renaissance.

Suggestions for Further Reading

The Renaissance has spawned an immense, scholarly bibliography, much of which is of interest chiefly to specialists. The following suggestions for further readings are very highly selective, keyed to the general topics and figures covered in this volume, and limited to works in English.

Charles G. Nauert, Jr., has written an excellent survey, *Humanism and the Culture of Renaissance Europe* (Cambridge: Cambridge University Press, 1995), which places the scholarly debates of this volume in their broadest historical context. In addition, his bibliography is both judicious and reasonably up-to-date. Those interested in exploring questions of originality and continuity in the Renaissance should begin by consulting Wallace K. Ferguson's classic study, *The Renaissance in Historical Thought: Five Centuries of Interpretation* (Boston, Mass.: Houghton Mifflin, 1948). Although dated, his account provides a ready guide to interpretations of the Renaissance from the humanist tradition in Italy to World War II, with special emphasis on the fate of Jacob Burckhardt's interpretation. Karl J. Weintraub provides the best introduction to Burckhardt's historical thought in Chapter 3 of his *Visions of Culture* (Chicago, Ill.: University of Chicago Press, 1966). Whereas Weintraub emphasizes the visual-pictorial quality of Burckhardt's cultural history, E. H. Gombrich sees Hegelian overtones in this pattern, as described in his *In Search of Cultural History* (Oxford: Oxford University Press, 1969). Weintraub also provides the best introduction to Johan Huizinga's historical thought in Chapter 5 of *Visions of Culture*, and his work on Huizinga has inspired the recent English translation of the 1919 Dutch edition of Huizinga's masterpiece, *The Autumn of the Middle Ages* (Chicago, Ill.: University of Chicago Press, 1996). Haskins's pioneering work on the twelfth-century Renaissance has been revisited, revised, and rejuvenated in *Renaissance and Renewal in the Twelfth Century*, eds. Robert L. Benson and Giles Constable (Cambridge, Mass.: Harvard University Press, 1982). Michael Ann Holly's *Panofsky and the Foundation of Art History* (Ithaca, N.Y.: Cornell University Press, 1984) provides a good introduction to the work of that art historian; in addition, one might also consult Sylvia Ferretti's *Panofsky and Warburg: Symbol, Art, and History*, trans. Richard Pierce (New Haven, Conn.: Yale University Press, 1989).

George M. Logan's "Substance and Form in Renaissance Humanism" (*Journal of Medieval and Renaissance Studies* 7 [1977]: 1–34) synthesizes the points made in our selections from Kristeller, Gray, Trinkaus, and Bouwsma about the nature of humanism and then tries to move beyond them, identifying the movement's general pattern of evolution. *The Impact of Humanism on Western Europe* (eds. Anthony Goodman and Angus MacKay [London: Longman, 1990]) provides several interesting topical and national studies of humanism, as does *The Cambridge Companion to Renaissance Humanism*, ed. Jill Kraye (Cambridge: Cambridge University Press, 1996). Albert Rabil, Jr.'s massive three-volume editorial effort, *Renaissance Humanism: Foundations, Forms, and Legacy* (Philadelphia, Pa.: University of Pennsylvania Press, 1988) offers a wealth of articles on the major aspects of the movement. And, of course, one should not forget to consult Paul Oskar Kristeller's various collections of essays on the subject, such as his *Renaissance Thought: The Classic, Scholastic, and Humanist Strains* (New York: Harper and Row, 1961) and *Renaissance Thought II: Papers on Humanism and the Arts* (New York: Harper and Row, 1965). Kristeller has also contributed to the study of women and humanism; see especially his "Learned Women of Early Modern Italy: Humanists and University Scholars," in *Beyond Their Sex: Learned Women of the European Past*, ed. Patricia H. Labalme (New York: New York University Press, 1980). Another important contribution is the second chapter of Anthony Grafton and Lisa Jardine's *From Humanism to the Humanities* (Cambridge, Mass.: Harvard University Press, 1986), provocatively entitled, "Women Humanists: Education for What?"

The theme of civic humanism is explored in Eugenio Garin, *Italian Humanism: Philosophy and Civic Life in the Renaissance*, trans. Peter Munz (New York: Harper and Row, 1965). First published in a German edition of 1947, Garin's book predates Hans Baron's famous work on the subject, although Baron had laid the foundation for his thesis about civic humanism in the 1920s and 1930s. The first major challenge to Baron's thesis was mounted by Jerrold E. Seigel, and the exchange of articles between Seigel and Baron constitutes a classic instance of academic debate. See Seigel's "'Civic Humanism' or Ciceronian Rhetoric? The Culture of Petrarch and Bruni," *Past and Present* 34 (1966): 3–46; and Baron's response, "Leonardo Bruni: 'Professional Rhetorician' or 'Civic

Humanist'?", *Past and Present* 36 (1967): 21–37. Also see Baron's collection of essays, *From Petrarch to Leonardo Bruni* (Chicago, Ill.: University of Chicago Press, 1968). Almost every modern historian of the Italian Renaissance has weighed in on this debate in works too numerous to mention. The major positions, however, are nicely summarized by Albert Rabil, Jr., in his essay, "The Significance of 'Civic Humanism' in the Interpretation of the Italian Renaissance," in Volume 1 of his edited collection, *Renaissance Humanism*. For a more recent postmortem, see James Hankins, "The 'Baron Thesis' after Forty Years and Some Recent Studies of Leonardo Bruni," *Journal of the History of Ideas* 56 (1995): 309–338. Nauert's defense of Baron in the equally recent *Humanism and the Culture of Renaissance Europe* indicates that the patient may not be quite dead yet. In addition to Anthony Grafton's attempts to advance beyond the terms of this debate, one should also consult James Hankins, "Humanism and the Origins of Modern Political Thought," in the above-cited *Cambridge Companion to Renaissance Humanism*.

Thomas M. Greene's work on *imitatio* is indebted to that of G. W. Pigman III; see especially his "Versions of Imitation in the Renaissance," *Renaissance Quarterly* 33 (1980): 1–32, and his "Imitation and the Renaissance Sense of the Past: The Reception of Erasmus' *Ciceronianus*," *Journal of Medieval and Renaissance Studies* 9 (1979): 155–177. For a broader analysis of the relation between reading and writing, see Terence Cave, *The Cornucopian Text: Problems of Writing in the French Renaissance* (Oxford: Oxford University Press, 1979). An excellent study of the commonplace books spawned by the doctrine of imitation is Ann Moss, *Printed Commonplace-Books and the Structuring of Renaissance Thought* (Oxford: Oxford University Press, 1996). Also see the classic essay by Walter J. Ong, S. J., "Commonplace Rhapsody: Ravisius Textor, Zwinger and Shakespeare," in *Classical Influences on European Culture* A.D. *1500–1700*, ed. R. R. Bolgar (Cambridge: Cambridge University Press, 1976). Ong has authored several works on Renaissance education; especially provocative is "Latin Language Study as a Renaissance Puberty Rite," in his collection, *Rhetoric, Romance, and Technology: Studies in the Interaction of Expression and Culture* (Ithaca, N.Y.: Cornell University Press, 1971). One should also consult his magisterial *Ramus, Method, and the Decay of Dialogue: From the Art of Discourse to the Art of Reason* (Cambridge, Mass.: Harvard University Press, 1958). William Harrison Woodward's *Vittorino da Feltre and Other Humanist Educators* (Cambridge: Cambridge University Press, 1897; reprint ed.,

New York: Columbia University Press, 1963) and his *Studies in Education During the Age of the Renaissance* (Cambridge: Cambridge University Press, 1906; reprint ed., New York: Russell and Russell, 1965) are still useful, though Woodward tends to conflate the theory and practice of humanist education. By contrast, R. R. Bolgar's *The Classical Heritage and Its Beneficiaries* (Cambridge: Cambridge University Press, 1954) more fully distinguishes practice from theory, describing the narrow range of readings students actually encountered in humanist schools. In addition to Grafton and Jardine's *From Humanism to the Humanities* and Paul F. Grendler's *Schooling in Renaissance Italy* (Baltimore, Md.: Johns Hopkins University Press, 1989), one should also consult R. A. Houston, *Literacy in Early Modern Europe: Culture and Education, 1500–1800* (London: Longman, 1988), which situates humanist education within a broader historical context.

The link between the theory of imitation and the idea of historical anachronism is discussed in the above-cited articles by Pigman. Also see Chapter 1 of Thomas M. Greene's *The Light in Troy* (New Haven, Conn.: Yale University Press, 1982). For a more general study of the relation between rhetoric and history, see Nancy S. Struever, *The Language of History in the Renaissance: Rhetoric and Historical Consciousness in Florentine Humanism* (Princeton, N.J.: Princeton University Press, 1970). On humanist philology, see Bolgar's *Classical Heritage*, Rudolf Pfeiffer, *History of Classical Scholarship, 1300–1850* (Oxford: Oxford University Press, 1976), and L. D. Reynolds and N. G. Wilson, *Scribes and Scholars: A Guide to the Transmission of Greek and Latin Literature*, 2nd ed. (Oxford: Oxford University Press, 1974). In addition to these general studies, one should also consult Chapter 1 of Anthony Grafton's *Joseph Scaliger: A Study in the History of Classical Scholarship*, vol. 1 (Oxford: Oxford University Press, 1983), and Grafton's *Defenders of the Text: Traditions of Scholarship in an Age of Science, 1450–1800* (Cambridge, Mass.: Harvard University Press, 1991), especially Chapter 2. The best introduction to legal humanism and its historiographical implications is still the first chapter of J. G. A. Pocock's *The Ancient Constitution and the Feudal Law* (Cambridge: Cambridge University Press, 1957; reissued with a retrospective, 1987). Also see Myron P. Gilmore, *Humanists and Jurists: Six Studies in the Renaissance* (Cambridge, Mass.: Harvard University Press, 1963). The French historical school of law and its effect on historical scholarship has been assessed most judiciously in Julian H. Franklin, *Jean Bodin and the Sixteenth-Century*

Revolution in the Methodology of Law and History (New York: Columbia University Press, 1963); it has been analyzed most exhaustively in Donald R. Kelley, *Foundations of Modern Historical Scholarship: Language, Law, and History in the French Renaissance* (New York: Columbia University Press, 1970); and it has been described most enthusiastically in George Huppert, *The Idea of Perfect History: Historical Erudition and Historical Philosophy in Renaissance France* (Urbana, Ill.: University of Illinois Press, 1970). These authors and others making similar claims are analyzed and criticized in the first half of Zachary S. Schiffman's article, "Renaissance Historicism Reconsidered," only the second half of which has been excerpted in this volume. Schiffman's *On the Threshold of Modernity: Relativism in the French Renaissance* (Baltimore, Md.: Johns Hopkins University Press, 1991) represents an attempt to advance beyond debates about Renaissance historicism. For the distinction between the ideas of development and unfolding, see the classic account of the eighteenth-century origins of historicism by Friedrich Meinecke, *Historism: The Rise of a New Historical Outlook,* trans. J. E. Anderson (New York: Herder and Herder, 1972).

Credits

Part I

p. 27:   Copyright © Johan Huizinga from *The Waning of the Middle Ages* by Johan Huizinga. Reprinted with permission of St. Martin's Press, LLC.

p. 36:   Reprinted by permission of the publisher from *The Renaissance of the Twelfth Century* by Charles Homer Haskins, Cambridge, Mass.: Harvard University Press, Copyright © 1927 by Charles Homer Haskins, renewed 1955 by Clare Allen Haskins.

p. 41:   Edited text excerpt, "Renaissance and Renascences in Western Art (1960)" by Erwin Panofsky from *Renaissance and Renascences in Western Art* by Erwin Panofsky, Harper & Row, © 1969, pp. 82–86, 100–103, 106–113; published by arrangement with Almquist and Wiksells, © 1960. Reprinted by permission of Perseus Books Group.

Part II

p. 59:   From Kristeller, Paul Oskar; *Renaissance Thought: The Classic, Scholastic, and Humanist Strains*, Copyright 1961 by Princeton University Press. Reprinted by permission of Princeton University Press.

p. 70:   Text excerpt from Gray, Hanna H. "Renaissance Humanism: The Pursuit of Eloquence," Journal of the History of Ideas 24 (1963), 497–514. © Journal of History of Ideas, Inc. Reprinted by permission of the Johns Hopkins University Press.

p. 83:   Excerpted from Charles Trinkaus, *In Our Image and Likeness: Humanity and Divinity in Italian Humanist Thought*, 2 Vols. (Chicago, Ill.: University of Chicago Press, 1970). Reprinted by permission.

p. 92:   From *Itinerarium Italicum: The Profile of the Italian Renaissance in the Mirror of its European Transformations*, ed. Heiko A. Oberman with Thomas A. Brady, Jr. E. J. Brill, © 1975, pp. 3–60. Reprinted by permission of Brill Academic Publishers, The Netherlands.

p. 114:   Excerpted from "Book-Lined Cells: Women and Humanism in the Early Italian Renaissance (1980)" by Margaret L. King from *Beyond Their Sex: Learned Women of the European Past*, ed. Patricia H. Labalme, New York University Press, © 1980, pp. 71–81. Reprinted by permission of New York University Press.

Part III

p. 127:   From Baron, Hans; *The Crisis of the Early Italian Renaissance*, rev. ed., Copyright © 1966 by Princeton University Press, © 1966, pp. 3–11, pp. 459–462. Reprinted by permission of Princeton University Press.

p. 135:   From Seigel, Jerrold; *Rhetoric and Philosophy in Renaissance Humanism*, Copyright © 1968 by Princeton University Press. Reprinted by permission of Princeton University Press.

p. 143:   Excerpted from *The Foundations of Modern Political Thought, Vol. 1: The Renaissance* by Quentin Skinner, pp. 69–101. Copyright © 1978 Cambridge University Press. Reprinted with the perimssion of Cambridge University Press.

p. 157:   Edited text excerpt, "Humanism and Political Theory (1991)" by Anthony Grafton, from *The Cambridge History of Political Thought, 1450–1700*, ed. J. H. Burns, Cambridge University Press, © 1991, pp. 20–29. Reprinted with the permission of Cambridge University Press.

Part IV

p. 171:   From *The Light in Troy: Imitation and Discovery in Renaissance Poetry* by Thomas M. Greene, Yale University Press, © 1982, pp. 28–47. Reprinted by permission of Yale University Press.

p. 183:   Edited text excerpt, "From Humanism to the Humanities (1986)" by Anthony Grafton and Lisa Jardine, from *From Humanism to the Humanities* by Anthony Grafton and Lisa Jardine © 1986. Reprinted by permission of Gerald Duckworth & Co. Ltd.

p. 195:   From Grendler, Paul F. *Schooling in Renaissance Italy: Literacy and Learning, 1300–1500*, pp. 403–410. © 1989 Johns Hopkins University Press. Reprinted with the permission of The Johns Hopkins University Press.

Part V

p. 206:   Edited text excerpted from "Petrarch's Conception of the 'Dark Ages' (1942)" by T. E. Mommsen from *Speculum 17*, Copyright © 1942 Medieval Academy of America, pp. 226–242. Reprinted by permission.

p. 211:   Edited text excerpt, "The Renaissance Conception of the Lessons of History 1959" by Myron P. Gilmore, from *Facets of the Renaissance*, ed. William H. Werkmeister, Harper & Row, 1963, 73–98. Gilmore essay Harvard University Press, © 1963, pp. 73–98. Reprinted by permission of Ayer Co. Publishers.

p. 225:   Edited text excerpt, "Guillaume Budé and the First Historical School of Law (1967)" by Donald R. Kelley from *American Historical Review 72*, American Historical Association, © 1967, pp. 807–834. Reprinted by permission of the author.

p. 240:   Excerpted from, "Renaissance Historicism Reconsidered" (1985) from *History and Theory 24*, Blackwell Publishers, © 1985, pp. 178–182. Reprinted by permission of Blackwell Publishers, UK.